THE PRESIDENTIAL SCANDALS: FROM JOHN KENNEDY TO DONALD TRUMP

Dr. NASSER AFIFY

2019

Table of Contents

INTRODUCTION

States based on principles and ethics always expect their leaders and politicians to respect these principles and morals and to set an example for the people and for other countries, especially if these leaders occupy the highest position in the country, which is the position of president. Although there are some say that politics has no morality and that it depends only on interests and that the ends justify the means, it has been proven through many historical events that these statements are incorrect and that those who stick to them end a tragic end and perhaps a scandal echoed over time.

The Constitution of the United States is one of the most powerful and most effective constitutions in the world. This Constitution has helped to create a balanced government. The balance between the federal and state governments has been maintained. The flexibility of the Constitution has been maintained and developed to put some restrictions to protect it from hasty changes.

Politician includes not only those elected, but also party officials, candidates for office, their staffs and appointees.

Every president directly selects, appoints or hires several thousand people. Private citizens should only be mentioned when they are closely linked to the scandal or politician. This list also does not include crimes that occur outside the politician's tenure unless they specifically stem from acts made while in office and discovered later.

Scandal is defined as "loss of or damage to reputation caused by actual or apparent violation of morality or propriety". Scandals are separate from 'controversies', which implies two differing points of view and 'unpopularity'. Many decisions are controversial, many decisions are unpopular, and that alone does not make them scandals. Breaking the law is a scandal. The finding of a court is the sole method used to determine a violation of law, but it is not the sole method of determining a scandal. Also included as scandals are politicians who resign, quit, run, or commit suicide while being investigated or threatened with investigation.

Notoriety is a major determinant of a scandal, that is, the amount of press dedicated to it. Misunderstandings, breaches of ethics, unproven crimes or cover-ups may or may not result in inclusion depending on the standing of the accused, the amount of publicity generated, and the seriousness of the crime, if any. Drunk driving may be a conviction, but is usually too minor and too common to mention unless there are multiple convictions and/or jail time.

Given the political nature of congress in which the leading party has determining power, politicians who are rebuked, admonished, condemned, suspended, reprimanded, found in contempt, found to have acted improperly or used poor judgment, are *not* included unless the scandal is exceptional or leads to expulsion or conviction.

The history of American presidents is full of scandals ranging from sexual, financial and political scandals, some of which may amount to treason, when an external force is used to intervene in the elections in favor of a particular candidate against another candidate because this candidate will be indebted to that external force and demanding that He pays a lot of bills at the expense of his country's interests.

CHAPTER ONE
JFK AND THE POOL OF PLEASURES

John F. Kennedy's maternal grandfather, and the man for whom JFK was named, John F. Fitzgerald was a two term mayor of Boston. His mayoral administration involved significant nepotism, patronage and graft. Fitzgerald was booted out of the U.S. House of Representatives for vote fraud (he had won that election by just over 1% of the votes cast). A major organizer for his corrupt campaign was his son-in-law; the ambitious Joseph P. Kennedy, Jack's father.

Joe Kennedy outlived three sons, Joe, Jack, and Bobby, and a daughter Kathleen (he had five other children). When he died in 1969, Joe Kennedy was one of the richest men in the U.S. with a net worth estimated at half a billion dollars. He made his fortune in the stock market, movies, and through various illicit means including bootlegging during Prohibition and partnering with organized crime. Joe had lofty political aspirations.

He made significant contributions to Franklin Delano Roosevelt's presidential election campaigns, but FDR, who didn't trust Joe, declined to offer him a cabinet position. Joe successfully lobbied President Roosevelt for the ambassadorship to England. The leverage he used was FDR's son James, whose friendship he solidified by supplying James with women. Joe was openly adulterous; at times flaunting it in front of his wife and their guests.

As ambassador, Joe Kennedy was reviled in England for his defeatism and regarded as a coward when, during Luftwaffe bombings in 1940, he left London to spend his nights at a country estate. While ambassador he engaged in profiteering; commandeering valued transatlantic cargo space for the continued importation of British Scotch and gin to his importing company. He was anti-Semitic and willingly ignorant of European history. He sought, without State Department approval, a personal meeting with Hitler with the intent of keeping the U.S. out of the war. Over the objection of the State Department and FDR, he met with a high-level Nazi official seeking to reach an agreement to pay the Nazis up to $1 billion for peace. Ambassador Kennedy once briefed a group of American journalists about a plot of dissident German generals to overthrow Hitler; even giving them the names of the dissidents jeopardizing their plotting and lives. He may have feared Communism more than Nazism.

Joe Kennedy used his contacts in the press to position himself for a presidential nomination in 1940. FDR isolated him from the American public by keeping him in London. Unfortunately for FDR, Kennedy had access to secret FDR-Churchill communications including those indicating FDR's willingness to assist England in war against Hitler. This was powerful blackmail material against FDR as the American people wanted to remain out of the war. When Kennedy returned to the U.S. in October 1940, 10 days before the presidential election, he was expected to endorse Republican Wilkie. After a private dinner with FDR, Kennedy agreed to endorse FDR in a radio speech. It is not known why but it was probably because both men had the goods on the other (FDR having access to Kennedy's tax returns and IRS problems and, through his friend J. Edgar Hoover, FBI information on Kennedy). Kennedy's speech included the lie that no secret commitments had been made and that FDR was not trying to involve the country in war.

Three days after FDR won re-election, Kennedy self-destructed. He claimed Hitler had won the war and that democracy was finished in England and perhaps in the U.S. His public support collapsed and his dreams of high public office ended. He resigned as ambassador to England a few months later and he never served in public office again. He refocused his considerable energies on his two oldest sons, Joe and Jack. When Joe Jr., a naval aviator, died in 1944, the emphasis shifted almost entirely to Jack. Joe purposely moved to the background to protect his sons from any damage his tainted reputation may cause them. Still, Joe remained a commanding and demanding force in the lives of his sons. A private phone was installed in the White House through which Joe and his son, President John F. Kennedy, would frequently communicate—at least until Joe's stroke in December 1961 left him unable to speak.

Since these conversations were always held in private and the two principals are dead--having apparently left no record of the subject matter of their talks--no one knows how strongly Joe Kennedy influenced or directed Jack's presidency, especially during that first year. It would be surprising if the influence were not substantial, given Joe's ambitiousness, desire for power, longtime political aspirations, and his money, connections, and energy being critical to JFK's election and given Jack's loyalty and devotion to his father.

John Kennedy seemed to have it all; looks, charm, intelligence, a sense of humor, power, and the Kennedy fortune. He was a man's man and a woman's man. He was also impatient, self-absorbed, zealously loyal to his family, a womanizer, an adulterer, physically unhealthy, dishonest, and extremely reckless. John Kennedy was a notorious penny-pincher who never carried cash and thus was never able to pay his share of a restaurant or bar bill.

JFK adored his father and maternal grandfather, his brother Bobby was his closest friend, but he had little time or use for his mother nor for women as peers in general. He often called women he knew "kid" because he couldn't remember their names; even the names of his lovers. Hersh speculates that JFK's craving for women and compulsive need to shower (as often as five times a day) may have been linked to a lack of mothering.

He not only considered women as less than equals, he often referred to the poor, the blacks, and the Jews, as "poor bastards". He showed almost no empathy and, like the majority of people of his time, accepted inequalities based on race, gender, and religious belief.

Though he won a Pulitzer Prize for his autobiography *Profiles in Courage*, it is likely the book was largely ghostwritten and it is the case that his dad's money kept it on the bestseller list and Joe's connections won it the Pulitzer.

JFK had an undistinguished legislative output in the Senate, but his looks and personal appeal and Joe Kennedy's planning, connections, and money were behind marketing efforts that made him a national celebrity.

During JFK's presidency, his desire and demand for loyalty resulted in his capable staff serving him poorly as they preferred to please him rather than enlighten him. What the public saw in JFK was an attractive, glamorous, hardworking President devoted to country, wife and family. Four former secret service men who were assigned the Kennedy presidential detail reported they saw a president obsessed with sex, willing to take enormous risks to gratify that obsession, a president who came late many times to the Oval Office and who was not readily available for hours during the day.

Jack Kennedy had a severe case of Addison's disease; an often fatal disease that weakens the immune system. He was given last rites on four occasions but recovered each time.

He was often sick as an infant. He nearly died from scarlet fever at age 2, at 4 he missed two thirds of his nursery school days due to illness, at 13 he almost died due to appendicitis, and in college he suffered a back injury playing football that led him to wear a back brace much of the rest of his life. He was born with one leg slightly longer than the other so he had back problems even before the football injury.

JFK had been treated since his early twenties for a series of often painful venereal diseases. He was repeatedly reinfected and presumably infecting his wife and many other sex partners.

Basically, pain was a constant in JFK's life. To deal with it, he enlisted the services of Dr. Max Jacobson. Dr. Jacobson was known to the secret service agents as "Dr. Feelgood". He often treated the president with "painkillers" (apparently a combination of cortisone and amphetamines), and provided drugs and hypodermic needles for self-administration.

There were periods during his presidency when JFK would get an injection every six hours. He received treatments shortly before one of the televised debates with Nixon, during Presidential travels to Europe, moments before a summit meeting with Soviet premier Nikita Khruschev, and during the tense moments of the October 1962 missile crisis. Dr. Jacobson's license to practice medicine was revoked in 1975 for misuse of amphetamines.

President Kennedy once told a friend, "You know, I get a migraine headache if I don't get a strange piece of ass every day." Apparently he didn't have many headaches. His affairs were legion. He even slept with one of his long time lovers in the Georgetown home he shared with his wife and two children the night before his inauguration. He and this woman began their affair when she was a 19 year old Radcliffe College student and he was a 42 year old Senator running for president. Their four year affair lasted through the election and into his presidency during which time she was a member of the White House staff.

JFK, at 24, had a torrid affair with a married journalist, Inga Marie Arvadi. The former Danish beauty queen had earlier socialized with Hitler. FBI surveillance, wire-tapping, and searches found no evidence of illegal doings; just lovers at play.

Kennedy's affair with Marilyn Monroe, an open secret in Hollywood, began before the 1960 election and continued after he went to the White House. Alicia Darr, who was to become an expensive call girl, had an affair with JFK in the spring of 1960 and tried to extort money from the Kennedys, though there is no record of money ever having been paid.

JFK told one of his lovers during the 1960 presidential primary that he would divorce his wife if he didn't win the election. A Georgetown housewife, obsessed with exposing the womanizing JFK, became a public nuisance to the 1960 Kennedy presidential campaign but the general public did not care to hear or believe her evidence.

President Kennedy did not have affairs in the White House when his wife was also staying there, but she spent most of her time with their children at a family retreat in Virginia. When returning to the White House earlier than expected, she would typically call ahead, presumably to enable the coast to be cleared before her arrival. It seems "plausible deniability" was important to the first lady as well as her husband.

According to a Secret Service agent who was on the Kennedy presidential detail, when she (Jackie) was there, it was no fun. He just had headaches. You really saw him droop because he wasn't getting laid. He was like a rooster getting hit with a water hose."

Secret service agents were frustrated by the many "unknown" women who were brought to the President for one-night stands. The women were not searched before meeting the President. The agents feared that one of these women would blackmail or even kill JFK.

This was not the only way the agents felt derelict in their duty, they also allowed crimes to go unreported. When travelling, oftentimes local officials would bring call girls and hookers (often more than one at a time) to the President. The agents, rather than arresting the President or his aides, friends and supporters for procuring prostitutes, would say nothing. There were many budding Hollywood starlets brought to the White House for their "services" with it made clear that sex with the President could help a career but news of the affair would end it. JFK's skinny-dipping lunchtime pool parties at the White House with two young female staff aides (Fiddle and Faddle) sometimes included his brothers Bobby and Teddy.

Judith Campbell (now known as Judith Exner) was a gorgeous California socialite, 25 years old when she was introduced to JFK by Frank Sinatra in early 1960. One month later they become lovers. A month after that, JFK asked Campbell to carry a satchel containing at least $250,000 ("for the [presidential primary] campaign") to Mafia kingpin Sam Giancana; who was also recently introduced to Campbell by Sinatra. She became a conduit between Kennedy and Giancana during the primaries and remained so during the general election and the Kennedy administration.

She carried money and documents on the "elimination" of Castro from JFK to Giancana and arranged meetings between the two. Throughout her years with JFK, Campbell was under intense FBI surveillance due to her association with Giancana. The surveillance revealed to the FBI her relationship with JFK. Hoover chose not to make this information public at least in part because revealing it would indicate the extent of his illegal bugging and would damage his and the FBI's reputations.

By the fall of 1962, Campbell was out of JFK's life. The FBI surveillance and JFK's waning passion for her (he'd brought another woman to their bed much to Campbell's dismay) left her heartbroken. Exner (Campbell) claims to have gotten pregnant from JFK during their last sexual encounter. According to Exner, JFK told her not to keep the baby and to seek help from Giancana, who had also become her lover, in terminating the pregnancy.

In 1963, German born Ellen Rometsch became one of the White House pool party girls. Rometsch was 27, beautiful, and a prostitute when she met JFK. As a youth and young adult she was a member of the Communist Party. Other call girls from Communist countries, Maria Novtny (a Czech) and Suzy Chang (a Chinese) serviced JFK (their relationship preceded his election). These latter two women were also involved with a British prime minister of war, getting answers to questions about British nuclear policy being fed them by a Soviet naval attaché. When that dalliance became known, prime minister Harold Macmillan resigned and his government was shortly voted out of office.

Some reporters knew about the link between these call girls and JFK but their story was suppressed by publishing mogul Bill Hearst. The FBI learned of the Rometsch-Kennedy connection and began to investigate her as a possible spy. The Kennedys had her deported to Germany and paid her to keep her mouth shut.

In September 1963, while frolicking poolside with one of his sexual partners, JFK tore a groin muscle. He had to wear a stiff shoulder-to-groin brace that locked his body in a rigid upright position. It was far more constraining than his usual back brace, which he continued to wear. The two braces made it impossible for JFK to bend in reflex when he was struck in the neck by a bullet fired by Lee Harvey Oswald. The president remained erect for the fatal shot from Oswald.

The first election JFK won was his grandfather Honey Fitz's congressional seat. Critical to the win was Joe's money. It didn't hurt when a second Joseph Russo was placed on the ballot. The first Joseph Russo was a leading contender for the House seat but the two

Russo names split his vote total. JFK's election to the U.S. Senate was again largely the result of Joe's money and connections. Bobby Kennedy was his brother's official campaign manager.

During the Democratic primaries for the 1960 presidential election, JFK's most important victory came in West Virginia. Large sums of Kennedy money--at least $2 million ($11 million in today's dollars) and possibly twice that--bought votes. The paymasters included JFK's brothers, Bobby and Ted Kennedy. The primary was effectively stolen from Hubert Humphrey.

At the democratic convention, JFK came in with enough delegates for a first ballot nomination. He made a surprise choice of Lyndon Johnson as a running mate. No one, including JFK, had wanted Johnson on the ticket. LBJ was a close friend of J. Edgar Hoover, who had provided him with much information about JFK's personal life. JFK admitted in private that he chose Johnson because, "those bastards are trying to frame me."

Prior to the 1960 election, the CIA had unassailable evidence of a Nixon bribe; a copy of a check for $100,000 that had been deposited in Nixon's checking account in a California bank. This was given by a former business partner of Albert Göring (brother of Field Marshall Hermann Göring). The men in the upper echelons of the CIA disliked the dishonorable Nixon—who had publicly and vehemently disavowed ever accepting any bribes—and strongly favored JFK in the election.

In the 1960 presidential election, Joe Kennedy made a deal with Sam Giancana. This former Al Capone hit man was the most influential gangster in the powerful organized crime syndicate in Chicago. The deal was for Giancana to get out the JFK vote among the rank and file in the mob controlled unions and siphon campaign funds from the corrupt Teamster's union fund. What Giancana would get in return is unknown. JFK's stolen win in Illinois was crucial to his narrow general election victory of less than one tenth of one percent of the popular vote.

In 1960, Hoover was five years short of the mandatory retirement age for government workers. Through illegal wiretaps, he knew the election corruption went far beyond Illinois. Allegations of fraud were filed in eleven states. The day after the election, JFK announced he would reappoint Hoover as FBI director. Another JFK appointment was his brother Bobby as Attorney General. This choice was forced on Jack by his dad. With his brother the Attorney General, the investigation into election fraud was stopped in its tracks. Nothing was done after the Justice Department forwarded a report to the Attorney General that the Illinois election was stolen.

During the election, JFK railed against the "missile gap", a supposed shortcoming of U.S. nuclear missile capability compared to that of the Soviet Union. Through briefings with high ranking officials Kennedy knew no such gap existed, but it became an issue to the electorate worried about nearby Cuba. JFK was more vocal in bashing Cuba than his opponent, Vice President Richard Nixon.

Both of them knew of Eisenhower's top secret plans to assassinate Cuban leader Fidel Castro and to invade Cuba though Nixon, as VP, couldn't bash Cuba too much or it would jeopardize that plan.

Eisenhower and Nixon had hoped that the Castro overthrow would occur prior to the 1960 election. Under the direction of the Eisenhower administration, the CIA involved the Mafia in plotting the assassination of Fidel Castro as early as August 1960. The CIA contact, Johnny Rosselli (believed to be personally responsible for 13 Mafia murders), was a top man directly responsible to Sam Giancana. Giancana was supposed to arrange the Castro hit in October 1960 for Eisenhower and Nixon while he was also working to steal the election for Kennedy. Giancana made no attempt to kill Castro before the election.

Castro was preparing for an invasion based on JFK's tough talk, his awareness of invasion plans, and the expected Republican response to JFK's accusations that they were soft on Cuba. Nixon believed JFK's manipulation of the Cuba issue beat him in the election. He saw Kennedy men as "the most ruthless group of political operatives." In his memoirs, Nixon wrote: From this point on I had the wisdom and wariness of someone who had been burned by the power of the Kennedys and their money and by the license they were given by the media. I vowed that I would never again enter an election at a disadvantage by being vulnerable to them – or anyone – on the level of political tactics.

The lesson he learned appears to have led Nixon to the presidency, a re-election, and the disgrace of a forced resignation. The Kennedys planned to have Jack as president for two terms followed by Bobby as president for two terms. To move Bobby closer to the presidency for the 1968 election, the Kennedys planned to dump Vice President Lyndon Johnson from the 1964 ticket. In 1963, they supplied documents about Johnson and some of his illegal financial dealings to Republicans.

Just prior to assuming office, JFK asked CIA director Richard Bissell to create a formal capacity for political assassination. He picked up where the Eisenhower administration left off; in plotting the assassination of three foreign leaders: Fidel Castro of Cuba,

Patrice Lumumba of the Congo, and Rafael Trujillo of the Dominican Republic. Well-versed in "plausible deniability", there are no papers tying JFK to the use of the word "assassination", but the evidence for his directives is overwhelming. In mid-January 1961, Lumumba was murdered. In May 1961, Trujillo was murdered by assassins using CIA supplied weapons and ammunition.

Over a three year period, dozens of plans to assassinate Castro were developed by the Eisenhower and Kennedy administrations, the CIA, and the Mafia under Sam Giancana. None of those plans was successfully executed. On November 22, 1963, as Oswald was shooting JFK in Dallas, an undercover CIA agent was meeting with a former follower of Castro and delivering to him an assassination device for use against Castro.

There was at least one more successful assassination by unknown killers. Mafia kingpin Sam Giancana was brutally murdered in his home the night before he was to meet with a lawyer for the Church Committee, the Congressional committee established in 1975 to investigate CIA assassination plots.

JFK also continued the Eisenhower plan to invade Cuba. Though the plan was to assassinate Castro just prior to the invasion, the invasion proceeded with Castro still in control. It was a disaster. On April 17, 1961, three months after Kennedy took office, Castro's army routed the 1,400 Cuban exiles that landed at the Bay of Pigs. The Cuban exiles were recruited, trained, and armed by the CIA. On the eve of the invasion, JFK personally cancelled a scheduled second airstrike intended to destroy the Cuban air force.

The first bombing, carried out two days earlier by 8 unmarked WWII B-26's, failed to complete their mission. Kennedy thought a second attempt would more likely implicate the U.S.. His cancellation of that mission had inevitable deadly consequences when the landing proceeded into the teeth of superior air power.

Four U.S. pilots in Nicaragua secretly training Cubans ignored the President's orders not to do the second air strike and took off with two bombers on their own to fight Castro. They did heavy damage before being shot down. JFK had denied any U.S. involvement inside Cuba so he hoped the pilots were dead--hence avoiding the type of embarrassment

Eisenhower endured when downed U-2 pilot Francis Gary Powers was displayed in Moscow after Eisenhower denied any such missions were in effect. The Kennedy administration initially refused to pay the families of those pilots military pensions because of the possible political fallout of how they died. The families eventually got part of the pensions.

In public, JFK took responsibility for the Bay of Pigs fiasco. His popularity soared to an 83% approval rating. In private, he blamed the CIA and the military brass for the debacle and drew the circle of decision-makers ever tighter around himself and Bobby. Though inexperienced in foreign policy, the Kennedys began back channel communications with Soviet Premier Nikita Khruschev and spent the next 18 months negotiating foreign policy secretly. Bobby Kennedy, just 35 years old, within the first six months of JFK's presidency had become the president's legal advisor, political advisor, protector, best friend, and most influential foreign affairs advisor.

Kennedy was devastated by the humiliating failure in Cuba and sought revenge on Castro. He paused in dealing with Cuba to turn his attention elsewhere. Less than two months after the Bay of Pigs, JFK approved a series of clandestine actions to escalate the war in Vietnam.

The Kennedys continued to lean heavily on the CIA to murder Fidel Castro and overthrow his government. CIA leadership bristled at the pressure; feeling the Kennedys were carrying out a family vendetta against Castro since the

Bay of Pigs (for which the Kennedys blamed the CIA). The Mafia was again enlisted and again unsuccessful.

Attorney General Bobby Kennedy was publicly out to destroy the Mafia while privately using them for information about and dirty work in Cuba. Ultimately more than $100 million was spent by the Kennedy administration trying to assassinate Castro and overthrow his regime. In anticipation of a successful CIA and Mafia initiated revolt in Cuba (scheduled for October 1962; just before the midterm elections), the Pentagon had been ordered to begin prepositioning troops and matériel for a massive invasion of Cuba.

Hundreds of thousands of American soldiers and sailors took part in military exercises in the Caribbean. This activity was observed by Cuban and Soviet intelligence. Khruschev responded by moving Soviet missiles and launchers into Cuba triggering the missile crisis of October 1962.

The Soviets were already capable of launching missiles from submarines against any coastal U.S. city, a few more in Cuba wouldn't make much difference to U.S. security (the United States had ten times the number of warheads and missile launchers as the Soviets). Despite his awareness of these facts, President Kennedy brought the world to the brink of nuclear war. He had already mobilized a vast army of men and matériel in preparation for an invasion of Cuba.

He refused to believe U.S. intelligence reports that the Soviets were placing missiles in Cuba preferring to believe the lies he was receiving from Khruschev through their secret back channel communications. On October 16, 1962, Kennedy was given irrefutable U-2 photographic evidence of a Soviet ballistic site in Cuba. The President, angered by the Khruschev lies, eschewed diplomacy and played a terrifying game of nuclear chicken.

A year earlier, JFK approved operational status for U.S. nuclear missiles stationed in Turkey, just across the Black Sea from Russia. This deployment in the Soviet Union's backyard coupled with the continued U.S. threat to Cuba prompted Khruschev to gamble on deploying missiles in Cuba. On October 22, 1962, JFK told the American people about the Soviet missiles in Cuba. A U.S. naval blockade was established to keep Soviet ships from reaching Cuba. When the Soviet vessels reached the blockade, they stopped then returned to the Soviet Union. The public record is that JFK won the missile crisis by negotiating through strength. The resolution of the crisis was actually the result of a secret arrangement made by the U.S. to give Khruschev what he wanted; a promise that the U.S. would not invade Cuba and the removal of U.S. missiles from Turkey.

JFK was a hero to the uninformed American people. Nine days after the missile crisis ended, the Democrats had a successful midterm election (Ted Kennedy won his first term in the Senate.) The missile crisis did not deter the Kennedys in their quest to rid themselves of Castro and his regime. Anti-Castro exile groups continued to be provided with funds, arms, and intelligence by the CIA.

JFK's enduring legacy as president was the war in Vietnam. JFK had personal responsibility for the November 2, 1963, overthrow and murder of his friend Ngo Dinh Diem, the president of South Vietnam. Diem's fall is considered to be the turning point in converting a Vietnamese war into an American one with the eventual loss of 58,000 American lives and many more thousands of Vietnamese lives. In 1963, Diem had begun secret talks with North Vietnam to reach a peaceful settlement to establish a neutral regime in the South and to get the 16,500 Americans out. Kennedy did not want to lose South

Vietnam to communism (his administration had inherited the inevitable loss of Laos to communism), and that was the expected result of an agreement between North and South Vietnam. However, there was strong support for communism among the South

Vietnamese (the Viet Cong), who despised Diem's influential brother Nhu. To avoid the South settling with the North, JFK had the CIA help South Vietnamese General Minh plot a coup against Diem knowing the Vietnamese president and his brother would be murdered in the coup. JFK had planned to get the U.S. out of Vietnam, but not until after his re-election in November 1964. An earlier settlement between North and South, brokered in part by the French, would jeopardize his re-election as he would have appeared to lose another country to communism. Apparently JFK's policy was not to save South Vietnam from communism, but to delay that conversion until after his re-election.

His public proclamations of the need to stem the tide of communism lest more countries fall like dominoes drove America's foreign policy in Vietnam even after JFK's death.

In June of 1961, at a summit in Vienna between the leaders of the United States and Soviet Union, Khruschev bullied and threatened Kennedy over the status of Berlin. Many of the most capable and intelligent people in East Germany were leaving that country and communist rule through Berlin for the freedom of the West. To stop the exodus, it appeared Khruschev might take over all of Berlin by force.

The following month Kennedy announced a series of military escalations; tripling draft calls, increasing defense spending and extending tours of duty, canceling leaves, placing elements of the Strategic Air Command on heightened alert, and increasing military hardware and munitions shipments to Europe. The U.S. population rallied around him. On August 13, 1961, Khruschev had the city of Berlin split in two with the erection of the Berlin Wall. The Kennedy administration did nothing to stop its construction. The way Kennedy saw it, "Better a wall than a war."

In October 1961, Dr. Cheddi Jagan, the recently elected Prime Minister of the tiny Latin American country of British Guiana visited the White House seeking American foreign aid. As he was a socialist, he didn't get any money. Further, Kennedy ordered the CIA to unseat Prime Minister Jagan. Within months, CIA men in Guianan triggered race and labor riots which resulted in the burning of the capital. The CIA also financed new radio stations and phony newspaper stories to heighten unrest. Jagan clung to power for nearly three more years before being unseated by a strong anticommunist.

JFK sought to enlist the Soviet Union's help in destroying China's ability to create nuclear weapons. How this could be carried off was still under investigation by the Kennedy administration at JFK's death.

The Kennedy administration accomplished little in domestic legislation. For the first two years of his administration, Kennedy did not respond to calls from black leaders for passing comprehensive civil rights legislation. The Democrats held a narrow majority in Congress and many of the Democratic seats were held by Southerners who opposed such legislation. JFK needed the white Southern vote to win re-election in 1964 so his approach to civil rights was a cautious, noncommital one.

In February 1963 Kennedy submitted a watered down civil rights package to Congress, but he did little to promote its passing and it quickly expired. Anguished by the (televised) violence of Southern segregationists against those promoting civil rights, Kennedy announced on June 11, 1963 that he would send comprehensive civil rights legislation to Congress. The legislation had not yet passed when JFK was assassinated. Kennedy's efforts to cut taxes and increase funding for education died in Congress, leaving his administration with a legacy in which no significant legislation was passed. (Note: This material was drawn largely from PBS's website as Hersh had little to write about regarding legislation pushed or passed through Congress by Kennedy.)

During Kennedy's presidency, there were many potential scandals that didn't erupt. One that almost did was JFK's first marriage. John Kennedy secretly wed Palm Beach socialite Durie Malcolm in early 1947 before his high-society wedding to Jacqueline Bouvier in 1953. Joe Kennedy was livid about his son's non-Catholic wedding to a twice any divorce. Evidently JFK and Malcolm, who would marry twice more, were bigamists.

Rumors of his first marriage broke in 1957 and persisted into his presidency. They were finally put to bed when journalist Ben Bradlee, trying to ingratiate himself with the Kennedys, agreed to collaborate with the White

House in "debunking" the Durie Malcolm marriage story once and for all. His widely published story repudiated the rumor and exposed the hate groups and gossip columnists who were continuing to spread it.

Paul Corbin, a campaign worker in the Democratic National Committee was also a whistle blower. In late 1963, he collected evidence of the skimming of campaign funds by JFK's friend and appointments secretary Kenny O'Donnell. This eventually reached the president who took no action. It might have been that at least some of the skimming was going for payoffs or to pay bribes for JFK.

Kennedy's mistress, Judith Campbell Exner, in addition to transporting papers and money from JFK to Mafia kingpin Giancana, also became a conduit for bribes paid to the President. Campbell passed along money from California businessmen to JFK for three different contract proposals.

The Kennedy-Campbell relationship became known to executives at General Dynamics Corporation, one of two defense firms competing for the right to manufacture a new combat plane. The FBI, monitoring Campbell's apartment, watched as the sons of the General Dynamics executive in charge of security broke into her apartment. A few months later the Kennedy administration made the surprising choice of awarding the huge contract for the combat plane to General Dynamics over the more highly regarded Boeing. This choice was so controversial that a Senate committee was formed to investigate why it was made. The committee was not told what the FBI knew about the Campbell break-in and it shut down its investigation after JFK was assassinated. It seems quite possible that JFK was blackmailed by a desperate corporation. Billions of American taxpayer dollars would be spent on an aircraft that became renowned as a failure.

Bobby Kennedy was convinced JFK's assassination was done as part of a domestic conspiracy. He believed it had a Mafia tie-in but his connections in Chicago could not find any evidence in support of this conspiracy theory. Bobby Kennedy did not testify before the Warren Commission. He did nothing to pursue the truth behind his brother's death in 1964. The price of an investigation, making public the truth about President Kennedy and the Kennedy family was too high. By early morning the day after JFK was killed, all his papers had been moved to the most secure room of the White House complex and placed under 24 hour guard. The papers and secret recordings made by the president were screened, edited, and in some cases destroyed. The remaining papers and tapes were passed to the Kennedy presidential library for further screening.

A few days after the assassination of JFK, Jackie Kennedy related in an interview how she and her husband would lay in bed listening to a recording of the musical Camelot.

CHAPTER TWO
WATERGATE SCANDAL AND NEXON'S RESIGNATION

The Watergate scandal was one of the worst political scandals in American history. It resulted in the resignation of the president, Richard M. Nixon, under threat of impeachment and the conviction of several high-ranking members of his administration. Watergate takes its name from the break-in at the Democratic National Committee (DNC) headquarters in the Watergate apartment and office complex in Washington, D.C., in June 1972, but the scandal spread, as other illegal activities were made public.

This scandal continued until the summer of 1974, when Nixon resigned from office. The activities that would fall under the umbrella term "Watergate" began early in the Nixon administration. In 1969, Nixon approved wiretaps on the phones of government officials and reporters in an attempt to discern the source of news leaks about activities in Vietnam. In 1971 a special investigations unit was formed to plug news leaks. Dubbed the "plumbers," they broke into the office of Dr.

Also in 1971, Attorney General John N. Mitchell and John Dean, counsel to the president, met to discuss the need to obtain political intelligence for the Committee for the Re-Election of the President (CREEP). In 1972 Mitchell resigned as attorney general to accept the position as director of the committee. Shortly thereafter a plan was approved to break into the DNC headquarters to secure campaign strategy documents and other materials.

The deputy director of the committee, Jeb Magruder, later testified that Mitchell had approved a plan developed by G. Gordon Liddy, the chief plumber, to break into the Watergate complex. Mitchell denied this. It has never become clear who ordered the operation or what the conspirators hoped to find.

On June 17, 1972, five men were arrested at the DNC headquarters, including the security coordinator for the committee, James McCord. The burglars were adjusting surveillance equipment they had installed in May when they were caught. Immediately a cover-up began. Magruder destroyed documents and gave false testimony to investigators. The White House blocked an FBI inquiry, declaring that it was a national security operation undertaken by the CIA.

Mitchell resigned from his post on July 1, 1972, citing personal reasons. From the original investigation only the five burglars, plus Liddy and E. Howard Hunt, were indicted. In January all seven were convicted, but the cover-up was beginning to unravel. In March 1973 U.S. District Court judge John Sirica received a letter from McCord charging that witnesses had committed perjury at the trial. He went on to implicate Dean and Magruder.

Dean and Magruder broke under questioning and offered testimony that implicated White House and Nixon campaign officials. Dean testified that Mitchell had approved the break-in with the knowledge of White House domestic adviser John Ehrlichman and chief of staff H. R. Haldeman. In May 1973 Senator Sam Ervin (D-N.C.) opened a special Senate committee investigation into the affair.

At the same time, Attorney General Elliot L. Richardson appointed Archibald Cox, Jr., as special prosecutor to investigate the entire affair. Cox soon uncovered widespread evidence of political espionage, illegal wiretaps, and influence peddling. In July 1973 it was revealed that Nixon had secretly recorded conversations in the White House since 1971. Cox sued to obtain the tapes.

On October 20, 1973, Nixon ordered Richardson to fire the special prosecutor. Richardson refused and resigned; his assistant, William Ruckelshaus, refused and was fired. Finally, Solicitor General Robert Bork fired Cox. This became known as the "Saturday Night Massacre."

It led to calls for Nixon's impeachment, and the House of Representatives began an impeachment investigation. Following Nixon's firing of Special Prosecutor Archibald Cox, in April 1974 Nixon appointed a new special prosecutor, Leon Jaworski. Upon assuming office, Jaworski subpoenaed 64 tapes needed for the trials resulting from the indictments. Nixon refused to comply with the subpoena and proposed a compromise in which he offered to provide edited transcripts in place of the actual tapes. The 1,254 pages of transcripts contained embarrassing material, including a large number of presidential deleted expletives; they were also inaccurate and incomplete. The inaccuracies were exposed when the House Judiciary Committee released its version of the tapes.

U.S. District Court judge John Sirica, who had issued the original subpoena, rejected the transcripts as unacceptable and reissued an order for the original tapes.

James St. Clair, the head of Nixon's Watergate defense team, appealed Sirica's ruling to the Court of Appeals. Jaworski, wishing to expedite the process, appealed directly to the Supreme Court.

The Court agreed to hear the case, United States v. Nixon, on July 8, 1974. Nixon's case rested on two issues. First, the administration questioned the judiciary's jurisdiction in subpoenaing the tapes, citing separation of powers. Second, the administration cited executive privilege, the need for the protection of communication between high government officials and their advisers. The Court unanimously rejected both claims in a ruling on July 24, 1974.

On the first point, the Court cited Marbury v. Madison (1803), which affirmed the power of judicial review. As for the second point, Chief Justice Warren Burger argued that neither separation of powers nor the need for confidential communication allowed for absolute presidential privilege of immunity from the judicial process. On August 5, 1974, the transcripts were released, including one particularly damaging to Nixon, in which he discussed using the CIA to obstruct the FBI investigation of the Watergate break-in. These tapes led to the indictments of Haldeman, Ehrlichman, Mitchell, Charles Colson, Robert Mardian, and Kenneth Parkinson for conspiring to cover up the Watergate scandal. Colson pleaded guilty to charges stemming from the Fielding break-in and the cover-up charges were dropped. Ultimately, Haldeman, Ehrlichman, and Mitchell were found guilty.

Facing a congressional vote on impeachment, Nixon announced his resignation on the evening of August 8, 1974, to be effective the next day at noon.

The Watergate scandal was a major political scandal that occurred in the United States during the early 1970s, following a break-in by five men at the Democratic National Committee (DNC) headquarters at the Watergate office complex in Washington, D.C. on June 17, 1972, and President Richard Nixon's administration's subsequent attempt to cover up its involvement. After the five burglars were caught, and the conspiracy was discovered—chiefly through the work of a few journalists, Congressional staffers and an election-finance watchdog official. Watergate was investigated by the United States Congress. Meanwhile, Nixon's administration resisted its probes, which led to a constitutional crisis.

The term Watergate, by metonymy, has come to encompass an array of clandestine and often illegal activities undertaken by members of the Nixon administration. Those activities included such dirty tricks as bugging the offices of political opponents and people of whom Nixon or his officials were suspicious. Nixon and his close aides also ordered investigations of activist groups and political figures, using the Federal Bureau of Investigation (FBI), the Central Intelligence Agency (CIA), and the Internal Revenue Service (IRS) as political weapons. The scandal led to the discovery of multiple abuses of power by members of the Nixon administration, an impeachment process against the president that led to articles of impeachment, and Nixon's resignation. The scandal also resulted in the indictment of 69 people, with trials or pleas resulting in 48 being found guilty, many of whom were top Nixon officials.

The affair began with the arrest of five men for breaking into the DNC headquarters at the Watergate complex on Saturday, June 17, 1972. The FBI investigated and discovered a connection between cash found on the burglars and a slush fund used by the Committee for the Re-Election of the President (CRP), the official organization of Nixon's campaign. In July 1973, evidence mounted against the president's staff, including testimony provided by former staff members in an investigation conducted by the Senate Watergate Committee. The investigation revealed that Nixon had a tape-recording system in his offices and that he had recorded many conversations.

After a series of court battles, the Supreme Court of the United States unanimously ruled that the president was obligated to release the tapes to government investigators. The tapes revealed that Nixon had attempted to cover up activities that took place after the break-in, and to use federal officials to deflect the investigation. Facing virtually certain impeachment in the House of Representatives and equally certain conviction by the Senate, Nixon resigned the presidency on August 9, 1974, preventing the House from impeaching him. On September 8, 1974, his successor Gerald Ford, pardoned him.

The name "Watergate" and the suffix "-gate" have since become synonymous with political and non-political scandals in the United States, and some other parts of the world.

On January 27, 1972, G. Gordon Liddy, Finance Counsel for the Committee for the Re-Election of the President (CRP) and former aide to John Ehrlichman, presented a campaign intelligence plan to CRP's Acting Chairman Jeb Stuart Magruder, Attorney General John Mitchell, and Presidential Counsel John Dean that involved extensive illegal activities against the Democratic Party. According to Dean, this marked "the opening scene of the worst political scandal of the twentieth century and the beginning of the end of the Nixon presidency".

Mitchell viewed the plan as unrealistic. Two months later, he was alleged to have approved a reduced version of the plan, including burgling the Democratic National Committee's (DNC) headquarters at the Watergate Complex in Washington, D.C. — ostensibly to photograph campaign documents and install listening devices in telephones. Liddy was nominally in charge of the operation, but has since insisted that he was duped by both Dean and at least two of his subordinates, which included former CIA officers E. Howard Hunt and James McCord, the latter of whom was serving as then-CRP Security

Coordinator after John Mitchell had by then resigned as Attorney General to become the CRP chairman.

In May, McCord assigned former FBI agent Alfred C. Baldwin III to carry out the wiretapping and monitor the telephone conversations afterward. McCord testified that he selected Baldwin's name from a registry published by the FBI's Society of Former Special Agentsto work for the Committee to re-elect President Nixon. Baldwin first served as bodyguard to Martha Mitchell - John Mitchell's wife, who was living in Washington. Baldwin accompanied Martha Mitchell to Chicago.

On May 11, McCord arranged for Baldwin, who investigative reporter Jim Hougan described as "somehow special and perhaps well known to McCord", to stay at the Howard Johnson's motel across the street from the Watergate complex. Room 419 was booked in the name of McCord's company. At behest of G. Gordon Liddy and E. Howard Hunt, McCord and his team of burglars prepared for their first Watergate break-in, which began on May 28.

Two phones inside the DNC headquarters' offices were said to have been wiretapped. One was Robert

Spencer Oliver's phone. At the time, Oliver was working as the executive director of the Association of State Democratic Chairmen. The other phone belonged to DNC chairman Larry O'Brien. The FBI found no evidence that O'Brien's phone was bugged; however, it was determined that an effective listening device was installed in Oliver's phone.

Despite successfully installing the listening devices, the Committee agents soon determined that they needed repairs. They planned a second "burglary" in order to take care of the situation.

Sometime after midnight on Saturday, June 17, 1972, Watergate Complex security guard Frank Wills noticed tape covering the latches on some of the complex's doors leading from the underground parking garage to several offices, which allowed the doors to close but stay unlocked. He removed the tape, thinking nothing of it. When he returned a short time later and discovered that someone had retaped the locks, he called the police.

Responding to the call was an unmarked car with three plainclothes officers working the overnight "bum squad" - dressed as hippies and on the lookout for drug deals and other street crimes. The burglars' sentry across the street, Alfred Baldwin, was distracted watching TV and didn't notice the arrival of the police car in front of the hotel or the plainclothes officers investigating the DNC's sixth floor suite of 29 offices. By the time Baldwin noticed unusual activity on the sixth floor and radioed the burglars, it was already too late.

The police apprehended five men, later identified as Virgilio Gonzalez, Bernard Barker, James McCord, Eugenio Martínez, and Frank Sturgis. They were charged with attempted burglary and attempted interception of telephone and other communications. The Washington Post reported that "police found lock-picks and door jimmies, almost $2,300 in cash, most of it in $100 bills with the serial numbers in sequence.   a short wave receiver that could pick up police calls, 40 rolls of unexposed film, two 35 millimeter cameras and three pen-sized tear gas guns.

The following morning, Sunday, June 18th, G. Gordon Liddy called Jeb Magruder in Los Angeles and informed him that "the four men arrested with McCord were Cuban freedom fighters, whom Howard Hunt recruited." Initially, Nixon's organization and the White House quickly went to work to cover up the crime and any evidence that might have damaged the president and his reelection.

Three months later, on September 15th, a grand jury indicted the five office burglars, as well as Hunt and Liddy, for conspiracy, burglary, and violation of federal wiretapping laws. The burglars were tried by a jury, with Judge John Sirica officiating, and pled guilty or were convicted on January 30, 1973.

E. Howard Hunt and G. Gordon Liddy, who led the Watergate break-in team, were stationed in a Watergate Hotel room while the burglary was underway. A lookout was posted across the street at the Howard Johnson Hotel .Bruce Givner was a 21-year old intern working at the DNC's 6th floor offices in the Watergate Hotel Complex when his prolonged stay on that floor precluded the burglars from entering the offices to correct their earlier wiretap work. During the break-in, Hunt and Liddy would remain in contact with each other and with the burglars by radio. These Chapstick tubes outfitted with tiny microphones were later discovered in Hunt's White House office safe.

Within hours of the burglars' arrest, the FBI discovered E. Howard Hunt's name in Barker and

Martínez's address books. Nixon administration officials were concerned because Hunt and Liddy were also involved in a separate secret activity known as the "White House Plumbers", which was set up to stop security "leaks" and investigate other sensitive security matters. Dean later testified that top Nixon aide John Ehrlichman ordered him to "deep six" the contents of Howard Hunt's White House safe. Ehrlichman subsequently denied this. In the end, Dean and the FBI's Acting Director L. Patrick Gray (in separate operations) destroyed the evidence from Hunt's safe.

Nixon's own reaction to the break-in, at least initially, was one of skepticism. Watergate prosecutor James Neal was sure that Nixon had not known in advance of the break-in. As evidence, he cited a conversation taped on June 23 between the President and his Chief of Staff, H. R. Haldeman, in which Nixon asked, "Who was the asshole that did?" However, Nixon subsequently ordered Haldeman to have the CIA block the FBI's investigation into the source of the funding for the burglary.

A few days later, Nixon's Press Secretary, Ron Ziegler, described the event as "a third- rate burglary attempt." On August 29, at a news conference, Nixon stated that Dean had conducted a thorough investigation of the incident, when Dean had actually not conducted any investigations at all. Nixon furthermore said, "I can say categorically that no one in the White House staff, no one in this Administration, presently employed, was involved in this very bizarre incident." On September 15, Nixon congratulated Dean, saying, "The way you've handled it, it seems to me, has been very skillful, because you—putting your fingers in the dikes every time that leaks have sprung here and sprung there."

On June 19, 1972, the press reported that one of the Watergate burglars was a Republican Party security aide. Former Attorney General John Mitchell, who at the time was the head of the CRP, denied any involvement with the Watergate break-in or knowledge of the five burglars. On August 1, a $25,000 ($146,000 today) cashier's check was found to have been deposited in the US and Mexican bank accounts of one of the Watergate burglars, Bernard Barker. Made out to the Finance Committee of the Committee to Reelect the President, the check was a 1972 campaign donation by Kenneth H. Dahlberg. This money (and several other checks which had been lawfully donated to the CRP) had been directly used to finance the burglary/wiretapping team's expenses, hardware, and supplies.

Mr. Barker's multiple national and international businesses all had separate bank accounts, which he was found to have attempted to use to disguise the true origin of the monies being paid to the burglars. The donor's checks demonstrated the burglar's' direct link to the finance committee of the CRP.

Donations totaling $86,000 ($503,000 today) were made by individuals who thought they were making private donations by certified and cashier's checks for the president's re-election. Investigators' examination of the bank records of a Miami company run by Watergate burglar Barker revealed an account controlled by him personally had deposited a check and then transferred it (through the Federal Reserve Check Clearing System.

The banks that had originated the checks were keen to ensure the depository institution used by Barker had acted properly in ensuring the checks had been received and endorsed by the check's payee, before its acceptance for deposit in Bernard Barker's account. Only in this way would the issuing banks not be held liable for the unauthorized and improper release of funds from their customers' accounts.

The investigation by the FBI, which cleared Barker's bank of fiduciary malfeasance, led to the direct implication of members of the CRP, to whom the checks had been delivered. Those individuals were the Committee bookkeeper and its treasure, Hugh Sloan.

As a private organization, the committee followed normal business practice in allowing only duly authorized individuals to accept and endorse checks on behalf of the Committee. No financial institution could accept or process a check on behalf of the committee unless a duly authorized individual endorsed it. The checks deposited into Barker's bank account were endorsed by Committee treasurer Hugh Sloan, who was authorized by the Finance Committee. However, once Sloan had endorsed a check made payable to the Committee, he had a legal and fiduciary responsibility to see that the check was deposited only into the accounts named on the check. Sloan failed to do that. When confronted with the potential charge of federal bank fraud, he revealed that committee deputy director Jeb Magruder and finance director Maurice Stans had directed him to give the money to Gordon Liddy.

Liddy, in turn, gave the money to Barker, and attempted to hide its origin. Barker tried to disguise the funds by depositing them into accounts in banks outside of the United States. What Barker, Liddy, and Sloan did not know was that the complete records of all such transactions were held for roughly six months. Barker's use of foreign banks in April and May 1972, to deposit checks and withdraw the funds via cashier's checks and money orders, resulted in the banks keeping the entire transaction records until October and November 1972.

All five Watergate burglars were directly or indirectly tied to the 1972 CRP, thus causing Judge Sirica to suspect a conspiracy involving higher-echelon government officials.

On September 29, 1972, the press reported that John Mitchell, while serving as Attorney General, controlled a secret Republican fun used to finance intelligence-gathering against the Democrats. On October 10, the FBI reported the Watergate break-in was part of a massive campaign of political spying and sabotage on behalf of the Nixon re-election committee. Despite these revelations, Nixon's campaign was never seriously jeopardized; on November 7, the President was re-elected in one of the biggest landslides in American political history.

The connection between the break-in and the re-election committee was highlighted by media coverage—in particular, investigative coverage by The Washington Post, Time, and The New York Times. The coverage dramatically increased publicity and consequent political and legal repercussions. Relying heavily upon anonymous sources, Post reporters Bob Woodward and Carl Bernstein uncovered information suggesting that knowledge of the break-in, and attempts to cover it up, led deeply into the upper reaches of th Justice Department, FBI, CIA, and the White House. Woodward and Bernstein interviewed Judy Hoback Miller, the bookkeeper for Nixon, who revealed to them information about the mishandling of funds and records being destroyed.[

Chief among the Post's anonymous sources was an individual whom Woodward and Bernstein had nicknamed Deep Throat; 33 years later, in 2005, the informant was identified as William Mark Felt, Sr., deputy director of the FBI during that period of the 1970s, something Woodward later confirmed. Felt met secretly with Woodward several times, telling him of Howard Hunt's involvement with the Watergate break-in, and that the White House staff regarded the stakes in Watergate as extremely high.

Felt warned Woodward that the FBI wanted to know where he and other reporters were getting their information, as they were uncovering a wider web of crimes than the FBI first disclosed. All of the secret meetings between Woodward and Felt took place at an underground parking garage somewhere in Rosslyn over a period from June 1972 to January 1973. Prior to resigning from the FBI on June 22, 1973, Felt also anonymously planted leaks about Watergate with Time magazine, the Washington Daily News and other publications.

During this early period, most of the media failed to grasp the full implications of the scandal, and concentrated reporting on other topics related to the 1972 presidential election. Most outlets ignored or downplayed Woodward and Bernstein's scoops; the crosstown Washington Star-News and the Los Angeles Times even ran stories incorrectly discrediting the Post's articles. After the Post revealed that H.R. Haldeman made payments from the secret fund, newspapers like the Chicago Tribune and the Philadelphia Inquirer failed to publish the information, but did publish the White House's denial of the story the following day.[39] The White House also sought to isolate the Post's coverage by tirelessly attacking that newspaper while declining to criticize other damaging stories about the scandal from the New York Times and Time Magazine.

After it was learned that one of the convicted burglars wrote to Judge Sirica alleging a high-level cover-up, the media shifted its focus. Time magazine described Nixon as undergoing "daily hell and very little trust." The distrust between the press and the Nixon administration was mutual and greater than usual due to lingering dissatisfaction with events from the Vietnam War. At the same time, public distrust of the media was polled at more than 40%.

Nixon and top administration officials discussed using government agencies to "get" (or retaliate against) those they perceived as hostile media organizations. Such actions had been taken before. At the request of Nixon's White House in 1969, the FBI tapped the phones of five reporters. In 1971, the White House requested an audit of the tax return of the editor of Newsday, after he wrote a series of articles about the financial dealings of Charles "Bebe" Rebozo, a friend of Nixon.

The Administration and its supporters accused the media of making "wild accusations", putting too much emphasis on the story, and of having a liberal bias against the Administration. Nixon said in a May 1974 interview with supporter Baruch Korff that if he had followed the liberal policies that he thought the media preferred, "Watergate would have been a blip."

The media noted that most of the reporting turned out to be accurate; the competitive nature of the media guaranteed widespread coverage of the far-reaching political scandal. Applications to journalism schools reached an all-time high in 1974.

Rather than ending with the conviction and sentencing to prison of the five Watergate burglars on January 30, 1973, the investigation into the break-in and the Nixon Administration's involvement grew broader. Nixon's conversations in late March and all of April 1973 revealed that not only did he know he needed to remove Haldeman, Ehrlichman, and Dean to gain distance from them, but he had to do so in a way that was least likely to incriminate him and his presidency. Nixon created a new conspiracy—to effect a cover- up of the cover-up—which began in late March 1973 and became fully formed in May and June 1973, operating until his presidency ended on August 9, 1974.[42] On March 23, 1973, Judge Sirica read the court a letter from Watergate burglar James McCord, who alleged that perjury had been committed in the Watergate trial, and defendants had been pressured to remain silent. Trying to make them talk, Sirica gave Hunt and two burglars provisional sentences of up to 40 years.

On March 28, on Nixon's orders, aide John Ehrlichman told Attorney General Richard Klein said that nobody in the White House had prior knowledge of the burglary. On April 13, Magruder told U.S. attorneys that he had perjured himself during the burglars' trial, and implicated John Dean and John Mitchell.

John Dean believed that he, Mitchell, Ehrlichman, and Haldeman could go to the prosecutors, tell the truth, and save the presidency. Dean wanted to protect the president and have his four closest men take the fall for telling the truth. During the critical meeting between Dean and Nixon on April 15, 1973, Dean was totally unaware of the president's depth of knowledge and involvement in the Watergate cover-up. It was during this meeting that Dean felt that he was being recorded. He wondered if this was due to the way Nixon was speaking, as if he were trying to prod attendees' recollections of earlier conversations about fundraising. Dean mentioned this observation while testifying to the Senate Committee on Watergate, exposing the thread of what were taped conversations that would unravel the fabric of the conspiracy.

Two days later, Dean told Nixon that he had been cooperating with the U.S. attorneys. On that same day, U.S. attorneys told Nixon that Haldeman, Ehrlichman, Dean, and other White House officials were implicated in the cover-up. On April 30, Nixon asked for the resignation of Haldeman and Ehrlichman, two of his most influential aides. They were later both indicted, convicted, and ultimately sentenced to prison.

He asked for the resignation of Attorney General Kleindienst, to ensure no one could claim that his innocent friendship with Haldeman and Ehrlichman could be construed as a conflict. He fired White House Counsel John Dean, who went on to testify before the Senate Watergate Committee and said that he believed and suspected the conversations in the Oval Office were being taped. This information became the bombshell that helped force Richard Nixon to resign rather than be impeached.

Writing from prison for New West and New York magazines in 1977, Ehrlichman claimed Nixon had offered him a large sum of money, which he declined.

The President announced the resignations in an address to the American people:

In one of the most difficult decisions of my Presidency, I accepted the resignations of two of my closest associates in the White House, Bob Haldeman, John Ehrlichman, two of the finest public servants it has been my privilege to know. Because Attorney General Kleindienst, though a distinguished public servant, my personal friend for 20 years, with no personal involvement whatsoever in this matter has been a close personal and professional associate of some of those who are involved in this case, he and I both felt that it was also necessary to name a new Attorney General. The Counsel to the President, John Dean, has also resigned.

On the same day, Nixon appointed a new attorney general, Elliot Richardson, and gave him authority to designate a special counsel for the Watergate investigation who would be independent of the regular Justice Department hierarchy. In May 1973, Richardson named Archibald Cox to the position.

On February 7, 1973, the United States Senate voted 77-to-0 to approve 93 S .Res. 60 and establish a select committee to investigate Watergate, with Sam Ervin named chairman the next day. The hearings held by the Senate committee, in which Dean and other former administration officials testified, were broadcast from May 17 to August 7, 1973. The three major networks of the time agreed to take turns covering the hearings live, each network thus maintaining coverage of the hearings every third day, starting with ABC on May 17 and ending with NBC on August 7.

On Friday, July 13, 1973, during a preliminary interview, deputy minority counsel Donald Sanders asked White House assistant Alexander Butterfield if there was any type of recording system in the White House. Butterfield said he was reluctant to answer, but finally stated there was a new system in the White House that automatically recorded everything in the Oval Office, the Cabinet Room and others, as well as Nixon's private office in the Old Executive Office Building.

On Monday, July 16, 1973, in front of a live, televised audience, chief minority counsel Fred Thompson asked Butterfield whether he was "aware of the installation of any listening devices in the Oval Office of the President." Butterfield's revelation of the taping system transformed the Watergate investigation. Cox immediately subpoenaed the tapes, as did the Senate, but Nixon refused to release them, citing his executive privilege as president, and ordered Cox to drop his subpoena. Cox refused.

On October 20, 1973, after Cox refused to drop the subpoena, Nixon ordered Attorney General Elliot Richardson to fire the special prosecutor. Richardson resigned in protest rather than carry out the order. Nixon then ordered Deputy Attorney General William Ruckelshaus to fire Cox, but Ruckelshaus also resigned rather than fire him. Nixon's search for someone in the Justice Department willing to fire Cox ended with the Solicitor General Robert Bork. Though Bork said he believed Nixon's order was valid and appropriate, he considered resigning to avoid being "perceived as a man who did the President's bidding to save my job." Bork carried out the presidential order and dismissed the special prosecutor.

These actions met considerable public criticism. Responding to the allegations of possible wrongdoing, in front of 400 Associated Press managing editors at Disney's Contemporary Resort on November 17, 1973, Nixon stated emphatically, "I'm not a crook." He needed to allow Bork to appoint a new special prosecutor; Bork chose Leon Jaworski to continue the investigation.

On March 1, 1974, a grand jury in Washington, D.C., indicted several former aides of Nixon, who became known as the "Watergate Seven"—H. R. Haldeman, John Ehrlichman, John N. Mitchell, Charles Colson, Gordon C. Strachan, Robert Mardian, and Kenneth Parkinson—for conspiring to hinder the Watergate investigation. The grand jury secretly named Nixon as an unindicted co- conspirator. The special prosecutor dissuaded them from an indictment of Nixon, arguing that a President can only be indicted after he leaves office.

John Dean, Jeb Stuart Magruder, and other figures had already pled guilty. On April 5, 1974, Dwight Chapin, the former Nixon appointments secretary, was convicted of lying to the grand jury. Two days later, the same grand jury indicted Ed Reinecke, the Republican Lieutenant Governor of California, on three charges of perjury before the Senate committee.

The Nixon administration struggled to decide what materials to release. All parties involved agreed that all pertinent information should be released. Whether to release unedited profanity and vulgarity divided his advisers. His legal team favored releasing the tapes unedited, while Press Secretary Ron Ziegler preferred using an edited version where "expletive deleted" would replace the raw material. After several weeks of debate, they decided to release an edited version. Nixon announced the release of the transcripts in a speech to the nation on April 29, 1974. Nixon noted that any audio pertinent to national security information could be redacted from the released tapes.

Initially, Nixon gained a positive reaction for his speech. As people read the transcripts over the next couple of weeks, however, former supporters among the public, media and political community called for Nixon's resignation or impeachment. Vice President Gerald Ford said, "While it may be easy to delete characterization from the printed page, we cannot delete characterization from people's minds with a wave of the hand." The Senate Republican Leader Hugh Scott said the transcripts revealed a "deplorable, disgusting, shabby, and immoral" performance on the part of the President and his former aides. The House Republican Leader John Jacob Rhodes agreed with Scott, and Rhodes recommended that if

Nixon's position continued to deteriorate, he "ought to consider resigning as a possible option."

The editors of The Chicago Tribune, a newspaper that had supported Nixon, wrote, "He is humorless to the point of being inhumane. He is devious. He is vacillating. He is profane. He is willing to be led. He displays dismaying gaps in knowledge. He is suspicious of his staff. His loyalty is minimal."

The Providence Journal wrote, "Reading the transcripts is an emetic experience; one comes away feeling unclean." This newspaper continued that, while the transcripts may not have revealed an indictable offense, they showed Nixon contemptuous of the United States, its institutions, and its people. According to Time magazine, the Republican Party leaders in the Western U.S. felt that while there remained a significant number of Nixon loyalists in the party, the majority believed that Nixon should step down as quickly as possible. They were disturbed by the bad language and the coarse, vindictive tone of the conversations in the transcripts.

The issue of access to the tapes went to the United States Supreme Court. On July 24, 1974, in United States v. Nixon, the Court ruled unanimously (8 to 0) that claims of executive privilege over the tapes were void. The Court ordered the President to release the tapes to the special prosecutor. On July 30, 1974, Nixon complied with the order and released the subpoenaed tapes to the public.

The tapes revealed several crucial conversations that took place between the President and his counsel, John Dean, on March 21, 1973. In this conversation, Dean summarized many aspects of the Watergate case, and focused on the subsequent cover-up, describing it as a "cancer on the presidency." The burglary team was being paid hush money for their silence and Dean stated: "That's the most troublesome post-thing, because Bob [Haldeman] is involved in that; John [Ehrlichman] is involved in that; I am involved in that; Mitchell is involved in that. And that's an obstruction of justice." Dean continued, saying that Howard Hunt was blackmailing the White House demanding money immediately. Nixon replied that the money should be paid: "... just looking at the immediate problem, don't you have to have—handle Hunt's financial situation damn soon? ...you've got to keep the cap on the bottle that much, in order to have any options."

At the time of the initial congressional proceedings, it was not known if Nixon had known and approved of the payments to the Watergate defendants earlier than this conversation. Nixon's conversation with Haldeman on August 1, 1972, is one of several that establishes he did. Nixon said: "Well ... they have to be paid. That's all there is to that. They have to be paid." During the congressional debate on impeachment, some believed that impeachment required a criminally indictable offense. Nixon's agreement to make the blackmail payments was regarded as an affirmative act to obstruct justice.

On December 7, 1973, investigators found that an 18 1/2-minute portion of one recorded tape had been erased. Rose Mary Woods, Nixon's longtime personal secretary, said she had accidentally erased the tape by pushing the wrong pedal on her tape player when answering the phone. The press ran photos of the set-up, showing that it was unlikely for Woods to answer the phone while keeping her foot on the pedal. Later forensic analysis in 2003 determined that the tape had been erased in several segments—at least five, and perhaps as many as nine.

Nixon's position was becoming increasingly precarious. On February 6, 1974, the House of Representatives approved H. Res. 803 giving the Judiciary Committee authority to investigate impeachment of the

President. On July 27, 1974, the House Judiciary Committee voted 27-to-11 to recommend the first article of impeachment against the president: obstruction of justice. The Committee recommended the second article, abuse of power, on July 29, 1974. The next day, on July 30, 1974, the Committee recommended the third article: contempt of Congress. On August 20, 1974, the House authorized the printing of the Committee report H. Rep. 93–1305, which included the text of the resolution impeaching Nixon and set forth articles of impeachment against him.

On August 5, 1974, the White House released a previously unknown audio tape from June 23, 1972. Recorded only a few days after the break-in, it documented the initial stages of the cover-up: it revealed Nixon and Haldeman had conducted a meeting in the Oval Office where they discussed how to stop the FBI from continuing their investigation of the break-in, as they recognized that there was a high risk that their position in the scandal may be revealed.

Haldeman introduced the topic as follows: the Democratic break-in thing, we're back to the—in the, the problem area because the FBI is not under control, because

Gray doesn't exactly know how to control them, and they have ... their investigation is now leading into some productive areas ... and it goes in some directions we don't want it to go.

After explaining how the money from CRP was traced to the burglars, Haldeman explained to Nixon the cover-up plan: "the way to handle this now is for us to have Walters [CIA] call Pat Gray [FBI] and just say, 'Stay the hell out of this ... this is ah, business here we don't want you to go any further on it.'

Nixon approved the plan, and after he was given more information about the involvement of his campaign in the break-in, he told Haldeman: "All right, fine, I understand it all. We won't second-guess Mitchell and the rest." Returning to the use of the CIA to obstruct the FBI, he instructed Haldeman: "You call them in. Good. Good deal. Play it tough. That's the way they play it and that's the way we are going to play it."

Nixon denied that this constituted an obstruction of justice, as his instructions ultimately resulted in the CIA truthfully reporting to the FBI that there were no national security issues. Nixon urged the FBI to press forward with the investigation when they expressed concern about interference.

Before the release of this tape, Nixon had denied any involvement in the scandal. He claimed that there were no political motivations in his instructions to the CIA, and claimed he had no knowledge before March 21, 1973, of involvement by senior campaign officials such as John Mitchell. The contents of this tape persuaded Nixon's own lawyers, Fred Buzhardt and James St. Clair, that "the President had lied to the nation, to his closest aides, and to his own lawyers—for more than two years." The tape, which Barber Conable referred to as a "smoking gun," proved that Nixon had been involved in the cover-up from the beginning.

The release of the "smoking gun" tape destroyed Nixon politically. The ten congressmen who had voted against all three articles of impeachment in the House Judiciary Committee announced they would all support the impeachment article accusing Nixon of obstructing justice when the articles came up before the full House.

On the night of August 7, 1974, Senators Barry Goldwater and Hugh Scott and Congressman John Jacob Rhodes met with Nixon in the Oval Office. Scott and

Rhodes were the Republican leaders in the Senate and House, respectively; Goldwater was brought along as an elder statesman. The three lawmakers told Nixon that his support in Congress had all but disappeared. Rhodes told Nixon that he would face certain impeachment when the articles came up for vote in the full House. Goldwater and Scott told the president that there were enough votes in the Senate to convict him, and that no more than 15 Senators were willing to vote for acquittal.

Realizing that he had no chance of staying in office and that public opinion was not in his favor, Nixon decided to resign. In a nationally televised address from the Oval Office on the evening of August 8, 1974, the president said, in part:

In all the decisions I have made in my public life, I have always tried to do what was best for the Nation. Throughout the long and difficult period of Watergate, I have felt it was my duty to persevere, to make every possible effort to complete the term of office to which you elected me. In the past few days, however, it has become evident to me that I no longer have a strong enough political base in the Congress to justify continuing that effort. As long as there was such a base, I felt strongly that it was necessary to see the constitutional process through to its conclusion, that to do otherwise would be unfaithful to the spirit of that deliberately difficult process and a dangerously destabilizing precedent for the future….

I would have preferred to carry through to the finish whatever the personal agony it would have involved, and my family unanimously urged me to do so. But the interest of the Nation must always come before any personal considerations. From the discussions I have had with Congressional and other leaders, I have concluded that because of the Watergate matter I might not have the support of the Congress that I would consider necessary to back the very difficult decisions and carry out the duties of this office in the way the interests of the Nation would require.

I have never been a quitter. To leave office before my term is completed is abhorrent to every instinct in my body. But as President, I must put the interest of America first. America needs a full-time President and a full-time Congress, particularly at this time with problems we face at home and abroad. To continue to fight through the months ahead for my personal vindication would almost totally absorb the time and attention of both the President and the Congress in a period when our entire focus should be on the great issues of peace abroad and prosperity without inflation at home. Therefore, I shall resign the Presidency effective at noon tomorrow. Vice President Ford will be sworn in as President at that hour in this office.

The morning that his resignation took effect, the President, with Mrs. Nixon and their family, said farewell to the White House staff in the East Room. A helicopter carried them from the White House to Andrews Air Force Base in Maryland. Nixon later wrote that he thought, "As the helicopter moved on to Andrews, I found myself thinking not of the past, but of the future. What could I do now?" At Andrews, he and his family boarded Air Force One to El Toro Marine Corps Air Station in California, and then were transported to his home La Casa Pacifica in San Clemente.

With Nixon's resignation, Congress dropped its impeachment proceedings. Criminal prosecution was still a possibility both on the federal and state level. Nixon was succeeded by Vice President Gerald Ford as President.

Nixon proclaimed his innocence until his death in 1994. In his official response to the pardon, he said that he "was wrong in not acting more decisively and more forthrightly in dealing with Watergate, particularly when it reached the stage of judicial proceedings and grew from a political scandal into a national tragedy."

Some commentators have argued that pardoning Nixon contributed to President Ford's loss of the presidential election of 1976. Allegations of a secret deal made with Ford, promising a pardon in return for Nixon's resignation, led Ford to testify before the House Judiciary Committee on October 17, 1974.

In his autobiography A Time to Heal, Ford wrote about a meeting he had with Nixon's Chief of Staff, Alexander Haig. Haig was explaining what he and Nixon's staff thought were Nixon's only options. He could try to ride out the impeachment and fight against conviction in the Senate all the way, or he could resign. His options for resigning were to delay his resignation until further along in the impeachment process, to try and settle for a censure vote in Congress, or to pardon himself and then resign.

Haig told Ford that some of Nixon's staff suggested that Nixon could agree to resign in return for an agreement that Ford would pardon him.

Haig emphasized that these weren't his suggestions. He didn't identify the staff members and he made it very clear that he wasn't recommending any one option over another. What he wanted to know was whether or not my overall assessment of the situation agreed with his [emphasis in original] ... Next he asked if I had any suggestions as to courses of actions for the President. I didn't think it would be proper for me to make any recommendations at all, and I told him so - .Gerald Ford, A Time to Heal

Charles Colson pled guilty to charges concerning the Daniel Ellsberg case; in exchange, the indictment against him for covering up the activities of the Committee to Re-elect the President was dropped, as it was against Strachan. The remaining five members of the Watergate Seven indicted in March went on trial in October 1974. On January 1, 1975, all but Parkinson were found guilty. In 1976, the U.S. Court of Appeals ordered a new trial for Mardian; subsequently, charges against him were dropped.

Haldeman, Ehrlichman, and Mitchell exhausted their appeals in 1977. Ehrlichman entered prison in 1976, followed by the other two in 1977. Since Nixon and many senior officials involved in Watergate were lawyers, the scandal severely tarnished the public image of the legal profession.

To defuse public demand for direct federal regulation of lawyers (as opposed to leaving it in the hands of state bar associations or courts), the American Bar Association (ABA) launched two major reforms. First, the ABA decided that its existing Model Code of Professional Responsibility (promulgated 1969) was a failure. In 1983 it replaced it with the Model Rules of Professional Conduct. The MRPC have been adopted in part or in whole by 49 states (and is being considered by the last one, California). Its preamble contains an emphatic reminder that the legal profession can remain self-governing only if lawyers behave properly. Second, the ABA promulgated a requirement that law students at ABA-approved law schools take a course in professional responsibility (which means they must study the MRPC). The requirement remains in effect.

On June 24 and 25, 1975, Nixon gave secret testimony to a grand jury. According to news reports at the time, Nixon answered questions about the18 1/2-minute tape gap, altering White House tape transcripts turned over to the House Judiciary Committee, using the Internal Revenue Service to harass political enemies, and a $100,000 contribution from billionaire Howard Hughes. Aided by the Public Citizen Litigation Group, the historian Stanley Kutler, who has written several books about Nixon and Watergate and had successfully sued for the 1996 public release of the Nixon White House tapes, sued for release of the transcripts of the Nixon grand jury testimony.

On July 29, 2011, U.S. District Judge Royce Lamberth granted Kutler's request, saying historical interests trumped privacy especially considering that Nixon and other key figures were deceased, and most of the surviving figures had testified under oath, have been written about, or were interviewed. The transcripts were not immediately released pending the government's decision on whether to appeal. They were released in their entirety on November 10, 2011, although the names of people still alive were redacted.

Texas A&M University–Central Texas professor Luke Nichter wrote the chief judge of the federal court in Washington to release hundreds of pages of sealed records of the Watergate Seven. In June 2012 the U.S. Department of Justice wrote the court that it would not object to their release with some exceptions. On November 2, 2012, Watergate trial records for G. Gordon Liddy and James McCord were ordered unsealed by Federal Judge Royce Lamberth.

According to Thomas J. Johnson, a professor of journalism at University of Texas at Austin, Secretary of State Henry Kissinger predicted during Nixon's final days that history would remember Nixon as a great president and that Watergate would be relegated to a "minor footnote."

When Congress investigated the scope of the president's legal powers, it belatedly found that consecutive presidential administrations had declared the United States to be in a continuous open-ended state of emergency since 1950. Congress enacted the National Emergencies Act in 1976 to regulate such declarations. The Watergate scandal left such an impression on the national and international consciousness that many scandals since then have been labeled with the sfuifx "-gate".

Disgust with the revelations about Watergate, the Republican Party, and Nixon strongly affected results of the November 1974 Senate and House elections, which took place three months after Nixon's resignation. The Democrats gained five seats in the Senate and forty-nine in the House (the newcomers were nicknamed "Watergate Babies"). Congress passed legislation that changed campaign financing, to amend the Freedom of Information Act, as well as to require financial disclosures by key government officials (via the Ethics in Government Act). Other types of disclosures, such as releasing recent income tax forms, became expected, though not legally required. Presidents since Franklin D. Roosevelt had recorded many of their conversations but the practice purportedly ended after Watergate. In 1977, Nixon arranged an interview with British journalist David Frost in the hopes of improving his legacy. Based on a previous interview in 1968, he believed that Frost would be an easy interviewer and was taken aback by Frost's.

In the aftermath of Watergate, "follow the money" became part of the American lexicon and is widely believed to have been uttered by Mark Felt to Woodward and Bernstein. The phrase was never used in the 1974 book

All the President's Men and did not become associated with it until the movie of the same name was released in 1976.

The parking garage where Woodward and Felt met in Rosslyn still stands. Its significance was noted by Arlington County with a historical marker in 2011. In 2017 it was announced that the garage would be demolished as part of construction of an apartment building on the site; the developers announced that the site's significance would be memorialized within the new complex.

Despite the enormous impact of the Watergate scandal, the purpose of the break-in of the DNC offices has never been conclusively established. Records from the United States v. Liddy trial, made public in 2013, showed that four of the five burglars testified that they were told the campaign operation hoped to find evidence that linked Cuban funding to Democratic campaigns. The longtime hypothesis suggests that the target of the break-in was the offices of Larry O'Brien, the DNC Chairman. However, O'Brien's name was not on Alfred C. Baldwin III's list of targets that was released in 2013. Among those listed were senior DNC official R. Spencer Oliver, Oliver's secretary Ida "Maxine" Wells, co-worker Robert Allen and secretary Barbara Kennedy.

Based on these revelations, Texas A&M history professor Luke Nichter, who had successfully petitioned for the release of the information, argued that Woodward and Bernstein were incorrect in concluding, based largely on Watergate burglar James McCord's word, that the purpose of the break-in was to bug O'Brien's phone to gather political and financial intelligence on the Democrats. Instead, Nichter sided with late journalist J. Anthony Lukas of the New York Times, who had concluded that the committee was seeking to find evidence linking the Democrats to prostitution, as it was alleged that Oliver's office had been used to arrange such meetings. However, Nichter acknowledged that Woodward and Bernstein's theory of O'Brien as the target could not be debunked unless information was released about what Baldwin heard in his bugging of conversations.

In 1968, O'Brien was appointed by Vice President Hubert Humphrey to serve as the national director of Humphrey's presidential campaign and, separately, by Howard Hughes to serve as Hughes' public-policy lobbyist in Washington. O'Brien was elected national chairman of the DNC in 1968 and 1970. In late 1971, the president's brother, Donald Nixon, was collecting intelligence for his brother at the time and asked John H. Meier, an adviser to Howard Hughes, about O'Brien. In 1956, Donald Nixon had borrowed $205000 from Howard Hughes and had never repaid the loan. The loan's existence surfaced during the 1960 presidential election campaign, embarrassing Richard Nixon and becoming a political liability. According to author Donald M. Bartlett, Richard Nixon would do whatever was necessary to prevent another family embarrassment. From 1968 to 1970, Hughes withdrew nearly half a million dollars from the Texas National Bank of Commerce for contributions to both Democrats and Republicans, including presidential candidates Humphrey and Nixon. Hughes wanted Donald Nixon and Meier involved but Nixon opposed this.

Meier told Donald that he was sure the Democrats would win the election because they had considerable information on Richard Nixon's illicit dealings with Hughes that had never been released, and that it resided with Larry O'Brien. According to Fred Emery, O'Brien had been a lobbyist for Hughes in a Democrat-controlled Congress, and the possibility of his finding out about Hughes' illegal contributions to the Nixon campaign was too much of a danger for Nixon to ignore. James F. Neal, who prosecuted the Watergate 7, did not believe Nixon had ordered the break-in because of Nixon's surprised reaction when he was told about it.

CHAPTER THREE
THE IRAN-CONTRA AFFAIR AND
REGAN'S MISBEHAVIOR

During the administrations of President Jimmy Carter (1977-1981) and President Ronald Reagan (1981-1989), the United States witnessed an increase in Communist uprisings and governments in Latin America, as well as turmoil and the growth of Islamic extremism in parts of the Middle East.

In 1979 in the Middle Eastern country of Iran, a revolution, led by the Islamic religious leader, Ayatollah Ruhollah Khomeini, overthrew Shah Mohammad Reza Pahlavi. Ayatollah Khomeini sought to remove all Western influences within the country and establish an Islamic Republic. In an act of deliberate aggression against the United States, the new Iranian government captured and held 52 Americans for 444 days.

Many historians agree that the inability of the Carter administration to resolve the crisis was instrumental to the election of Ronald Reagan in 1980. Negotiations were, in fact, secretly underway, but the release of the hostages would not come until Reagan was sworn into office in January 1981. The United States broke off relations with Iran and instituted a series of economic sanctions in an attempt to weaken the theocratic government.

In Central America in July 1979, a Cuban-backed Marxist organization, called the Sandinistas, took control of the government of Nicaragua. Communism and the Soviet Union appeared to be an ever-growing challenge to the United States and to the new Reagan administration. Reagan, a hardcore "Cold Warrior," who had used tough anti-Communist rhetoric during the presidential campaign, was incensed by the further encroachment of Soviet-Marxist influence in the Western Hemisphere.

Reagan was determined to support the opposing Contra rebel forces in Nicaragua to remove the Sandinistas from the government and military. In December 1981, Reagan authorized funding for the
Central Intelligence Agency (CIA) to conduct covert operations in Nicaragua by training the Contras as a paramilitary force. He regarded this as the best way to put pressure on the Sandinista government.

Congress, however, disagreed and drafted the (first) Boland Amendment, barring the use of funds for the specific purpose of overthrowing the government of Nicaragua. Reagan signed the bill into law in December 1982. A second Boland Amendment was signed into law in August 1984 stating again that no funds could be used against the Nicaraguan government.

Meanwhile, in 1984 and 1985, Hezbollah, an Islamic terrorist group with links to the Iranian regime, abducted seven Americans in the Middle Eastern country of Lebanon. Among the hostages was William F. Buckley, the CIA chief in Beirut, the capital of Lebanon.
In 1984, President Reagan was re-elected to a second term in a landslide victory, winning 49 of 50 states.

With a strong mandate, he announced during his State of Union Address in February 1985, his foreign policy stance, known as the Reagan Doctrine, saying "we must not break our faith with those who are risking their lives – on every continent from Afghanistan to Nicaragua – to defy Soviet aggression and Educational materials developed through the Baltimore County History Labs Program, a partnership between Baltimore County Public Schools and the UMBC Center for History Education.

Reagan also needed to secure the release of the hostages in Lebanon and was therefore open to negotiating with Iran, despite his hardline public stance against it. Iran was embroiled in war with the nation of Iraq at the time and was willing to turn to sworn enemies, like the United States, for military arms.

In June 1984, Reagan met with Vice President George H.W. Bush and his other chief aides to begin discussing other ways to support the Contra rebels. In March 1985, Lieutenant Colonel Oliver North, a member of the National Security Council, proposed to National Security Advisor Robert McFarlane the possibility of using "third-party" donors, like Saudi Arabia and Brunei in the Middle East, and Panama in Latin America, as intermediaries between the United States, Iran, and the Contras.

In April 1985, President Reagan called the President of Honduras, Roberto Suazo Córdova, and insisted that the United States was committed to helping the Contras even if Congress would not provide financial assistance.

In the summer of 1985, Lt. Col. Oliver North began raising funds for the secret operations in Nicaragua by meeting with officials from Brunei and Panama. In August 1985, Reagan approved an arms deal to allow Israel to sell U.S.-made weapons to Iran. The profits were then sent to support the Contras. The operation, known as "Enterprise," raised about $16 million in profits from arms sales to Iran. Over $3.5million was then sent to the Contras in Nicaragua. In return for the arms shipments, Iran agreed to broker the release of the hostages, however the exchange for all of the hostages did not occur as planned, and their release was sporadic.

In August 1986, North met with General Manuel Noriega, the military dictator of Panama and a knowndrug trafficker, to organize an arrangement between the United States and Panama. In a message to the National Security Advisor, John Poindexter, North stated that Noriega suggested that if the United States helped "clean up his image" and lifted a ban on foreign missile sales, he "would undertake to 'take care of' the Sandinista leadership for us."

By 1986, the arms-for-hostages deal had been exposed. On November 26, 1986, President Reagan appointed the Tower Commission, under the leadership of former Senator John Tower of Texas, to investigate. Lawrence Walsh, a former judge and deputy attorney general in the Eisenhower Administration, was appointed the independent counsel for the investigation. Walsh brought charges

against 14 employees of the National Security Council (NSC), the Department of Defense, the Department of State, and the Central Intelligence Agency, and private individuals.

Following the Congressional investigation, numerous members of the Reagan administration were charged with providing false testimony, conspiracy, and diversion. In January 1989, Oliver North was charged with sixteen counts. North had been fired by the administration in November 1986, as the story of the deal with Noriega became public. In November 1986, North shredded documents and attempted to obstruct the joint committee investigation.

During the trial, the defense's witnesses portrayed North as a hero and savior, while the prosecution relied on testimony that depicted North as a thief and liar. North admitted to altering documents and misinforming Congress about the events related to the Contras; however, he insisted that it was not unlawful because he was carrying out orders. Some have claimed that the trial became about whether or not Oliver North was a "pawn or knight errant."

In the end, the jury found North guilty of "aiding and abetting the preparation of the false testimony for the Congressional testimony…destruction of NSC documents, and…acceptance of illegal gratuity." He was sentenced to two years probation, fined $150,000, and required to perform 1,200 hours of community service.

The Iran-Contra Affair of 1984-1987 was not one, but two separate covert foreign policy issues concerning two different problems, in two separate countries, that were dealt in two very different ways. Under the management of the same few officials, both the Iran and the Contra policies intersected at certain important points giving rise to the singular title, Iran-Contra Affair.

The first covert foreign policy initiative was the continued support for the democratic rebel Contras against the communist Sandinistas in Nicaragua in a time when Congress had cut off funds to the Contras. The second covert foreign policy initiative was the selling of arms to Iran in exchange for the release of American hostages held by Iranian allies in Lebanon. The two policies intersected when profits from the arms sales to Iran were used to support the Nicaraguan Contras through third parties and private funds.

The National Security Council ("NSC") and the Central Intelligence Agency ("CIA") developed in such a way that structurally allowed each to work around Congress and have the Executive Branch and third party actors implement and frame the foreign policy of the entire Unites States. To understand how, one must look historically at the evolution of these two groups. The beginning starts with the National Security Act of July 26, 1947. Truman signed this piece of legislation that gave birth simultaneously to both the National Security Council and the Central Intelligence Agency.

The NSC was not originally founded to facilitate presidential decision making, but it evolved with each administration until it became structured and powerful enough to perform covert operations. During Eisenhower's administration in the mid 1950's the NSC became a "virtual adjunct of the presidency."1 The NSC staff was now under a special assistant to the President and not the NSC directly, turning the Presidency into a bureaucracy itself. The Kennedy administration's changes to the NSC were driven by the Bay of Pigs incident that left Kennedy skeptical of the traditional departments and led him to prefer a more direct and personal style of executing policies. It was under Kennedy that the "distinction between planning and operation" was altered.2 Whereas the NSC was previously a planning entity, Kennedy made i also function operationally. This allowed the executive branch to avoid the State Department and furthered a trend of inflating the Office of the President through its replication of the rest of the government. The Office of the President grew in ways that sometimes supported, sometimes competed with, and other times ignored other governmental agencies and offices.

The inflationary trend continued with the Reagan administration. The NSC became further professionalized with a staff of about forty-five under the National Security Advisor Robert McFarlane and more than 200 people in support.3 It became further structured in reflection of the State Department under Robert McFarlane's successor, John Poindexter when it was organized into twelve directorates i.e. the African office, European Office, etc. The person most hurt, and most undermined by this trend was the Secretary of State, George Shultz during the Reagan administration, because now the president was performing similar duties, with similar staff support from his own office. The NSC was now "large and varied enough to carry out the president's wishes covertly- even from the rest of the government."

Lieutenant Colonel Oliver North, deputy director of political-military affairs for the National Security Council staff was deeply involved in both the Iran and Contra affairs.

Like the NSC, the CIA evolved with the different Presidential administrations. Under Eisenhower, the 1955 NSC directive outlined the spectrum of the CIA's covert operations in an effort to turn the CIA into a "virtual Cold War machine against Communism-" to "create and exploit troublesome problems for international Communism…reduce international Communist control over any areas of the world" and "develop underground resistance and facilitate covert and guerilla operations."5 Eisenhower did qualify that the covert operations had to be consistent with U.S. foreign and military policies. The War Powers Resolution, which was created as a
check on presidential power by Congress did not include a check of covert wars and paramilitary activities that the CIA was authorized to conduct. The CIA director during the Reagan administration was William Casey.

The U.S. has long intervened in Nicaraguan affairs, aiming to keep its political developments amicable with and aligned to American interests. As early as 1912 the U.S. has utilized military force to quell rebellions against American approved leaders or to help overthrow unwanted regimes. Therefore, when U.S. trained head of the Nicaraguan National Guard, Somoza García, forcefully took power in 1936, the U.S. made no move to protect the current administration under Augusto César Sandino. Sandino's murder marked the beginning of the Somoza dynastic rule which lasted for the next 43 years. In 1961, the Sandinista National Liberation Front ("FSLN"), named in honor of Sandino, was created in opposition to the Somoza dynasty.

Ideologically, the Sandinistas saw themselves as a Marxist-Leninist organization with aims of turning Nicaragua into a socialist state. Inspired by and closely connected to Cuba, the Sandinistas worked to create and consolidate their power in the context of a cold war era where socialist revolutions and uprisings were gaining in worldwide popularity.

In 1967, Anastasio Somoza Debayle, son of Somoza García, became president. He became notorious in

Nicaragua for suppressing opposition and focusing on self-enrichment while in power. For example, in 1972, when an earthquake struck Managua, the capital of Nicaragua,

Somoza exercised "emergency powers" to address the earthquake which in actuality resulted in him and his close friends confiscating the majority of international aid sent to help rebuild

Nicaragua. This event consolidated the Nicaraguan's disapproval of Anastasio Somoza Debayle, especially among the Sandinistas.

In 1974, the Sandinistas kidnapped several Nicaraguan elites at a Christmas Party. Somoza responded to the affair by declaring a state of siege which spiraled into a series of serious human rights violations and guerilla attacks on peasants. In response, the United States, hyper-sensitive to the threat of communism and in conjunction with a contemporaneous trend of protecting human rights victims, began to pay attention to Nicaraguan affairs for the first time since the Somoza dynasty commenced in 1936. President Jimmy Carter's foreign policy was shaped not only by a consciousness of human rights, but also by a fatigue of foreign intervention due to the Vietnam War. President Carter cut off all aid to the Nicaraguan government until it improved its human rights violations. Somoza responded by lifting the state of siege. This was met by the Sandinistas re-initiating and expanding their attacks which were now supported by business elites including Alfonso Robelo, and academics, including Adolfo Calero.

On July 19, 1979, the Sandinista uprising culminated in their gaining full power in Nicaragua. The Sandinistas first move as new political leaders was to declare a state of emergency and expropriate land and businesses owned by the old dynastic family and friends,
nationalize banks, mines, and transit systems, abolish old courts, denounce churches, and nullify the constitution, laws, and elections. A socialist state was born in Nicaragua. President Carter immediately sent $99 million in aid to the FSLN in an attempt to keep the new regime pro-U.S.

Simultaneously, however, Cuban officials were advising the FSLN on foreign and domestic policy and the FSLN sought an alliance with the Soviet bloc which they reached by March 1980 signing economic, cultural, technological, and scientific agreements with the USSR. Deliveries of Soviet weapons from Cuba began almost immediately after the signing of these agreements.

It was mid-1980 when José Cardenal and Enrique Bermúdez founded what would become the Nicaraguan Democratic Force, or FDN, the main contra group ("the Contras"). The Contras found support among the populations disaffected by Sandinista policies – i.e. protestant evangelicals, farmers, Nicaraguan Indians, Creoles, and other disgruntled and disenfranchised parties. The Argentinean government was the first to support the Contras. They directly oversaw the Contras, trained the military forces, and chose the Contra leadership whereas the U.S. took on the role of supplying money and arms. Many worried that the Contras were a continuation of the Somoza regime because of their use of brutal tactics against noncombatants and their alleged human rights abuses.

Once it became clear to Washington that the FSLN would not moderate its policies, President Carter authorized the CIA to support resistance forces in Nicaragua including propaganda efforts, but not including armed action. The Sandinistas supported expanding socialism abroad, including sending weapons to leftist rebels in El Salvador beginning in 1980 and continuing for the next ten years. Some argue that this international support from Nicaragua was also in effort to insure that the Soviets would fully support and protect Nicaragua in case of a U.S. attack or intervention. Sandinista support for the Salvadoran rebels had a profound impact on U.S.-Nicaragua relations throughout the 80's politics. He quickly cut off all aid to FSLN indefinitely due to the Sandinista's continued support of Salvadoran rebels. In response, the Sandinistas consolidated power and expanded arrests of perceived dissidents under the belief that the U.S. would invade. On December 1, 1981, Reagan signed an order that allowed the CIA to support the Contras with arms, equipment, and money.

This order was implemented in conjunction with an overall strengthening of U.S. presence in Central America and the belief that covert activities are the most effective way to put pressure on a regime. This shift of foreign policy away from the Carter administration's non-intervention culminated in June 1982 with the Reagan Doctrine which called for supporting democratization everywhere. It was at this point that the goal of the covert operations in Nicaragua shifted away from one of simply interdicting arms to one of supporting a change in government. Iran-Contra historian Theodore Draper, among others, argued, that this was the real goal all the long.

To help popularize the foreign policy changes of the Reagan administration certain propaganda and media initiatives were implemented to sway public and congressional opinion.

In January of 1983, National Security Decisions Directive was signed, entitled "Management of Public Diplomacy Relative to National Security," institutionalizing public diplomacy. In effect, it was a special planning group within the NSC to coordinate public diplomacy campaigns. This group was America's first peacetime propaganda ministry. Every administration tries to influence public opinion, but not until Reagan was it so institutionalized. Another use of "white propaganda," which Richard Miller described as "actually putting out [the] truth, straight information, not deception," was the State Department's Group of Latin American Public Diplomacy (S/LPD).

This group, in actuality, reported directly to the NSC despite being housed within the State Department. Both committees utilized a variety of media propaganda and control efforts. A fourteen page memorandum dated March

20, 1985 from North to National Security Advisor Robert McFarlane explained over 80 publicity stunts to influence public and congressional opinion before upcoming Contra aid votes.8 The public diplomacy officials also leaked select pieces of information that they wanted made public to journalists who favored Reagan. Strategic leaking and declassification of documents allowed the Executive Branch to manage the public perceptions of the American efforts in South America.

Despite all the propaganda efforts, a series of high-profile articles began to divide the Executive Branch and the Legislature over the topic of Nicaragua and Contra support. In 1982, the CIA gained a more prominent role in the training and funding of the Contras. This attracted the attention of *Newsweek,* whose cover story on November 8, 1982 was entitled "America's Secret War: Nicaragua." The story outlined America's efforts to "undermine the Sandinista government," 9 and prompted a heated editorial response in *The Boston Globe.* This response article sparked Massachusetts Representative Edward P. Boland to lead a congressional effort to end all funding of Nicaraguan efforts.

The first Congressional legislation aimed at preventing funding came on December 21, 1982 with the first Boland Amendment which barred "the use of funds 'for the purpose of' overthrowing the government of Nicaragua or provoking a war between Nicaragua and Honduras." In a joint session of Congress, President Reagan said, "The Congress shares both the power and the responsibility for our foreign policy," but by the time Congress exercised said shared power by passing Boland I, the Reagan administration had already committed itself to supporting the Contras unconditionally and at any cost- even if that meant defying Congress.

Open defiance was impossible, so covert defiance was adopted as the Executive Branch's new normal. Boland I left a loophole that the Reagan administration quickly utilized- as long as the U.S. itself did not intend to overthrow the Nicaraguan government, the U.S. could support the Contras under a different guise such as humanitarian aid or by the solicitation of money from third-party funds and private actors. Thus, Boland I had no real impact on the conduct of the war in Nicaragua.

During the second half of 1983, the CIA helped the Contras to conduct air strikes on Sandino airport near

Managua in addition to other targets. The CIA used its own assets to implement some of the covert actions in Nicaragua, including destroying several fuel tanks. The CIA also placed mines in Nicaraguan harbors on January 7, 1984 and February 29, 1984,damaging several ships. The Contras initially took credit for the mining, but it was later revealed by *The Wall Street Journal* that the mines were placed by the CIA. Furthermore, *The Wall Street Journal* disclosed that Lieutenant Colonel Oliver North, a U.S. Marine who worked on the National Security Council staff at the Reagan White House, had knowledge of and encouraged such actions. Oliver North would become an integral figure in the Iran-Contra Affair.

Also at this time, National Security advisor Robert McFarlane began meeting with Israeli counterpart David Kimche inquiring to whether or not Israel would help support the Contras.

The solicitation of Israel proved unsuccessful, but a few months later, McFarlane secured money from Saudi Arabia in support of the Contras. McFarlane would later argue that he had not solicited the funds, but simply mentioning the loss of the Contra aid was enough to insight the Saudis to provide money for the cause. McFarlane was able to secure over $32 million from Saudi Arabia from 1984-1986. North added on another $2 million from Taiwan throughout the affair. Later in 1984, some people within Reagan's administration began toying with the idea of setting up a private tax-exempt organization to raise money for the Contras. Carl "Spitz" Channell led this effort to secure private funds, many of the larger donors meeting with Oliver North and even President Reagan directly. Realizing the ineffectiveness of Boland I, Congress, still determined to stop the flow of funds to Nicaragua, passed a second Boland Amendment on October 12, 1984 which reads:

"During fiscal year 1985, no funds available to the Central Intelligence Agency, the Department of Defense, or any other agency or entity of the United States involved intelligence activities may be obligated or expended for the purpose or which would have the effect of supporting directly or indirectly, military or paramilitary operations in Nicaragua by any nation, group, organization, movement or individual."

Boland II left two loopholes for getting money to the Contras. The first loophole, like that of Boland I, was to solicit third-party funds from private donors or third party countries to give money to the Contras. The second loophole was to use the NSC which is "the President's principal forum for considering national security and foreign policy matters with his senior national security advisors and cabinet officials" based on the logic that the NSC is not covered under Boland. Oliver North, on loan to the NSC from the Marine Corps, began to undertake this activity. President Reagan trusted that North, in conjunction with McFarlane, would make sure to keep the Contras together "body and soul." The passage of Boland II led to creative means of operational support of the contras: arms deals, air supply ops and intelligence support, and further solicitation of additional third party funds.

Arms Deals: In addition to seeking alternative funding, North and others sought to provide the contras with arms and supplies. Oliver North worked with Richard Secord- a retired Air Force General, and Albert Hakim an Iranian businessmen to supply the Contras with arms. In November 1984 the three solidified their first agreement and by the end of the following summer over $11 million in arms were given to the Contras via private funds.

In 1985, North worked with Secord to "build and oversee an air resupply operation for the contras." A privately funded airstrip was built in Costa Rica in order to carry out this operation which was functional and successfully delivering arms to the Contras by May 1986. October 5, 1986 marked the end of the air supply operations when an aircraft was shot down by the Sandinistas, and crewmember Eugene Hasenfus was captured. This would eventually lead to the full exposure of the operation.

When private funding and third party governments did not provide as much support as North wanted for the Contras, North came upon the idea of overcharging the Iranians for weapons sold to them by Americans "and using the surplus to fund the Contra resupply operation and other covert activities." North wrote what would later be infamously known as the Diversion Memo to the new National Security Advisor John Poindexter and President Reagan in which he outlined how $12 MM of the profit Secord and Hakim made from the sale of arms to Iran "will be used to purchase critically needed supplies for the Nicaraguan Democratic Resistance Forces." Of all of the events of the Iran-Contra Affairs, it was this diversion scheme that was the most controversial and explosive.

Secord and Hakim were motivated by the potential to profit from the activities they engaged in, thus the Contras did not receive all the money given to their cause. As Kagan writes, "For all the controversy raised about the diversion, the Contras were fortunate if they received $2million worth of tangible benefits [between January and October 1986,] an amount that paled in comparison to the far less controversial $32 million they ultimately received from Saudi Arabia." With government funding, 100% of the money goes directly to the beneficiary. With third party and private actors, a portion of that will be allocated as profit.

Congress changed its position on Contra funding with a series of amendments and provisions that resulted in the loosening of the Boland language. The Boland Amendments originally aimed to prevent all funds from flowing into Nicaragua, but from 1985-1986 Congress began qualifying which funds and for what purposes was acceptable. In August 1985, Congress passed a provision which allocated $14 million directly to the Contras for humanitarian assistance. Later that year, in December 1985, as part of the Intelligence Authorization Act, Congress outlawed most U.S. government departments and agencies, except for the State Department, from soliciting money from third-party countries to fund the Contras for "humanitarian assistance only." The State Department was allowed to solicit funds provided that the money donated was from the countries' own funds and that the U.S. did not enter into "any express or implied arrangement making U.S. provision of assistance to the third country contingent on the third country's assistance to the contras."

The amendment also included a no "quid pro quo" statement between the U.S. and the third country. In 1986, The Intelligence Authorization Bill allowed the CIA to provide training and intelligence to the Contras as long as it did not "amount to participation in the planning for execution of military or paramilitary operations" or participation in "logistics activities integral to such operations." In the summer of 1986, Congress passed a provision allocating $100MM of their own budget in aid to the Contras.

As an oil rich nation, Iran is a country that the U.S. has long held foreign policy interest in. The U.S. maintained favorable relations with Iran throughout the Shah, Mohammad Reza Shah Pahlavi's, secular, yet authoritarian, rule. During those years, Iran was one of the

United States' strongest allies in the Middle East. It was this close relationship with the U.S. and its foundation in the Shah's secularism that ultimately served as an impetus for riots and demonstrations to break out across Iran in 1978.

These demonstrations grew in strength and number culminating in the Shah leaving Iran in January 1979 and Ayatollah Ruhollah Khomeini naming Iran an Islamic Republic. Ayatollah Khomeini immediately severed all ties with the U.S. and declared Israel an illegitimate country. He ruled Iran as a religious leader, further consolidating his power. Iran shifted from the U.S.'s most powerful and valued ally in the Middle East to an American enemy virtually overnight.

The U.S., wary of losing its oil rich friend, and desperate to keep Soviets from influencing the region, quickly moved to "normalize relations" with Iran. Despite these efforts, the Muslim Followers of the line of the Imam, a fundamentalist, anti-imperialist group made up predominately of young radical revolutionaries, seized the U.S. embassy in Tehran on November 4, 1979, symbolizing the end of cordial diplomacy between the two nations. Fifty-three hostages were taken by this group and the Iranian government and general public supported their actions further antagonizing relations between the two former allies. Although these hostages were eventually released the day of President Reagan's inauguration, more hostages would soon be taken, and relations would further be galvanized.

Iran's need for weapons during the Iran-Iraq war from 1980-1990 complicated the Iranian-American relations. In the beginning of the Iran-Iraq war, the U.S. actively engaged in an arms embargo against Iran called Operation Staunch and religious fundamentalist group Islamic Holy War took more U.S. hostages beginning in March 1984. It was Iran's need for weapons, and the United States' desire to re-open diplomatic relations that in 1985 led Manucher Ghorbanifar, an Iranian businessman working with the U.S., and Adnan Khashoggi, a Saudi Arabian arms dealer, to devise a skeleton plan for what would later become the Iran arms deal.

This deal would alter Iranian-American relations and lead to the most controversial piece of the Iran-Contra scandal: the diversion of funds from the sale of weapons to Iran to supporting the Nicaraguan Contras.

On July 1, 1985, the *New York Times* quoted President Ronald Reagan saying, "The United States gives terrorists no rewards. We make no concessions, we make no deals." Three days later, McFarlane met with Israeli David Kimche (who had previously met with Khashoggi and Ghorbanifar) and the arms-for-hostages deal was first outlined as both a means to obtain the release of American hostages in addition to an attempt to improve diplomatic relations. Thirteen days after Reagan denounced bartering with terrorists on July 16, 1985, McFarlane visited President Reagan and his Chief of Staff Donald Regan while the President was in the hospital recovering from abdominal surgery. McFarlane proposed their recently outlined arms-for hostages deal that specifically called for the selling of 100 American made TOW antitank missiles to Iran via Israel in exchange for some if not all American hostages and open communications with Iran. America would also send replacement TOWs to Israel. There are conflicting accounts of what was said and agreed to at this meeting.

Regan remembered McFarlane saying to the President, "they had been approached by the Israelis, who had had contact that they would put us in touch with that could lead to a breakthrough in reaching elements in the Government of Iran" and "that this could lead to some help in the hostage situation because we suspected that the Iranians were in some way connected in to the group who had abducted the Americans."

McFarlane gave multiple versions of what the President said in the hospital. One version that McFarlane relayed to Poindexter was that Reagan "was all for letting the Israelis do anything they wanted." Another version McFarlane gave was that "As Irecall [Reagan] said that he could understand how people who were trying to overthrown a government would need weapons, but we weren't yet sure about whether they were legitimate.

So he said that we, the United States, could not do it." President Reagan also gave multiple stories of that day. In 1987 he said that he did not remember meeting with McFarlane at all, but in 1990 he agreed that during the meeting he first became aware of the arms-for hostage initiative in Iran.

Khashoggi provided "bridge financing," posting $1 million of his private funds until Iran paid Israel for the weapons.16 The deal was wholly managed through private actors- Ghorbanifar for Iran and Schwimmer and Nimrodi for Israel. Lt. Colonel Oliver North was brought into the Iran affair by McFarlane to manage logistics in the interest of the United States. North continued to stay involved in Iran when Poindexter succeeded McFarlane. On September 15, 1985, American hostage Benjamin Weir was released after 408 more TOWs were shipped to Iran. Any profits from the deal went to Ghorbanifar, Schwimmer or Nimrodi.

Major General Richard Secord was brought into the Iran affair by North to help resupply Israel's weapon store and organize logistical issues such as moving "sensitive material" between Israel and Iran. In November 1985, a second load of missiles was sold to Iran. The second sale provided the first funds that were diverted to the Nicaraguan Contras. To complete the diversion covertly, and without the knowledge of Congress, Secord and Hakim established a company called the Stanford Technology Trading Group International which was commonly known as "The Enterprise." Israel transferred $1 million to an Enterprise-owned, Secord-Hakim Lake Resources Swiss bank account for the second arms shipment. This account had previously been used only for Nicaraguan Contra business.17 Of the $1 million, only $150,000 was spent on the weapons, the other $850,000 was diverted, by North, to be used to support the Contras.

Ordinarily the entire million would've been paid back to the Israelis, but in this instance, North "told them we used it for the purpose of the Contras, and they acknowledged that" –and they never asked for the money back.18 In January of 1986, the diversion scheme continued when Ghorbanifar suggested that any extra money made through the arms sales be diverted to aiding the Contras. McFarlane's successor, John Poindexter, approved this plan.

The Second shipment of arms-for-hostages mentioned briefly above was a logistical nightmare that North described as "a horror story."19 The original plan was that on November22nd, 1985, 120 Hawk missiles would be shipped from Israel to Portugal on an Israeli 747. In Portugal the weapons would be unloaded, stored, and reloaded on a non-Israeli plane and shipped to Iran in two intervals. First, eighty Hawks would be sent, followed by the release of hostages. Second, contingent upon the hostages' release, the remaining forty would then be sent to Iran.

Schwimmer, who was heading the Israeli operations, applied last minute to get the necessary special clearances to land the cargo of arms at the Portuguese airport in Lisbon. Schwimmer found the authorities hesitant to grant him permission. It was at this point that Oliver North got involved and met with Israeli Defense Minister Rabin in New York on November 18th about the operational logistics of shipping the "oil drilling equipment" to Iran. To help with logistics, North brought Secord on board rather than using someone from the U.S. government because Secord had close ties with leading Portuguese arms dealer, Defex.

"At the Poindexter trial, North said that Rabin had told him the number of missiles they were trying to ship and some overflight clearance problems they were having. ,North told Rabin he would get back to him after checking for authorization. Thus north knew at this time that the cargo was made up of missiles, not oil-drilling equipment." Draper

The first effort to get airport clearance was described to the Portuguese Foreign Ministry as Defex working with a retired American general to ship arms to Iran. This confused Portuguese officials because of what they understood as the United States' opposition to all shipments of arms to Iran under Operation Staunch. Portugal was now skeptical of the whole affair; especially in regards to who was making this arms shipment request- the United States Government, or a private citizen.

When that request was denied, North worked with Dewey R. Clarridge, Chief of the European division of the CIA, to help deal with the Lisbon airport crisis and try again to obtain airport clearance. Portugal firmly insisted on receiving a "formal acknowledgement they were being asked to help in a weapons shipment" as not to later be charged with violating Operation Staunch.

Ultimately North and Clarridge used an alternate plan utilizing "proprietary" airline flights to make the arms shipment. A proprietary airline is such that it is owned and controlled by the CIA but operates as if it were an ordinary commercial operation when not utilized for special CIA assignment. When Clarridge decided to go the proprietary route he informed the CIA controller in Frankfurt that "an urgent fight" that was "in the interest of the U.S. government" would need to be flown.23 This shipment method did not run smoothly either, running across problems in Cyprus, Turkey, and culminating in the realization that the wrong missiles had been sent once they reached Tehran. The horror story ended with the decision to immediately repeat the operation under U.S. instead of Israeli management, this time with more success.

After experiencing difficulties such as the second arms shipment and problems in securing the discussed exchanges with Iran, on January 17, 1986, President Reagan signed a Presidential Finding authorizing direct U.S. arms sales to Iran. Secord and the Enterprise would still be used as a third party to release the U.S. of any liability. Israel, would still serve as the base, but it would no longer buy and sell weapons. Now the Enterprise would buy and sell weapons directly on behalf of the United States.

After continuing difficulties in securing the release of hostages from Iran, North and Secord determined that the U.S. had to find an alternate channel for dealing with Iran, and put Hakim in charge of the effort. In August 1986, Hakim, with his new Iranian contact, Ali

Hashemi Bahramani, worked out a nine-point plan that compromised both his and the Iranians 'interests. The resulting agreement was that the U.S. would send Iran 1,500 TOWs in exchange for the release of "1 ½ hostages (1 definitely and the 2nd with all effective possible effort)."

Iran also offered to pay the U.S. $3.6 million in addition to releasing the hostages which meant more funds could be diverted to the Contras. Hakim, serving as a "U.S. representative," implemented his nine-point plan beginning in October 28, 1986 with the first shipment of arms. Of the $3.6 million Iran paid to the Enterprise, $2 million of this was given to the CIA who supplied the weapons, and the remaining $1.6 million was diverted to the Contras.

On November 3, 1986, two Lebanese newspapers broke the story of the Iran arms deal, and quickly thereafter the entire scandal began to unravel in the United States. The first two weeks following the newspaper leak were marked by an increasing crisis of confidence in the government as facts rapidly became public. By December 1986 everything from the Contra affair to the diversion scheme found its way into the press.

Nov. 13, 1986: President Ronald Reagan made his Address to the Nation on the Iran Arms and Contra Aid Controversy and again addressed the nation in a press conference on November 19th. On the 13th, Reagan said that the U.S. was working with the Iranian government, but on the 19th, he admitted to working with a "particular group,"24 implying he dealt with terrorist organizations.

Further contradictions were made during the press conference on the 19th when Reagan stated that, "we did not condone and do not condone the shipment of arms from other countries." This, however, was said after Chief of Staff Donald Regan had already admitted that the White House condoned an Israeli shipment of Arms to Iran in September 1985.

By the 19th, virtually everything about the Iran side of the affair had come out: missiles and spare parts to Iran, the role of Israel, McFarlane's mission to Tehran, North, Ghorbanifar, etc.26
Reagan's blunders during the November 19th conference set into motion public discourse on the President's credibility and role in the whole affair.

On November 21st, Oliver North engaged in what he would later be referred to as a "shredding party," destroying potentially incriminating documents, helped by his secretary Fawn Hall, in anticipation of the Justice Department lawyers coming to search his office the next day.

North did not, however, destroy the smoking gun of the connection between the Iran arms sales and the funding for the Nicaraguan contras, the Diversion Memo. After

Attorney General Meese, Assistant Attorney General Reynolds, and Chief of Staff to Attorney General Richardson interviewed North about the document, the Reagan administration raced to release this information to the public. Fearing accusations of a Watergate style cover-up and more seriously the possibility of impeachment, President Reagan himself publicly acknowledged diversion scheme of the arms deal to the public.

November 25, 1986 Reagan held a press conference where Attorney General Meese responded to the majority of questions. Meese said that the affair did not go any higher than Admiral Poindexter.28 This press conference was also the first time the possibility of legal charges was discussed and North, watching from a TV in his office, found out simultaneously with the general public that he could be facing criminal charges.29 That same day, Poindexter resigned as National Security Advisor, and North, who was only detailed to the NSC and appointed as assistant to the President was transferred back to the Marines.

Three mechanisms were established to uncover the truth of the Iran-Contra Affair in hopes of regaining public trust in addition to fully understand the scandal: a special review board appointed by Reagan, an independent counsel per-Meese's request, and the holding of immunized joint-congressional hearings.

On November 26, 1986, one day after President Reagan and Attorney General Edwin Meese held a press conference at which they publicized the diversions scheme, President Reagan appointed former US. Senator John Tower and others to a special review board known as the Tower Commission. The Tower Commission was created with the purpose of "evaluating the operation of the National Security Council in general and the role of the NSC staff in particular."

The Tower Commission released its findings on February 26, 1987, concluding that the NSC itself was sound, and placed a heavy amount of blame on Chief of Staff Regan and National Security Advisor Poindexter. Although the Tower Commission did not find Reagan "guilty" nor claimed that he knew more than he was leading on to, it did argue that Reagan should have been more informed, criticizing his managerial style of running the White House for causing him to act with neglect and lack of oversight.

Per Request of Attorney General Meese III, a panel of three judges appointed an Independent Counsel, Lawrence Walsh, to investigate the legal issues of the Iran-Contra affairs on December 19th, 1986. Walsh, a former judge and deputy attorney general under Eisenhower, requested an official appointment by the U.S. Department of Justice on March 5, 1987, in order to avoid challenges over the constitutionality of using an Independent Counsel (Note: *Morrison v. Olson* had not yet been decided). Walsh's job was made extremely difficult because of the immunity granted to the joint-committee hearings. These difficulties were formally presented to Congress in a report dated April 28, 1987.

Walsh also encountered a problem with graymail- the refusal to declassify documents even if necessary to conduct a fair trial. Only the Attorney General can overrule this refusal. The Legal Aftermath of the Iran-Contra fairs includes fourteen people that were criminally charged. Of those fourteen, four were convicted of felony charges, seven pleaded guilty to either felonies or misdemeanors, one case was dismissed, and two that were awaiting trial were pardoned by George H.W. Bush.

On March 5, 1987, the joint hearings of the House Select Committee to investigate Covert Arms Transactions with Iran and the Senate Select Committee on Secret Military Assistance to Iran and the Nicaraguan Opposition, later referred to simply as the Iran- Contra hearings, began and lasted for 41-days. Co-Chairman Inouye in his opening statements describes the purpose of the hearings:

"Our hearings are neither pro-Contra nor anti-Contra, neither pro-Administration nor anti-Administration. We are not prosecutors; and this is not an adversarial proceeding. We meet here as American citizens, united in a common effort to find the facts lest we repeat the mistakes."

The witnesses were granted immunity under the Fifth Amendment to prevent self-incrimination and in an effort to uncover all the facts. Of the thirteen key witnesses, this will highlight two:
Oliver North and the John Poindexter.

Oliver North's immunized testimony before the joint-congressional committee began on July 7th and lasted until the July 14th, 1987. Adorned in his military uniform complete with decorations of valor from Vietnam, the handsome soldier promised on the first day to tell the truth, "the good, the bad, and the ugly." North appeared to some a hero, to others a victim, (Reagan called him both in December 1986) but ultimately his favorability rating was 67% after his testimony.

During the hearings, North admitted to shredding documents because the Attorney General's people were coming to look through his office the next day:

"**Mr. NIELDS**: And you shredded documents before they got there?

Mr. NORTH: I would prefer to say that I shredded documents that day like I did on all other days, but perhaps with increased intensity; that's correct." North's testimony also revealed his willingness to engage in controversial, possibly illegal, covert activities:

"**Mr. NORTH.** I want you to know lying does not come easy to me. I want you to know that it doesn't come easy to anybody, but I think we all had to weigh in the balance the difference between lives and lies. I had to do that on a number of occasions in both these operations, and it is not an easy thing to do." The hearings' Majority Report concluded that "North's testimony demonstrates that he also lied to members of the Executive branch, including the Attorney General, and officials of the State Department, CIA and NSC." And also that "other officials lied repeatedly to Congress and to the American people about the Contra covert action and Iran arms sales, and that he altered and destroyed official documents"

The hearing's Majority Report referred to North as the central figure of the Iran-Contra Affair. It acknowledged that he did not and could not have acted alone, but it was his coordination and involvement in all activities and secret operations that made him the leading character. North explained that he "sought approval for every one of [his] actions and it is well documented. [He] assumed when [he] had approval to proceed from…Bud McFarlane or Admiral Poindexter, which they had indeed solicited and obtained the approval of the President."

The hearings committee Majority Report recognized this causal chain of command, but North admitted that simply following orders alone was not sufficient grounds for breaking the law.

"Both he and adm. Poindexter have argued," however "that their activities did not break the law because they did not use money appropriated by the Congress." The use of legal defenses was utilized again by North when he testified that he got a legal opinion from the staff counsel of the President's Intelligence Oversight Board ("IOB") - a group of civilians appointed by the President to act as an independent watchdog over intelligence organizations, that confirmed that the NSC was not violating Boland restrictions as long as the "solicitation, banking, and movement of supplies were done outside the United States."

The IOB staff counsel during the Reagan years had previously failed the bar exam four times before passing and had never written a legal opinion until his appraisal of the relevance of the Boland amendment to the NSC.34 No substantive legal advice was sought from the Justice Department, the State Department, the White House counsel, or any other administrative official within the government.

John Poindexter's immunized testimony immediately followed Oliver North's and lasted from July 15-17 to July 20-21, 1987. From an appearance standpoint, Poindexter provided a stark contrast to North. Wearing Civilian clothing because, as Poindexter said the first day of the hearings, "this issue is not a Navy issue," Poindexter was much more awkward, less dynamic, and not as handsome as North. The Watergate Scandal's legacy focused the hearings' questions to 'what did the President know and when did he know it?'36 These questions were addressed by Poindexter who took full responsibility for the affair. This is in direct contrast to the Watergate Scandal where John Dean turned against Nixon in the public hearings.

Poindexter testified that the "buck" stopped with him and that Reagan knew nothing about the dispersion plan. Poindexter cited three reasons for why he was justified in not informing the President: first, Poindexter, unlike McFarlane did not believe that the Boland

Amendment applied to the NSC, thereby Poindexter believed that the diversion of funds to the Contras was legal; second, he saw the diversion as a "detail" of the larger political goal of aiding the Contras; and third, "the president would have supported the policy had he known about it."

Chairman Hamilton criticized Poindexter for claiming the buck stops with him because "that is not where the buck is supposed to stop," arguing that Poindexter only wanted "to deflect responsibility from the President and that should not be done in our system of government."

Poindexter admitted during his testimony that he destroyed Reagan's signed finding that sent arms to Iran on

November 21, 1986 in order to avoid "political embarrassment," and he also claimed to "not recall" several key incidents. Two-thirds of those polled after Poindexter's testimony believed that he was "covering up" for others in the administration, and a majority said he was covering up for the President.

The Majority Report of the Congressional Committees Investigating the Iran-Contra Affair, released on November 18, 1987, like the Tower Commission, criticized Reagan for his blunders: "The President himself told the public that the U.S. Government had no connection to the Hasenfus airplane. He told the public that early reports of arms sales for hostages had 'no foundation.' He told the public that the United States had not traded arms for hostages.

He told the public that the United States had not condoned the arms sales by Israel to Iran, when in fact he had approved them and signed a Finding, later destroyed by Poindexter, recording his approval. All of these statements by the President were wrong." and his lack of oversight:

"Nevertheless, the ultimate responsibility for the events in the Iran-Contra Affair must rest with the President. If the President did not know what his National

Security Advisers were doing, he should have. It is his responsibility to communicate unambiguously to his subordinates that they must keep him advised of important actions they take for the Administration. The Constitution requires the President to 'take care that the laws be faithfully executed.' This charge encompasses a responsibility to leave the members of his Administration in no doubt that the rule of law governs."

The day before the hearings began, 63% of Americans felt that "it's time for the country to give the president the benefit of the doubt and put the Iran arms affair behind us." One-third of those questioned during the hearings said that they would care "a great deal" if Reagan had known about the diversion scheme. A few days after the hearings ended, 58% of those polled say that Congress spent too much time on the investigation. Ultimately, 58% said that the important questions had not even been answered. Indeed, the Iran-Contra Affair did leave the United States with several enduring issues.

CHAPTER FOUR

CLINTON AND MONICA: IMPEACHMENT OF THE PRESIDENT

The impeachment of Bill Clinton, the 42nd President of the United States, was initiated in December 1998 by the House of Representatives and led to a trial in the Senate on two charges, one of perjury and one of obstruction of justice. These charges stemmed from a sexual harassment lawsuit filed against Clinton by Paula Jones. Clinton was subsequently acquitted of these charges by the Senate on February 12, 1999. Two other impeachment articles – a second perjury charge and a charge of abuse of power – failed in the House.

Leading to the impeachment, Independent Counsel Ken Starr turned over documentation to the House Judiciary Committee. Chief Prosecutor David Schippers and his team reviewed the material and determined there was sufficient evidence to impeach the president. As a result, four charges were considered by the full House of Representatives; two passed, making Clinton the second president to be impeached, after Andrew Johnson in 1868, and only the third against whom articles of impeachment had been brought before the full House for consideration (Richard Nixon resigned from the presidency in 1974, while an impeachment process against him was underway

The trial in the United States Senate began right after the seating of the 106th Congress, in which the Republican Party held 55 Senate seats. A two-thirds vote (67 senators) was required to remove Clinton from office. 50 senators voted to remove Clinton on the obstruction of justice charge and 45 voted to remove him on the perjury charge; no member of his own Democratic Party voted guilty on either charge. Clinton, like Johnson a century earlier, was acquitted on all charges.

In 1994, Paula Jones filed a lawsuit accusing Clinton of sexual harassment when he was governor of Arkansas. Clinton attempted to delay a trial until after he left office, but in May 1997 the Supreme Court unanimously ordered the case to proceed and shortly thereafter the pre-trial discovery process commenced. Jones' attorneys wanted to prove that Clinton had engaged in a pattern of behavior with women that lent support to her claims. In late 1997, Linda Tripp began secretly recording conversations with her friend Monica Lewinsky, a former intern and

Department of Defense employee, in which Lewinsky divulged that she had had a sexual relationship with the President.

Tripp shared this information with Paula Jones' lawyers, who put Lewinsky on their witness list in December 1997. According to the Starr report, after Lewinsky appeared on the witness list Clinton began taking steps to conceal their relationship, including suggesting she file a false affidavit, suggesting she use cover stories, concealing gifts he had given her, and helping her obtain a job to her liking.

Clinton gave a sworn deposition on January 17, 1998, where he denied having a "sexual relationship", "sexual affair" or "sexual relations" with Lewinsky. He also denied that he was ever alone with her. His lawyer, Robert Bennet, stated with Clinton present that Lewinsky's affidavit showed that there was no sex in any manner, shape or form between Clinton and Lewinsky. The Starr Report states that the following day, Clinton "coached" his secretary Betty Curie into repeating his denials should she be called to testify.

After rumors of the scandal reached the news, Clinton publicly stated, "I did not have sexual relations with that woman, Miss Lewinsky." Months later, Clinton admitted that his relationship with Lewinsky was "wrong" and "not appropriate". Lewinsky engaged in oral sex with Clinton several times.

The judge in the Jones case later ruled the Lewinsky matter immaterial, and threw out the case in April 1998 on the grounds that Jones had failed to show any damages. After Jones appealed, Clinton agreed in November 1998 to settle the case for $850,000 while still admitting no wrongdoing.

The charges arose from an investigation by Ken Starr, an Independent Counsel. Originally dealing with Whitewater, Starr, with the approval of United States Attorney General Janet Reno, conducted a wide- ranging investigation of alleged abuses, including the Whitewater affair, the firing of White House travel agents, and the alleged misuse of FBI files.

On January 12, 1998, Linda Tripp, who had been working with the Jones lawyers, informed Starr that Lewinsky was preparing to commit perjury in the Jones case and had asked Tripp to do the same. She also said Clinton's friend Vernon Jordan was assisting Lewinsky. Based on the connection to Jordan, who was under scrutiny in the Whitewater probe, Starr obtained approval from Reno to expand his investigation into whether Lewinsky and others were breaking the law.

A much-quoted statement from Clinton's grand jury testimony showed him questioning the precise use of the word "is". Contending that his statement that "there's nothing going on between us" had been truthful because he had no ongoing relationship with Lewinsky at the time he was questioned, Clinton said, "It depends upon what the meaning of the word 'is' is. If the—if he—if 'is' means is and never has been, that is not—that is one thing. If it means there is none, that was a completely true statement".

Starr obtained further evidence of inappropriate behavior by seizing the computer hard drive and email records of Monica Lewinsky. Based on the president's conflicting testimony, Starr concluded that Clinton had committed perjury. Starr submitted his findings to Congress in a lengthy document (the so-called Starr Report), and simultaneously posted the report, which included descriptions of encounters between Clinton and Lewinsky, on the Internet. Starr was criticized by Democrats for spending $70 million on an investigation that substantiated only perjury and obstruction of justice.

Critics of Starr also contend that his investigation was highly politicized because it regularly leaked tidbits of information to the press in violation of legal ethics, and because his report included lengthy descriptions which were humiliating yet irrelevant to the legal case.

Since Ken Starr had already completed an extensive investigation, the House Judiciary Committee conducted no investigations of its own into Clinton's alleged wrongdoing, and it held no serious impeachment-related hearings before the 1998 midterm elections. Nevertheless, impeachment was one of the major issues in the election.

In November 1998, the Democrats picked up five seats in the House although the Republicans still maintained majority control. The results were a particular embarrassment for House Speaker Newt Gingrich, who, before the election, had been reassured by private polling that Clinton's scandal would result in Republican gains of up to thirty House seats. Shortly after the elections, Gingrich, who had been one of the leading advocates for impeachment, announced he would resign from Congress as soon as he was able to find somebody to fill his vacant seat; Gingrich fulfilled this pledge, and officially resigned from Congress on January 3, 1999.

Impeachment proceedings were initiated during the post-election, "lame duck" session of the outgoing 105th United States Congress. Unlike the case of the 1974 impeachment process against Richard Nixon, the committee hearings were perfunctory but the floor debate in the whole House was spirited on both sides. The Speaker-designate, Representative Bob Livingston, chosen by the Republican Party Conference to replace Gingrich as House Speaker, announced the end of his candidacy for Speaker and his resignation from Congress from the floor of the House after his own marital infidelity came to light.

In the same speech, Livingston also encouraged Clinton to resign. Clinton chose to remain in office and urged Livingston to reconsider his resignation. Many other prominent Republican members of Congress (including Dan Burton of Indiana, Helen Chenoweth of Idaho and Henry Hyde of Illinois, the chief House manager of Clinton's trial in the Senate) had infidelities exposed about this time, all of whom voted for impeachment. Publisher Larry Flynt offered a reward for such information, and many supporters of Clinton accused Republicans of hypocrisy.

On the passage of H. Res. 611, Clinton was impeached on December 19, 1998, by the House of Representatives on grounds of perjury to a grand jury (by a 228–206 vote) and obstruction of justice(by a 221–212 vote). Two other articles of impeachment failed – a second count of perjury in the Jones case (by a 205–229 vote) and one accusing Clinton of abuse of power (by a 148– 285 vote). Clinton thus became the second U.S. president to be impeached, following Andrew Johnson in 1868. (Clinton was the third sitting president against whom the House of Representatives initiated impeachment proceedings since 1789.

Five Democrats (Virgil Goode of Virginia, Ralph Hall of Texas, Paul McHale of Pennsylvania, Charles Stenholm of Texas and Gene Taylor of Mississippi) voted in favor of three of the four articles of impeachment, but only Taylor voted for the abuse of power charge. Five Republicans (Amo Houghton of New York, Peter King of New York, Connie Morella of Maryland, Chris Shays of Connecticut and Mark Souder of Indiana) voted against the first perjury charge.

Eight more Republicans (Sherwood Boehlert of New York, Michael Castle of Delaware, Phil English of

Pennsylvania, Nancy Johnson of Connecticut, Jay Kim of California, Jim Leach of Iowa, John McHugh of New York and Ralph Regula of Ohio), but not Souder, voted against the obstruction charge. Twenty-eight Republicans voted against the second perjury charge, sending it to defeat, and eighty-one voted against the abuse of power charge.

Article I charged that Clinton lied to the grand jury concerning:

1. The nature and details of his relationship with Lewinsky.
2. Prior false statements he made in the Jones deposition.
3. Prior false statements he allowed his lawyer to make characterizing Lewinsky's affidavit.
4. His attempts to tamper with witnesses.

Article III charged Clinton with attempting to obstruct justice in the Jones case by:

1. Encouraging Lewinsky to file a false affidavit.
2. Encouraging Lewinsky to give false testimony if and when she was called to testify.

3. Concealing gifts he had given to Lewinsky that had been subpoenaed.

4. Attempting to secure a job for Lewinsky to influence her testimony.

5. Permitting his lawyer to make false statements characterizing Lewinsky's affidavit.

6. Attempting to tamper with the possible testimony of his secretary Betty Curie.

7. Making false and misleading statements to potential grand jury witnesses Acquittal by the Senate.

The Senate trial began on January 7, 1999, with Chief Justice of the United States William Rehnquist presiding. Inspired by a character in a Gilbert and Sullivan operetta, Rehnquist chose to personalize his robes for the trial with four gold stripes on each sleeve. He continued to adorn his robes in this manner for the rest of his time on the bench. The first day consisted of formal presentation of the charges against Clinton, and of Rehnquist swearing in all argents in the trial.

Clinton was defended by Cheryl Mills. Clinton's counsel staff included Charles Ruff, David E. Kendall, Dale Bumpers, Bruce Lindsey, Nicole Seligman, Lanny A. Breuerand Gregory B. Craig. A resolution on rules and procedure for the trial was adopted unanimously on the following day; however, senators tabled the question of whether to call witnesses in the trial. The trial remained in recess while briefs were filed by the House (January 11) and Clinton (January 13).

The managers presented their case over three days, from January 14 to 16, with discussion of the facts and background of the case; detailed cases for both articles of impeachment (including excerpts from videotaped grand jury testimony that Clinton had made the previous August); matters of interpretation and application of the laws governing perjury and obstruction of justice; and argument that the evidence and precedents justified removal of the President from office by virtue of "willful, premeditated, deliberate corruption of the nation's system of justice through perjury and obstruction of justice."

The defense presentation took place from January 19–21. Clinton's defense counsel argued that Clinton's grand jury testimony had too many inconsistencies to be a clear case of perjury, that the investigation and impeachment had been tainted by partisan political bias, that the President's approval rating of more than 70 percent indicated that his ability to govern had not been impaired by the scandal, and that the managers had ultimately presented "an unsubstantiated, circumstantial case that does not meet the constitutional standard to remove the President from office". January 22 and 23 were devoted to questions from members of the Senate to the House managers and Clinton's defense counsel. Under the rules, all questions (over 150) were to be written down and given to Rehnquist to read to the party being questioned.

On January 25, Senator Robert Byrd of West Virginia moved for dismissals of both articles of impeachment for lack of merit. On the following day, Rep. Bryant moved to call witnesses to the trial, a question that the Senate had scrupulously avoided to that point. In both cases, the Senate voted to deliberate on the question in private session, rather than public, televised procedure.

On January 27, the Senate voted on both motions in public session; the motion to dismiss failed on a nearly party line vote of 56–44, while the motion to depose witnesses passed by the same margin. A day later, the Senate voted down motions to move directly to a vote on the articles of impeachment and to suppress videotaped depositions of the witnesses from public release, Feingold again voting with the Republicans.

Over three days, February 1–3, House managers took videotaped closed-door depositions from Monica Lewinsky, Clinton's friend Vernon Jordan, and White House aide Sidney Blumenthal. On February 4, however, the Senate voted 70–30 that excerpting these videotapes would suffice as testimony, rather than calling live witnesses to appear at trial. The videos were played in the Senate on February 6, featuring 30 excerpts of Lewinsky discussing her affidavit in the Paula Jones case, the hiding of small gifts Clinton had given her, and his involvement in procurement of a job for Lewinsky.

On February 8, closing arguments were presented with each side allotted a three-hour time slot. On the President's behalf, White House Counsel Charles Ruf declared:

There is only one question before you, albeit a difficult one, one that is a question of fact and law and constitutional theory. Would it put at risk the liberties of the people to retain the President in office? Putting aside partisan animus, if you can honestly say that it would not, that those liberties are safe in his hands, then you must vote to acquit.

On February 9, after voting against a public deliberation on the verdict, the Senate began closed-door deliberations instead. On February 12, the Senate emerged from its closed deliberations and voted on the articles of impeachment. A two-thirds vote, 67 votes, would have been necessary to convict and remove the President from office. The perjury charge was defeated with 45 votes for conviction and 55 against (Senator Arlen Specter of Pennsylvania voted "not proved" for both charges, which was considered by Chief Justice Rehnquist to constitute a vote of "not guilty".) The obstruction of justice charge was defeated with 50 for conviction and 50 against.

Senate votes

All 45 Democrats in the Senate voted "not guilty" on both charges. The five Republican senators who voted against conviction on both charges were John Chafee of Rhode Island, Susan Collins of Maine, Jim Jeffords of Vermont, Olympia Snowe of Maine, and Arlen Specter of Pennsylvania. Specter, who said he was not prepared to cast a guilty or not guilty vote, voted "not proved", which was counted as a not guilty vote. The additional five Republican senators who voted "not guilty" only on the perjury charge were Slade Gorton of Washington, Richard

Shelby of Alabama, Ted Stevens of Alaska, Fred Thompson of Tennessee, and John Warner of Virginia.

The robe worn by Chief Justice William Rehnquist during the proceedings won some media attention for the distinctive gold stripes, which were inspired by a costume from the Gilbert and Sullivan opera Iolanthe.

In April 1999, about two months after being acquitted by the Senate, Clinton was cited by Federal District Judge Susan Webber Wright for civil contempt of court for his "willful failure" to obey her repeated orders to testify truthfully in the Paula Jones sexual harassment lawsuit. For this citation, Clinton was assessed a $90,000 fine, and the matter was referred to the Arkansas Supreme Court to see if disciplinary action would be appropriate. Regarding Clinton's January 17, 1998,deposition where he was placed under oath, the judge wrote:

Simply put, the president's deposition testimony regarding whether he had ever been alone with Ms. (Monica) Lewinsky was intentionally false, and his statements regarding whether he had ever engaged in sexual relations with Ms. Lewinsky likewise were intentionally false.

On the day before leaving office in January 2001, President Clinton agreed to a five-year suspension of his Arkansas law license as part of an agreement with the independent counsel to end the investigation. Clinton was automatically suspended from the United States Supreme Court bar as a result of his law license suspension. However, as is customary, he was allowed 40 days to appeal an otherwise-automatic disbarment. The former President resigned from the Supreme Court bar during the 40-day appeals period.

Eventually, the court dismissed the Paula Jones harassment lawsuit, before trial, on the grounds that Jones failed to demonstrate any damages.

Polls conducted during 1998 and early 1999 showed that only about one-third of Americans supported Clinton's impeachment or conviction. However, one year later, when it was clear that House impeachment would not lead to the ousting of the President, half of Americans said in a CNN/USA Today/Gallup poll that they supported impeachment but 57% approved of the Senate's decision to keep him in office and two thirds of those polled said the impeachment was harmful to the country.

While Clinton's job approval rating rose during the Lewinsky scandal and subsequent impeachment, his poll numbers with regard to questions of honesty, integrity and moral character declined. As a result, "moral character" and "honesty" weighed heavily in the next presidential election. According to The Daily Princetonian, after the 2000 presidential election, "post-election polls found that, in the wake of Clinton-era scandals, the single most significant reason people voted for Bush was for his moral character." According to an analysis of the election by Stanford University:

A more political explanation is the belief in Gore campaign circles that disapproval of President Clinton's personal behavior was a serious threat to the vice president's prospects. Going into the election the one negative element in the public's perception of the state of the nation was the belief that the country was morally on the wrong track, whatever the state of the economy or world affairs. According to some insiders, anything done to raise the association between Gore and Clinton would have produced a net loss of support—the impact of Clinton's personal negatives would outweigh the positive impact of his job performance on support for Gore. Thus, hypothesis four suggests that a previously unexamined variable played a major role in 2000—the retiring president's personal approval.

The Stanford analysis, however, presented different theories and mainly argued that Gore had lost because he decided to distance himself from Clinton during the campaign. The writers of it concluded:

We find that Gore's oft-criticized personality was not a cause of his under-performance. Rather, the major cause was his failure to receive a historically normal amount of credit for the performance of the Clinton administration ... [and] failure to get normal credit reflected Gore's peculiar campaign which in turn reflected fear of association with Clinton's behavior.

According to the America's Future Foundation:

In the wake of the Clinton scandals, independents warmed to Bush's promise to 'restore honor and dignity to the White House'. According to Voter News Service, the personal quality that mattered most to voters was 'honesty'. Voters who chose 'honesty' preferred Bush over Gore by over a margin of five to one. Forty Four percent of Americans said the Clinton scandals were important to their vote. Of these, Bush reeled in three out of every four.

Political commentators have argued that Gore's refusal to have Clinton campaign with him was a bigger liability to Gore than Clinton's scandals. The 2000 US Congressional election also saw the Democrats gain more seats in Congress. As a result of this gain, control of the US Senate was split 50–50 between both parties, and Democrats would regain control over the US Senate after Republican Senator Jim Jeffords defected from his party in the spring of 2001 and agreed to caucus with the Democrats.

Al Gore reportedly confronted Clinton after the election, and "tried to explain that keeping Clinton under wraps [during the campaign] was a rational response to polls showing swing voters were still mad as hell over the Year of Monica". According to the AP, "during the one-on-one meeting at the White House, which lasted more than an hour, Gore used uncommonly blunt language to tell Clinton that his sex scandal and low personal approval ratings were a hurdle he could not surmount in his campaign ... [with] the core of the dispute was Clinton's lies to Gore and the nation about his affair with White House intern Monica Lewinsky." Clinton, however, was unconvinced by Gore's argument and insisted to Gore that he would have won the election if he had embraced the administration and its good economic record.

Of the 13 members of the House who managed Clinton's trial in the Senate, one lost to a Democrat in his 2000 bid for re-election (James E. Rogan, to Adam Schiff). Charles Canady retired from Congress in 2000, following through on a previous term limits pledge to voters, and Bill McCollum ran unsuccessfully for the U.S. Senate. Asa Hutchinson, after being re-elected in 2000, left Congress after being appointed head of the Drug Enforcement Administration by President George W. Bush.

In 2014, Hutchinson was elected governor of Arkansas. In 2002, two former House managers lost their seats after redistricting placed them in the same district as another incumbent (Bob Barr lost to John Linder in a Republican primary, and George Gekas lost to Democrat Tim Holden), while two more ran for the U.S. Senate (Lindsey Graham successfully, Ed Bryant unsuccessfully).

CHAPTER FIVE
DONALD TRUMP'S SCANDALS

Donald Trump, an American businessman and current President of the United States, has been accused of sexual assault and sexual harassment, including non-consensual kissing or groping, by at least nineteen women since the 1980s. Those accusations have resulted in three widely reported instances of litigation: his then-wife Ivana made a rape claim during their 1989 divorce litigation but later recanted that claim; businesswoman Jill Harth sued Trump in 1997 alleging breach of contract while also suing for nonviolent sexual harassment but withdrew the latter suit as part of a settlement for relating to the former suit; and, in 2017, former *Apprentice* contestant Summer Zervos filed a defamation lawsuit after Trump called her a liar.

Two of the allegations (by Ivana Trump and Jill Harth) became public before Trump's candidacy for president, but the rest arose after a 2005 audio recording was leaked during the 2016 presidential campaign. Trump was recorded bragging that a celebrity like himself "can do anything" to women, including "just start kissing them ... I don't even wait" and "grab them by the pussy". Trump subsequently characterized those comments as "locker room talk" and denied actually behaving that way toward women, and he also apologized for the crude language that was leaked. Many of his accusers stated that Trump's denials provoked them into going public with their allegations.

Another type of accusation was made, primarily after the audio recording surfaced, by several former Miss USA and Miss Teen USA contestants, who accused Trump of entering the dressing rooms of beauty pageant contestants. Trump, who owned the Miss Universe franchise, which includes both pageants, was accused of going into dressing rooms in 1997, 2000, 2001, and 2006, while contestants were in various stages of undress. During a 2005 interview on *The Howard Stern Show*, Trump said that he could "get away with things like that".

Donald (2015) and ex-wife Ivana Trump (2007) who alleged privately and legally he raped her in 1989. After the divorce, she has publicly stated "but I do not want my words to be interpreted in a literal or criminal sense", and that the claim was "without merit." A confidentiality clause also prevents her discussing the marriage or the divorce.

Sexual misconduct allegations have been made against Trump by at least 19 women. Trump has denied the allegations, saying that

he has been the victim of media bias, conspiracies, and a political smear campaign. In October 2016, Trump publicly vowed to sue all of the women who have made allegations of sexual assault (i.e. non-consensual kissing or groping) or sexual harassment against him, as well as to sue the *New York Times* for publishing allegations, but as yet has not followed through.

Ivana Trump and Donald Trump married in 1977. Ivana stated in a deposition taken in 1989, during their divorce proceedings, that Donald had visited her plastic surgeon following which he had expressed anger and ripped out hair from her scalp. Donald said the allegation was "obviously false". The 1993 book *Lost Tycoon: The Many Lives of Donald Trump*, by Harry Hurt III, described the alleged attack as a "violent assault" during which Donald attacked Ivana sexually. According to the book, Ivana later confided to some of her friends that Donald had raped her. In a statement given just before the publication of Hurt's book, and included in the book, Ivana said:

[O]n one occasion during 1989, Mr. Trump and I had marital relations in which he behaved very differently toward me than he had during our marriage. As a woman, I felt violated, as the love and tenderness, which he normally exhibited towards me, was absent. I referred to this as a "rape," but I do not want my words to be interpreted in a literal or criminal sense.

— Ivana Trump.

The Trumps' divorce was granted in December 1990 on grounds that Donald's treatment of Ivana, including his affair with Marla Maples, was "cruel and inhuman". According to Trump's lawyer, Jay Goldberg, this was based on Trump having been seen in public with Marla Maples in 1990. Their settlement[a] had a confidentiality clause preventing Ivana discussing the marriage or

the divorce. In 1992, Trump sued Ivana for not honoring a gag clause in their divorce agreement by disclosing facts about him in her best-selling book, and Trump won a gag order.

Years later, Ivana said that she and Donald "are the best of friends". In a July 2015 campaign endorsement, Ivana said: "I have recently read some comments attributed to me from nearly 30 years ago at a time of very high tension during my divorce from Donald. The story is totally without merit."

Jill Harth alleges that Trump assaulted her several times. Harth has stated that in December 1992, while dining with Trump and her then-boyfriend George Houraney, Trump attempted to put his hands between her legs. Harth and Houraney visited Trump's Mar-a-Lago estate in Florida in January 1993 for a contract-signing celebration. Trump, according to Harth, offered her a tour before pulling her into the empty bedroom of his daughter Ivanka. "I was admiring the decoration, and next thing I know he's pushing me against a wall and has his hands all over me.

He was trying to kiss me. I was freaking out." Harth says she desperately protested against Trump's advances and eventually managed to run out of the room. She and her boyfriend left rather than stay the night, as they had intended. After she became engaged, Harth alleges, Trump began to stalk her.

Harth filed a lawsuit in 1997 in which she accused Trump of non-consensual groping of her body, among them her "intimate private parts", and "relentless" sexual harassment. The suit was withdrawn after Houraney settled with Trump for an undisclosed amount in a lawsuit that claimed that Trump backed out of a business deal. She still claims to have been sexually assaulted and although he was never violent with her she says his actions were "unwanted and aggressive, every sexually aggressive".

Following the incident, Harth said she received "a couple years of therapy". In 2015 she reached out to Trump's campaign to get a job as a makeup artist and sell her men's cosmetic product line. She later said, "Yes, I had moved on but had not forgotten the pain [Trump] brought into my life. I was older, wiser. Trump was married to Melania and I had hoped he was a changed man."

She worked at one of Trump's rallies as a makeup artist. Of the experience, she said: "I'm a makeup artist. The guy is a mess, OK? He really needed my services, and I'm a makeup artist that needs a job. Why would, if I was on friendly terms, why wouldn't I try to get that job?"

Hearth's lawsuit was first published in February 2016 by LawNewz.com. Her case was first published in May 2016 in the *New York Times* article "Crossing the Line". Trump characterized her story in the *Times* as "false, malicious and libelous" and stated that he "strongly denies the claims". Harth stood by her charges in a July 2016 interview with *The Guardian*. In October 2016, she stated that, if sued by Trump, she intends to counter-sue.

Summer Zervos was a contestant on the fifth season of *The Apprentice*, which filmed in 2005 and aired in 2006. Subsequently, she contacted Trump in 2007, about a job after the show's completion, and he invited her to meet him at The Beverly Hills Hotel.

Zervos has said that Trump was sexually suggestive during their meeting, kissing her open-mouthed, groping her breasts, and thrusting his genitals on her. She also has said that his behavior was aggressive and not consensual. Zervos is being represented by attorney Gloria Allred.

John Barry, her cousin and a Trump supporter, has said that Zervos talked to her family and friends about Trump, promoting his candidacy and stating how Trump had helped her out in her life. Barry said that during the presidential primary campaign, Zervos invited Trump to her restaurant, and he declined. In October 2016, the Trump presidential campaign released an email by Zervos, sent to Trump's secretary in April 2016, in which she stated: "I would greatly appreciate reconnecting at this time. He will know my intentions are genuine." Zervos said that she had intended to confront Trump and give him the "opportunity to clear the air" She said that on April 21, she sent another email to Trump's assistant which she asked to be forwarded to Trump, in which she stated: "I have been incredibly hurt by our previous interaction."

On January 17, 2017, Zervos filed a defamation lawsuit against Trump, arising from his statement that she had lied about the allegations. Marc Kasowitz is defending Trump in the case. Zervos has filed a subpoena for "all documents concerning any woman who asserted that Donald J. Trump touched her inappropriately". On 21 March 2018, a New York Supreme Court judge decided to allow a defamation lawsuit against the President to go forward. On June 4, 2018, Manhattan Supreme Court Justice Jennifer Schecter ruled that Trump must be deposed by January 31, 2019.

As of September 9, 2018, Trump will provide written answers under oath in the defamation lawsuit. In May 2016, *The New York Times* published the article "Crossing the Line: How Donald Trump Behaved with Women in Private".

For the article, *Times* reporters Michael Barbaro and Megan Twohey conducted 50 interviews with women who had known Trump socially, during their professional career or while modeling or competing for a beauty pageant title.

Their accounts — many relayed here in their own words — reveal unwelcome romantic advances, unending commentary on the female form, a shrewd reliance on ambitious women, and unsettling workplace conduct, according to the interviews, as well as court records and written recollections. The interactions occurred in his offices at Trump Tower, at his homes, at construction sites and backstage at beauty pageants. They appeared to be fleeting, unimportant moments to him, but they left lasting impressions on the women who experienced them.

Other women interviewed for the story, a few of whom had worked for Trump, stated they had not received unwanted advances and "they had never known Mr. Trump to objectify women or treat them with disrespect." Jill Martin, a vice president and assistant counsel at the company, said that Trump was supportive of her and her role as a mother. Laura Kirilova Chukanov, a Bulgarian immigrant and 2009 Miss USA pageant contestant said that Trump helped her make connections for a documentary that she was working on about her home country.

Rowanne Brewer Lane, Trump's former girlfriend, was quoted at length in the article and was featured in the opening anecdote.

Following the article's publication, Brewer Lane accused *The Times* of taking her quotes out of context and said that she was "flattered" and not insulted by Trump. Trump spokesperson Barry Bennett responded to the story by stating: "They talked to 50 women and managed to put seven or eight in the story. Over half of them had great things to say. The one that had great things to say,
they twisted it and called her debased which is not how she feels." *The Times* defended the story and said Brewer Lane was "quoted fairly, accurately and at length".

Two days before the second 2016 presidential debate, the 2005 *Access Hollywood* tape was released, which records Trump having "an extremely lewd conversation about women" in which he described being able to kiss and grope women because he was "a star": "You know I'm automatically attracted to beautiful—I just start kissing them. It's like a magnet. Just kiss. I don't even wait. And when you're a star, they let you do it, you can do anything ... grab them by the pussy. You can do anything."

Many attorneys and media commentators have said that Trump's statements described sexual assault.

On October 7, Trump released a video statement in which he stated, "I said it, I was wrong, and I apologize." He called the development a distraction and attempted to deflect attention to the Clintons, and in particular sexual assault scandals involving Bill Clinton. Republican critics called on him to withdraw from the presidential race.

During the second debate, Anderson Cooper asked Trump if he understood that he had bragged about sexually assaulting women. Cooper used the Justice Department's sexual assault definition to include "any type of sexual contact or behavior that occurs without the explicit consent of the recipient."

Trump denied that he had said that he had sexually assaulted women. He claimed the comments were merely "locker room talk", then, after being asked three times whether he had ever kissed or groped any person without consent, he said "no I have not". Several of his subsequent accusers said this was the moment at which they were motivated to come forward.

Natasha Stoynoff, Mindy McGillivray, Jessica Leeds, and Rachel Crooks spoke out about their allegations in October 2016 after hearing Trump deny during the debate that he had ever assaulted women. The *Times* stated that they verified the stories with friends and family members of the accusers to ensure that the stories had been relayed to them earlier.

In the early 1980s, Leeds was a businesswoman at a paper company on a flight from the Midwest, returning to New York. A flight attendant offered her an empty seat in the first-class cabin next to Trump. Leeds alleged that about 45 minutes after takeoff, Trump lifted the armrest and began touching her, grabbing her breasts, and tried to put his hand up her skirt. "He was like an octopus," she said. "His hands were everywhere. It was an assault. " Leeds said she had sent a letter containing her allegations to the editor of *The New York Times*.

Trump spokesman Jason Miller responded to the allegation calling it "fiction." Miller stated the charges were politically motivated "for this to only become public decades later in the final month of a campaign for president should say it all." Trump publicly threatened to sue the *Times* over the newspaper's publication of the allegation, and demanded a retraction.

The *Times* rejected Trump's retraction demand, and Trump never followed through on his threat to take legal action against the company. An alleged witness to the case who claimed he saw "nothing untoward" upon the flight was former British Conservative county councilor from Gloucestershire, Antony Gilberthorpe. Gilberthorpe has previously made false allegations against politicians and has been previously accused of making "advances of an intimate nature" towards Conservative student.

On October 14, 2016, *The Washington Post* reported allegations by Kristin Anderson that Trump groped her beneath her skirt in a Manhattan nightclub in the early 1990s. An aspiring model at the time of the alleged incident, Anderson told the story to her friends, and decided to come forward after reading accounts of other women who had done so. Anderson believed that the alleged assault occurred at the China Club, a Manhattan nightclub that *Newsday* referred to as "Donald's Monday-night nest" due to his alleged habit of picking up women there.

In February 2016, Cathy Heller was interviewed off the record for an article for *The Guardian* in which she recounted how she was grabbed and kissed by Donald

Trump two decades earlier. Heller reports that, in 1997, she met Trump when she attended a Mother's Day brunch with her children, her husband, and her husband's parents at his Mar-a-Lago estate. Her parents-in-law were members of Mar-a-Lago. Heller was introduced to Trump, who became angry when she avoided a kiss. He then "grabbed" her and, when he tried to kiss her, she turned her head. Trump kissed her on the side of the mouth "for a little too long" and then he left her.

Heller's husband and children, who were present during the event, have corroborated her account. In the summer of 2015, the members of Heller's mahjong group heard Heller's account of the 1997 incident; this was not long after Trump announced his candidacy. She decided to go public after seeing the second presidential debate on October 9, 2016. Heller is a registered Democrat, and public supporter of Hillary Clinton.

Trump campaign spokesperson Jason Miller stated that Heller's account is "false" and "politically motivated" Temple Taggart McDowell, Miss Utah USA in 1997, publicly accused Trump of unwanted kisses and embraces that left McDowell and one of her chaperones so uncomfortable, according to McDowell, that she claimed she was instructed not to be left in a room alone with him again. According to McDowell, a chaperone had accompanied her to Trump's office. At the time, McDowell was 21 and was known as Temple Taggart. This incident occurred in Trump's first year of ownership of the Miss USA contest.

McDowell told her story initially to *The New York Times* in May 2016 which was published in the "Crossing the Line: How Donald Trump Behaved With Women in Private" article. She had not intended to speak publicly about the incidents again, but she received numerous calls recently due to the "Crossing the Line" article and felt, as a mother, that it is important to share a message about unwanted advances: "You have the right to say no. You have the right to get out of there. You have the right to leave, and you have the right to make them feel uncomfortable if they're making you feel uncomfortable," she said. Trump stated that he does not know her and denied McDowell's claims. He also told *The New York Times* that he is "reluctant to kiss strangers on the lips." Taggart McDowell stated that she is a Republican, and not coming out with the allegation in order to support Hillary Clinton.

At an October 2016 press conference with attorney Gloria Allred, yoga instructor and life coach Karena Virginia stated that in 1998, Trump grabbed her arm and touched her breast. Virginia, who was 27 years old at the time, was waiting for a ride after the US Open in Queens, New York. She stated that Trump, whom she had not met previously, approached her with a small group of other men, while commenting on her legs, then he grabbed her right arm. Virginia continued, "Then his hand touched the right side of my breast. I was in shock. I flinched. 'Don't you know who I am? Don't you know who I am?' – that's what he said to me. I felt intimidated and I felt powerless."

Trump campaign spokesperson Jessica Ditto responded to the allegation with a statement reading in part, "Discredited political operative Gloria Allred, in another coordinated, publicity seeking attack with the Clinton campaign, will stop at nothing to smear Mr. Trump."

In an article by *The Palm Beach Post*, Mindy McGillivray stated that in January 2003, when she was 23 years old, she was groped by Trump at his Mar-a-Lago estate. She said, "All of a sudden I felt a grab, a little nudge. I think it's [my friend Ken Davidoff's] camera bag that was my first instinct. I turn around and there's Donald. He sort of looked away quickly." Ken Davidoff, a photographer, corroborated McGillivray's account, saying he remembered her pulling him aside moments after the alleged incident to say "Donald just grabbed my ass!"

McGillivray said that she "chose to stay quiet" and never reported the incident to authorities. She had only shared details of the incident with close family and friends until she heard Trump deny such behavior during the second presidential debate on October 9, 2016. Hope Hicks, Trump's press secretary, stated that McGillivray's allegations lacked "any merit or veracity" and were untruthful.

Ken Davidoff's brother, Darryl Davidoff, said that he was also present at the time at Mar-a-Lago, and stated that in his opinion McGillivray is lying. According to Darryl: "I do not believe it really happened. Nobody saw it happen and she just wanted to be in the limelight."

In 2005, Rachel Crooks was a 22-year-old receptionist at Bayrock Group, a real estate investment and development company in Trump Tower in Manhattan. She says she encountered Trump in an elevator in the building one morning and turned to introduce herself. They shook hands, but Trump would not let go. Instead, he began kissing her cheeks, then directly on the mouth.

"It was so inappropriate," Crooks recalled in an interview. "I was so upset that he thought I was so insignificant that he could do that." Her story was printed by *The New York Times*, along with that of Jessica Leeds. Trump has disputed Crooks' claims, writing on Twitter, "Who would do this in a public space with live security cameras running?" Crooks is a public supporter and donor to Hillary Clinton's presidential campaign.

Canadian author and journalist Natasha Stoynoff, who wrote for *People* magazine and, previously, the *Toronto Star* and *Toronto Sun*, went to Trump's Florida estate in December 2005 to interview him and his wife, Melania. While there, Trump gave Stoynoff a tour of the Mar-a-Lago estate. She says that during this tour, he pushed her against a wall and forced his tongue into her mouth.

Stoynoff described the alleged episode, "We walked into that room alone, and Trump shut the door behind us. I turned around, and within seconds he was pushing me against the wall and forcing his tongue down my throat ... I was stunned. And I was grateful when Trump's longtime butler burst into the room a minute later, as I tried to unpin myself." Stoynoff composed herself and conducted the interview, after which she said Trump repeatedly told her, "We're going to have an affair, I'm telling you." Melania was also interviewed for that article.

Trump sent out a tweet on October 13, 2016, in which he said it had not happened and wondered why she had not mentioned the event in her *People* article of 2005. Stoynoff responded that she had become angry when Trump denied assaulting women during the presidential debate and was triggered by the release of the *Access Hollywood* recording in early October. Until that point, she said, she had conflicting emotions common among victims of assault, combined with embarrassment and confusion. J.D. Heyman,

People's deputy editor, said: "It was disorienting for her. She felt a great deal of worry and distress about it. Then she felt angry." That same day, Melania's lawyer demanded an apology from *People* magazine, stating that Melania did not say some or all of what was quoted in the *People* article by Stoynoff published on October 12, 2016; Melania specifically denied Stoynoff's claim that she'd run into her on Fifth Avenue following the article's publication.

In an interview with Anderson Cooper that aired October 17 on CNN, Melania again denied having crossed paths with Stoynoff on Fifth Avenue, as stated in Stoynoff's article. The following day, *People* published the account of Liza Herz. Herz said she witnessed the sidewalk encounter between Stoynoff and Melania Trump; Herz' account corroborated that of Stoynoff.

On October 18, *People* produced six corroborating witnesses who said Stoynoff had recounted the incident to them around the time that it occurred. The six witnesses were: "two editors from *People*, Mary Green and Liz McNeil; a professor of journalism, Paul McLaughlin; a co-worker; and two personal friends of Ms. Stoynoff".

Trump's former butler at Mar-a-Lago resort in Florida, Anthony Senecal, 85, was asked about the 2005 incident in which Stoynoff alleged that the butler "burst in" on Trump when she was pinned down by him; Senecal denied that ever happened, stating that as a butler "I don't burst in. I knock, then I go in, usually after someone says 'come in'," further alleging "And when I went in, there was nothing strange about where she was standing." According to Senecal, the alleged incident took place in a massage room with windows all around which made it unsuitable to grope anyone since there was no privacy.

In early December 2017, the reporter Juliet Huddy said that Trump kissed her on the lips while they were on an elevator in Trump Tower with Trump's security guard in 2005 or 2006. Regarding this incident, Huddy said "I was surprised that he went for the lips. But I didn't feel threatened... Whatever, everything was fine. It was a weird moment. He never tried anything after that, and I was never alone with him."

On October 22, 2016, Jessica Drake and attorney Gloria Allred held a news conference in which Drake accused Trump of having sexually assaulted her and two acquaintances nearly ten years prior. Drake, an adult film actress and sex education advocate, said that she met Trump at her company's booth during a charity golf tournament at Lake Tahoe in 2006. Drake claims that she was invited to meet with Trump, who was married at the time, at his hotel suite; she was "uncomfortable going alone" and brought two friends.

Describing the meeting with Trump, Drake recounted that "He grabbed each of us tightly, in a hug and kissed each one of us without asking permission." Drake stated that she and her friends left the suite after 30–45 minutes. Shortly thereafter, Drake claims she received phone calls from Trump or his associate, requesting that she join him in his suite for $10,000, and offering to fly her on his jet back to Los Angeles. She said she declined his offers.

During the news conference, Drake said, "I am not looking for monetary compensation. I do not need additional fame... I understand that I may be called a liar or an opportunist but I will risk that in order to stand in solidarity with women who share similar accounts." During the news conference, Gloria Allred held up a picture showing Trump and Drake standing together at the time.

In response to Drake's allegations, the Trump campaign stated that her story is "false and ridiculous", that "[t]he picture is one of thousands taken out of respect for people asking to have their picture taken with Mr. Trump" but Trump did not know Drake and "would have no interest in ever knowing her," and that the story was "just another attempt by the Clinton campaign to defame a candidate." Donald Trump appeared to dismiss the significance of the accusation because of Drake's line of work, saying, "Oh, I'm sure she's never been grabbed before."

Amanda Prestigiacomo, writing in *The Daily Wire*, has criticized Drake for suggesting that being greeted with a hug and a kiss without permission is "sexual assault". According to Prestigiacomo, if this were to be "sexual assault" then everyone has been "sexually assaulted" numerous times, and making such a claim does a disservice to women who have actually faced sexual assault.

Ninni Laaksonen, Miss Finland 2006, appeared with Trump on the *Late Show with David Letterman* on July 26, 2006. Laaksonen claims that before they went on the air, Trump grabbed her buttocks. As Laaksonen describes the interaction: "He really grabbed my butt. I don't think anybody saw it but I flinched and thought: "What is happening?" Someone later told Laaksonen that Trump liked her because she looked like his wife, Melania, when she was younger.

Laaksonen revealed her account to a local Finnish newspaper, *Ilta-Sanomat*, which had contacted her regarding the level of professionalism involved in Donald Trump's handling of his employees within the Miss Universe pageant. The story was published on October 27, 2016.

Rolling Stone and NPR have reported that Cassandra Searles, Miss Washington USA of 2013, was fondled by Trump during the Miss USA pageant of that year. Yahoo! News published an article in June 2016 stating that Searles had made Facebook postings that accused Trump of making unwanted advances. She said that he was "continually" groping her buttocks and had asked her to go "to his hotel room". Searles also asserted that Trump had "treated us like cattle". Trump and his campaign have not specifically responded to Searles' allegations.

Trump owned the Miss Universe franchise, which includes Miss USA and Miss Teen USA, from 1996 to 2015. Contestants of the shows have alleged that, during his tenure, Trump would enter the dressing rooms while they were in various stages of undress.

These incidents happened in 1997, 2000, 2001, and 2006 During a Howard Stern interview in 2005, Trump described his practice of walking in unannounced while beauty pageant contestants were naked or partially clothed: I'll go backstage before a show, and everyone's getting dressed and ready and everything else....You know, no men are anywhere. And I'm allowed to go in because I'm the owner of the pageant. And therefore I'm inspecting it.... *Is everyone OK*? You know, they're standing there with no clothes. And you see these incredible-looking women. And so I sort of get away with things like that .But no, I've been very good.

In the same interview with Stern, Trump declined to say whether he had slept with any contestants, stating "It could be a conflict of interest". Stern then imitated a foreign contestant ("Mr. Trump, in my country, we say hello with vagina"), and Trump jokingly responded: "Well, you could also say, as the owner of the pageant, it's your obligation to do that."

Mariah Billado, Miss Vermont Teen USA, is one of four women to mention such a dressing room visit incident in 1997. Billado said of the visit: "I remember putting on my dress really quick, because I was like, 'Oh my god, there's a man in here.' Trump, she recalled, said something like, 'Don't worry, ladies, I've seen it all before.'" Billado recalled talking to Ivanka, Trump's daughter, who responded "Yeah, he does that."

The dressing room had 51 contestants, each with their own stations. Eleven girls said that they did not see Trump enter the dressing room, though some said it was possible that he entered while they were somewhere else, or that they didn't notice. Of the 15 former contestants who were interviewed by Buzzfeed News, none alleged Trump said anything sexually explicit or made physical contact in the dressing room, and reportedly "Most of the former contestants were doubtful or dismissed the possibility that Trump violated their changing room privacy."

Allison Bowman, Miss Wisconsin Teen USA, expressed skepticism: "these were teenage girls. If anything inappropriate had gone on, the gossip would have flown." Trump's campaign stated the allegations of him entering the dressing room "have no merit and have already been disproven by many other individuals who were present."

In 2000, Bridget Sullivan was Miss New Hampshire USA. As she prepared for a television broadcast, Trump allegedly walked into the dressing room. She told *BuzzFeed* that he was coming to wish the contestants good luck, but they "were all naked". Some contestants that night do not remember him entering while the ladies prepared and other contestants mentioned that they had no negative experiences with Trump. A spokesman for Trump said that Sullivan's claims were "totally false".

Tasha Dixon, Miss Arizona USA 2001, told a CBS affiliate in Los Angeles that in 2001, "[Trump] just came strolling right in. There was no second to put a robe on or any sort of clothing or anything. Some girls were topless, other girls were naked." She said that having been walked in on when the women had little or no clothes put them in a "very physically vulnerable position, and then to have the pressure of the people that work for him telling us to go fawn all over him, go walk up to him, talk to him ..." Another contestant, Miss California USA Carrie Prejean Boller, told the same CBS affiliate it was wrong to paint Trump that way.

Trump's response, provided through spokeswoman Jessica Ditto, is that: "These accusations have no merit and have already been disproven by many other individuals who were present," Ditto adds that she believes that there is a political motivation behind the accusation.

An unnamed Miss USA contestant said that in 2001 Trump walked into her dressing room unannounced while she and another contestant were undressed. She told *The Guardian* that Trump "just barged right in, didn't say anything, stood there and stared at us .... He didn't walk in and say, 'Oh, I'm so sorry, I was looking for someone.' He walked in, he stood and he stared. He was doing it because he knew that he could." Another contestant told *The*

Guardian that the contestant spoke to others of this event at the time.

On October 14, 2016, Samantha Carol Holvey, Miss North Carolina USA 2006, related that "Trump's conduct was "creepy" around the women participating but never made an advance toward her." She also said that prior to pageant events, Trump had "moved into areas where she and other contestants were getting ready," and that she had "never been around men that were like that." More than a year after Trump was elected President, and after many high-profile men, such as Harvey Weinstein, had lost their jobs because of sexual harassment allegations, Holvey wrote: "You can't work in Hollywood if you're a sexual predator, but you can become the commander-in-chief?" She then related how Trump made her feel very uncomfortable at the 2006 Miss USA pageant:

"He eyed me like a piece of meat. I was shocked and disgusted. I have never felt so objectified. I left the meet-and-greet hoping that this would be my one and only encounter with him." She also described how he had come backstage unannounced, with Melania Trump: "I was shocked — again — by this violation of our personal space.

What was he doing, coming backstage when we were still getting dressed?"

Shaun R. Harper, executive director of the Penn Graduate Center for Education, has said that "many men talk like Donald Trump"; objectifying women and saying offensive things about them. He puts Trump in a class of men whose behavior sometimes includes sexual assault and degrading women. *The Economist* drew similar parallels, pointing to research that objectifying women can make sexual assault more likely.

NPR reported that Trump has exhibited questionable behavior in his treatment of women for some time, using offensive language to describe women including Megyn Kelly, Rosie O'Donnell, and former Miss Universe Alicia Machado. Arwa Mahdawi of *The Guardian* called his past remarks a "master class in rape culture", pointing to statements such as "26,000 unreported sexual assaults [sic] in the military-only 238 convictions. What did these geniuses expect when they put men & women together?" and "women, you have to treat them like shit."

On October 13, a transcript from a 1994 *Primetime Live* interview was unearthed where Trump states "I tell friends who treat their wives magnificently, get treated like crap in return, 'Be rougher and you'll see a different relationship.'"

Trump has presented himself as a political martyr in the face of these accusations. He declared "this is a conspiracy against you, the American people", saying "the Washington establishment and the financial and media corporations that fund it exist for only one reason: to protect and enrich itself" and that "the Clinton machine is at the center of this power structure." In his next speech, he said *New York Times* reporters are "corporate lobbyists" for minority shareholder Carlos Slim and Hillary Clinton, suggesting Slim's motivation is that he "comes from Mexico." Trump also said the accusers may instead have been motivated by fame or money. He went on to wonder why President Barack Obama had not been accused yet, and denied the Jessica Leeds allegation by saying "she would not be my first choice."

In the third presidential debate, Trump repeated his claims: "I think they want either fame or her campaign did it and I think it's her campaign." At a speech at Gettysburg outlining his vision for his first 100 days, he repeated his denials and stated "all of these liars will be sued after the election is over." To date, however, Trump has not filed suit against any of his accusers.

Melania Trump has responded to the allegations by charging Trump's accusers with lying. Melania has insisted that her husband is a "gentleman" and claimed that he had become a victim of a conspiracy involving the news media and the Clinton campaign. Although Ivanka Trump has claimed to be shocked over Trump's 2005 lewd *Access Hollywood* tapes, calling them "inappropriate and offensive", she has refused directly to address the issue of her father's alleged sexual assault. In contrast, Donald Trump Jr. described the 2005 comments as "a fact of life", and Eric Trump dismissed all allegations of assault as "dirty tricks" from the Clinton campaign.

Leeds's and Crooks' allegations, published by *The New York Times* on October 13, were disputed by Trump's campaign as having "no merit or veracity". The campaign alleged that the *Times* had a vendetta against Trump. The Trump campaign issued this statement through its spokesman Jason Miller.

This entire article is fiction, and for *The New York Times* to launch a completely false, coordinated character assassination against Mr. Trump on a topic like this is dangerous. To reach back decades in an attempt to smear Mr. Trump trivializes sexual assault, and it sets a new low for where the media is willing to go in its efforts to determine this election. It is absurd to think that one of the most recognizable business leaders on the planet with a strong record of empowering women in his companies would do the things alleged in this story, and for this to only become public decades later in the final month of a campaign for president should say it all. Further, the *Times* story buries the pro-Clinton financial and social media activity on behalf of Hillary Clinton's candidacy, reinforcing that this truly is nothing more than a political attack. This is a sad day for the *Times*.

Trump's campaign staff also stated that the Stoynoff and McGillivray accusations were without merit. Trump's attorneys demanded a retraction of the *Times* article and an apology for what they said was a "libelous article"—defamation designed to destroy Trump's run for president. David McCraw, assistant general counsel for the *Times*, responded on October 13, 2016, to the libel claims from Trump's attorney. He stated that Trump's reputation is damaged and "could not be further affected" due to his own statements, like those he made on the Howard Stern show.

McCraw continues, "it would have been a disservice not just to our readers but to democracy itself to silence [the accusers'] voices".

In response to the request to retract the story, McCraw said, "We decline to do so" and stated that Trump was free to pursue the matter in court. Trump's attorney, Michael D. Cohen, has defended Trump by saying that the accusers are not women Trump would find to be attractive.

In October 2017, White House press secretary Sarah Huckabee Sanders was asked if "the official White House position that all of these women are lying", in reference to the sexual harassment claims against Trump by at least 16 women. Sanders replied, "Yeah, we've been clear on that from the beginning, and the president's spoken on it". In November 2017, Trump criticized Senator Al Franken in the wake of sexual misconduct allegations against Franken. This resulted in Sanders describing "a very clear distinction" between the allegations against Trump and Franken: "Franken has admitted wrongdoing and the president hasn't".

In December 2017, after several of Trump's accusers called on Trump to resign, Sanders said that "the president has addressed these accusations directly and denied all of these allegations", which "took place long before he was elected". Since Americans elected Trump to office "at a decisive election", Sanders said, "we feel like these allegations have been answered through that process."

The hashtag #WhyWomenDontReport started trending on Twitter in response to the Trump campaign's statements that the accusers lack credibility. Many commentators disputed the claim that the timing of the allegations during the presidential campaign has a bearing on how likely the events were.

The range of reasons given for why women are reluctant to immediately report sexual assault included fear of reprisals, fear that no one will believe them, the low likelihood of obtaining justice against the assailant, and the traumatic experience of having to be reminded of the event. Liz Plank points out that Trump's accusers are now experiencing all of these factors since coming forward.

Civil rights lawyer Debra Katz and others point out that high-profile cases tend to encourage victims to speak up, even years later. Tom Tremblay, a police specialist in sexual assault, says: "Victims may wait days, weeks, months, years, decades ... When one victim comes forward, it's not at all uncommon to see other victims come forward, who are thinking, 'Well, they came forward; now it's not just my word.'"

Susan Dominus, writing for *The New York Times Magazine*, hopes this backlash against Trump will lead to more people believing women's stories in the future, *Washington Times* online opinion editor and Fox News contributor Monica Crowley said in October 2016 that the accusations come across as a "classical political hit job" on Trump.[140] *Fox and Friends* co-host Ainsley Earhardt said the allegations were "definitely coordinated" and questioned why the media had given more coverage to the allegations than the Podesta emails.

MSNBC host Joe Scarborough said that he was not skeptical of the stories, but said: "I think it's good to be skeptical when you have stories that are 30 years old that come out days before an election." Fox News Media analyst Howard Kurtz wrote in a column that it was "possible to find the allegations troubling while also questioning their timing and whether it's no accident that the women are breaking their silence a month before the election."

The day after *The New York Times* reported the allegations, First Lady Michelle Obama delivered a widely praised speech on women's experiences of sexism and sexually predatory behavior.

A survey conducted by YouGov in October 2016 found that 43 percent of respondents found the allegations to be credible. Republicans were least likely to find the allegations credible, and only 19 percent of Republicans thought sexual assault would disqualify Trump from the presidency. A year after the election, and after the Harvey Weinstein sexual abuse allegations, 86 percent of Clinton voters found the allegations credible, while only 6 percent of Trump voters did.

In addition to the sexual scandals, the Russian government interfered in the 2016 U.S. presidential election in order to increase political instability in the United States and to damage Hillary Clinton's presidential campaign by bolstering the candidacies of Donald Trump, Bernie Sanders and Jill Stein. A January 2017 assessment by the Office of the Director of National Intelligence (ODNI) stated that Russian leadership favored presidential candidate Trump over Clinton, and that Russian president Vladimir Putin personally ordered an "influence campaign" to harm Clinton's chances and "undermine public faith in the US democratic process".

On October 7, 2016, the ODNI and the Department of Homeland Security (DHS) jointly stated that the U.S. Intelligence Community was confident that the Russian Government directed recent hacking of emails with the intention of interfering with the U.S. election process. According to the ODNI's report on January 6, 2017, the Russian military intelligence service (GRU) had hacked the servers of the Democratic National Committee (DNC) and the personal Google email account of Clinton campaign chairman John Podesta and forwarded their contents to WikiLeaks. Although Russian officials have repeatedly denied involvement in any DNC hacks or leaks, there is strong forensic evidence linking the DNC breach to known Russian operations.

In January 2017, Director of National Intelligence James Clapper testified that Russia also interfered in the elections by disseminating fake news promoted on social media. On July 13, 2018, 12 Russian military intelligence agents were indicted by Special Counsel Robert Mueller for allegedly hacking the email accounts and networks of Democratic Party officials.

On October 31, 2016, President Barack Obama warned Putin via the "red phone" to stop interfering or face consequences. In December 2016, Obama ordered a report on hacking efforts aimed at U.S. elections since 2008, while U.S. Senators called for a bipartisan investigation. President-elect Trump rejected claims of foreign interference and said that Democrats were reacting to their election loss.

On December 29, 2016, the Obama Administration expelled 35 Russian diplomats, denied access to two Russia-owned compounds, and broadened existing sanctions on Russian entities and individuals. More sanctions were imposed against Russia by the Trump administration in March 2018, and on April 6, 2018, the Trump administration brought another new round of sanctions against Russia, targeting several oligarchs and high-ranking Russian officials.

In June 2018, the United States Department of the Treasury implemented new sanctions on several Russian entities and officials in connection to cyberattacks by Russia related to the 2016 election interference. Several countries in the European Union have also pursued a sanctions regime against Russia, accusing the state of supporting terrorism and interfering in their own election.

Investigations about Russian influence on the election include a counter-intelligence investigation by the FBI, hearings by the Senate Intelligence Committee and the House Intelligence Committee, and inquiries about possible links and financial ties between the Kremlin and Trump associates, notably targeting Paul Manafort, Carter Page and Roger Stone.

On May 9, 2017, Trump dismissed FBI Director James Comey, citing in part dissatisfaction with suspicions of his presidency because of "this Russia thing". On May 17, Deputy Attorney General, and Acting Attorney General for this investigation Rod Rosenstein appointed former FBI Director Robert Mueller as Special Counsel to oversee the investigation.

Last but not least, Trump was involved in supporting Saudi Crown Prince Mohammed bin Salman, whose hands were stained with the blood of Saudi journalist Jamal Khashoggi, citing strategic ties between the United States and Saudi Arabia.

In addition to Trump's support for dictators, in contrast to American values and principles, he has cast doubt on his personal and suspicious financial ties with the

Saudi crown prince, sparking widespread anger among members of Congress.

Trump's backing of Saudi Arabia following the murder of journalist Jamal Khashoggi has sparked a backlash from members of Congress who insist the US consider additional sanctions and further investigation into the killing. Both Republicans and opposition Democrats weighed in after Trump said he would stand by the US relationship with Saudi Arabia, citing the need for a strong ally in the Middle East, its partnership in the fight against terrorism and hundreds of billions of dollars of business deals.

Republican Senator Bob Corker, chairman of the Senate Foreign Relations Committee, said the position was akin to the White House acting as a public relations firm for Saudi Crown Prince Mohamed bin Salman (MbS), and said Congress would consider everything at its disposal to respond, including requiring by law the determination of Mohamed's role in the dissident Saudi's killing.

Corker joined with Senator Bob Menendez, a Democrat, in calling on Trump to clarify by February whether the crown prince is responsible for the murder, which took place in the Saudi consulate in Istanbul early last month.

Republican Senator Lindsey Graham also advocated "serious sanctions" against members of the Saudi royal family. Representative Eliot Engel, a Democrat on the House Foreign Affairs Committee, accused Trump of "trying to sweep bad acts under the rug". Engel also said Trump's backing of Saudi Arabia cast doubt on the ability of US intelligence, which has not yet issued its report on the Khashoggi murder.Trump, who is in Florida for the Thanksgiving holiday on Wednesday thanked Saudi Arabia, pointing to a drop in the price of oil and saying on Twitter it was "Like a big Tax Cut for America and the World". Meanwhile, Turkey accused the United States on Wednesday of trying to turn a blind eye to the murder of Khashoggi, and dismissed comments from Trump on the issue as "comic."

Of the possibility Prince Mohamed had a hand in the murder, Trump said: "Maybe he did, maybe he didn't". His comments contradicted the CIA, which believes Khashoggi's death was ordered directly by the crown prince, Saudi Arabia's de facto ruler. Numan Kurtulmus, the deputy chairman of President Tayyip Erdogan's AK

Party, dismissed Trump's assessment. "Wednesday's statement is a comic statement," he told state broadcaster TRT Haber.

CHAPTER SIX
RESPECT OF THE AMERICAN VALUES

America's population reflects remarkable ethnic diversity. More than 20 percent of the population of two major cities, Los Angeles and New York, were born in another country. In some other major cities (including San Francisco and Chicago) more than one of every ten residents is foreign born. Non-white people outnumber whites in several large cities. Newspapers commonly use such terms as "Asian American," "Italian American," and "Arab American" to reflect the persistence of various ethnic heritages within the United States. There are people whose skin is labeled white, black, brown, yellow and red.

America's population includes Catholics, Protestants of many denominations, Jews of several persuasions, Muslims, Buddhists, animists, and people who believe in no supreme being or higher power. There are people who have many years of formal education and people who have nearly none. There are the very rich as well as the very poor. There are Republicans, Democrats, Independents, Socialists, Communists, Libertarians, and adherents of other political views as well. There are lawyers, farmers, plumbers, teachers, social workers, immigration officers and people in thousands of other occupations. Some live in urban areas and some in rural ones. Given all this diversity, can one usefully talk about "Americans"? Probably so, if one is careful.

Americans do not usually see themselves, when they are in the United States, as representatives of their country. They see themselves as individuals who are different from all other individuals, whether those others are Americans or foreigners. Americans may say they have no culture, since they often conceive of culture as an overlay of arbitrary customs to be found only in other countries. Individual Americans may think they chose their own values, rather than having had their values and the assumptions on which they are based imposed on them by the society in which they were born. If you ask them to tell you something about "American culture," they may be unable to answer and they may even deny that there is an "American culture." At the same time, Americans will readily generalize about various subgroups within their own country. Northerners have stereotypes (generalized, simplified notions) about Southerners, and vice versa. There are stereotypes of people from the country, people from the city, people from the coasts, people from inland, people from the Midwest, minority ethnic groups, minority religious groups, Texans, New Yorkers, Californians, Iowans, and so on.

The most important thing to understand about American is probably their devotion to "individualism." They have been trained since very early in their lives to consider themselves as separate individuals who are responsible for their own situations in life and their own destinies. They have not been trained to see themselves as members of a close-knit, tightly interdependent family, religious group, tribe, nation, or other collectivity. It is this concept of themselves as individual decision-makers that blinds at least some Americans to the fact they share a culture with others. They have the idea as mentioned above, that they have independently made up their own minds about the values and assumptions they hold. The notion that social factors outside themselves have made them "just like everyone else" in important ways offends their sense of dignity. Foreigners who understand the degree to which Americans are imbued with the notion that the free, self-reliant individual is the ideal kind of human being will find it easier to understand many aspects of American behavior and thinking that otherwise might not make sense. Many Americans do not display the degree of respect for their parents people in more traditional or family-oriented societies commonly display. They have the conception it is a historical or biological accident that put them in the hands of particular parents. Parents fulfill their responsibilities to the children while the children are young, and when children reach "the age of independence" the close child-parent tie is loosened, if not broken. Closely associated with the value they place on individualism is the importance Americans assign privacy. Americans assume people "need some time to themselves" or "some time alone" to think about things or recover their spent psychological energy. Americans have great difficulty understanding foreigners who always want to be with another person and who dislike being alone.

Americans are also distinctive in the degree to which they believe in the ideal, as stated in their Declaration of Independence, that "all men are created equal." Although they sometimes violate the ideal in their daily lives, particularly in matters of interracial relationships, Americans have a deep faith that in some fundamental way all people (at least all American people) are of equal value, and no one is born superior to anyone else. "One man, one vote," they say, conveying the idea any person's opinion is as valid and worthy of attention as any other person's opinion. This is not to say Americans make no distinctions among themselves as a result of such factors as sex, age, wealth, or social position. They do. But the distinctions are acknowledged in subtle ways. Tone of voice, order of speaking, choice of words, seating arrangements-such are the means by which Americans acknowledge status differences among themselves.

Their notions of equality lead Americans to be quite informal in their general behavior and in their relationships with other people. People from societies where general behavior is more formal than in American are struck by the informality of American speech, dress, and posture. Idiomatic speech (commonly called "slang") is heavily used on most occasions, with formal speech reserved for public events and fairly formal situations. People of almost any station in life can be seen in public wearing jeans, sandals, or other informal attire. People slouch down in chairs or lean on walls or furniture when they talk, rather than maintaining an erect bearing.

Americans are generally less concerned about history and traditions than are people from older societies. "History doesn't matter," many of them will say. "It's the future that counts." They look ahead. This fundamental American belief in progress and a better future contrasts sharply with fatalistic (Americans are likely to us that term with a negative or critical connotation) attitude that characterizes people from many other cultures, notably Latin, Asian, and Arab, where there is a pronounced reverence for the past. In those cultures the future is considered to be in the hands of "fate," "God," or at least the few powerful people or families dominating society.

The future cannot be better if people are not fundamentally good and improvable. Americans assume that human nature is basically good, not basically evil. Foreign visitors will see them doing many things that are based on the assumption people are good and can make themselves better. "Where there's a will, there's a way," the Americans say. People who want to make things better can do so if only they have strong enough motivation.

For Americans, time is a "resource," like water or coal, which can be used well or poorly. "Time is money." "You only get so much time in this life, so you'd better use it wisely." The future will not be better than the past or the present, as Americans are trained to see things, unless people use their time for constructive, future-oriented activities. Thus, Americans admire a "well-organized" person, one who has a written list of things to do and a schedule for doing them. The ideal person is punctual (that is, arrives at the scheduled time for a meeting or event) and is considerate of other people's time (that is, does not "waste people's time" with conversation or other activity with no visible, beneficial outcome).The American attitude toward time is not necessarily shared by others, especially non-Europeans. They are more likely to conceive of time as something that is simply there around them, not something they can "use." One of the more difficult things to which many foreign businessmen and students must adjust in the States is the notion that time must be saved whenever possible and used wisely every day.

"He's a hard worker," one American might say in praise of another, or "she gets the job done." These expressions convey the typical American's admiration for a person who approaches a task conscientiously and persistently, seeing it through to a successful conclusion. More than that, these expressions convey an admiration for achievers, people whose lives are centered around efforts to accomplish some physical, measurable thing. Foreign visitors commonly remark that "Americans work harder than I expected them to." (Perhaps these visitors have been excessively influenced by American movies and television programs, which are less likely to show people working than to show them driving around in fast cars or pursuing members of the opposite sex.) While the so-called Protestant work ethic may have lost some of its hold on Americans, there is still a strong belief that the ideal person is a "hard worker." A hard worker is one who "gets right to work" on a task without delay, works efficiently, and completes the task in a way that meets reasonably high standards of quality.

Generally, Americans like action. They do indeed believe it is important to devote significant energy to their jobs or to other daily responsibilities. Beyond that, they tend to believe they should be doing something most of the time. They are usually not content, as people from many other countries are, to sit for hours and talk with other people. They get restless and impatient. They believe they should be doing something, or at least making plans and arrangements for doing something later.

Americans, as has been said before, generally consider themselves to be frank, open, and direct in their dealings with other people. Americans will often speak openly and directly to others about things they dislike. They will try to do so in a manner they call "constructive," that is, a manner which the other person will not find offensive or unacceptable. If they do not speak openly about what is on their minds, they will often convey their reactions in nonverbal way (without words, but through facial expressions, body positions, and gestures). Americans are not taught, as people in many Asian countries are, that they should mask their emotional responses.

Their words, the tone of their voices, or their facial expressions will usually reveal when they are feeling angry, unhappy, confused, or happy and content. They do not think it improper to display these feelings, at least within limits. Many Asians feel embarrassed around Americans who are exhibiting a strong emotional response to something. On the other hand, Latinos and Arabs are generally inclined to display their emotions more openly than Americans do, and to view Americans as unemotional and "cold."

But Americans are often less direct and open than they realize. There are in fact many restrictions on their willingness to discuss things openly. Despite these limitations, Americans are generally more direct and open than people from many other countries. They generally do not try to mask their emotions and are much less concerned with "face" - avoiding embarrassment to themselves or others. To them, being "honest" is usually more important than preserving harmony in interpersonal relationships. Americans use the words "pushy" or "aggressive" to describe a person who is excessively assertive in expressing opinions or making requests. The line between acceptable assertiveness and unacceptable aggressiveness is difficult to draw.

APPENDIX

THE CONSTITUTION OF THE UNITED STATES

(Preamble)

We the People of the United States, in Order to form a more perfect Union, establish Justice, insure domestic Tranquility, provide for the common defense, promote the general Welfare, and secure the Blessings of Liberty to ourselves and our Posterity, do ordain and establish this Constitution for the United States of America.

Article I (Article 1 - Legislative)

Section 1

All legislative Powers herein granted shall be vested in a Congress of the United States, which shall consist of a Senate and House of Representatives.

Section 2

1: The House of Representatives shall be composed of Members chosen every second Year by the People of the several States, and the Electors in each State shall have the Qualifications requisite for Electors of the most numerous Branch of the State Legislature.

2: No Person shall be a Representative who shall not have attained to the Age of twenty five Years, and been seven Years a Citizen of the United States, and who shall not, when elected, be an Inhabitant of that State in which he shall be chosen.

3: Representatives and direct Taxes shall be apportioned among the several States which may be included within this Union, according to their respective Numbers, which shall be determined by adding to the whole Number of free Persons, including those bound to Service for a Term of Years, and excluding Indians not taxed, three fifths of all other Persons.[2] The actual Enumeration shall be made within three Years after the first Meeting of the Congress of the United States, and within every subsequent Term of ten Years, in such Manner as they shall by Law direct. The Number of Representatives shall not exceed one for every thirty Thousand, but each State shall have at Least one Representative; and until such enumeration shall be made, the State of New Hampshire shall be entitled to chuse three, Massachusetts eight, Rhode-Island and Providence Plantations one, Connecticut five, New-York six, New Jersey four, Pennsylvania eight, Delaware one, Maryland six, Virginia ten, North Carolina five, South Carolina five, and Georgia three.

4: When vacancies happen in the Representation from any State, the Executive Authority thereof shall issue Writs of Election to fill such Vacancies.

5: The House of Representatives shall chuse their Speaker and other Officers; and shall have the sole Power of Impeachment.

Section 3

1: The Senate of the United States shall be composed of two Senators from each State, chosen by the Legislature thereof,[3] for six Years; and each Senator shall have one Vote.

2: Immediately after they shall be assembled in Consequence of the first Election, they shall be divided as equally as may be into three Classes. The Seats of the Senators of the first Class shall be vacated at the Expiration of the second Year, of the second Class at the Expiration of the fourth Year, and of the third Class at the Expiration of the sixth Year, so that one third may be chosen every second Year; and if Vacancies happen by Resignation, or otherwise, during the Recess of the Legislature of any State, the Executive thereof may make temporary Appointments until the next Meeting of the Legislature, which shall then fill such Vacancies.[4]

3: No Person shall be a Senator who shall not have attained to the Age of thirty Years, and been nine Years a Citizen of the United States, and who shall not, when elected, be an Inhabitant of that State for which he shall be chosen.

4: The Vice President of the United States shall be President of the Senate, but shall have no Vote, unless they be equally divided.

5: The Senate shall chuse their other Officers, and also a President pro tempore, in the Absence of the Vice President, or when he shall exercise the Office of President of the United States.

6: The Senate shall have the sole Power to try all Impeachments. When sitting for that Purpose, they shall be on Oath or Affirmation. When the President of the United States is tried, the Chief Justice shall preside: And no Person shall be convicted without the Concurrence of two thirds of the Members present.

7: Judgment in Cases of impeachment shall not extend further than to removal from Office, and disqualification to hold and enjoy any Office of honor, Trust or Profit under the United States: but the Party convicted shall nevertheless be liable and subject to Indictment, Trial, Judgment and Punishment, according to Law.

Section 4

1: The Times, Places and Manner of holding Elections for Senators and Representatives, shall be prescribed in each State by the Legislature thereof; but the Congress may at any time by Law make or alter such Regulations, except as to the Places of choosing Senators.

2: The Congress shall assemble at least once in every Year, and such Meeting shall be on the first Monday in December,[5] unless they shall by Law appoint a different Day.

Section 5

1: Each House shall be the Judge of the Elections, Returns and Qualifications of its own Members, and a Majority of each shall constitute a Quorum to do Business; but a smaller Number may adjourn from day to day, and may be authorized to compel the Attendance of absent Members, in such Manner, and under such Penalties as each House may provide.

2: Each House may determine the Rules of its Proceedings, punish its Members for disorderly Behaviour, and, with the Concurrence of two thirds, expel a Member.

3: Each House shall keep a Journal of its Proceedings, and from time to time publish the same, excepting such Parts as may in their Judgment require Secrecy; and the Yeas and Nays of the Members of either House on any question shall, at the Desire of one fifth of those Present, be entered on the Journal.

4: Neither House, during the Session of Congress, shall, without the Consent of the other, adjourn for more than three days, nor to any other Place than that in which the two Houses shall be sitting.

Section 6

1: The Senators and Representatives shall receive a Compensation for their Services, to be ascertained by Law, and paid out of the Treasury of the United States.[6] They shall in all Cases, except Treason, Felony and Breach of the Peace, be privileged from Arrest during their Attendance at the Session of their respective Houses, and in going to and returning from the same; and for any Speech or Debate in either House, they shall not be questioned in any other Place.

2: No Senator or Representative shall, during the Time for which he was elected, be appointed to any civil Office under the Authority of the United States, which shall have been created, or the Emoluments whereof shall have been increased during such time; and no Person holding any Office under the United States, shall be a Member of either House during his Continuance in Office.

Section 7

1: All Bills for raising Revenue shall originate in the House of Representatives; but the Senate may propose or concur with Amendments as on other Bills.

2: Every Bill which shall have passed the House of Representatives and the Senate, shall, before it become a Law, be presented to the President of the United States; If he approve he shall sign it, but if not he shall return it, with his Objections to that House in which it shall have originated, who shall enter the Objections at large on their Journal, and proceed to reconsider it. If after such Reconsideration two thirds of that House shall agree to pass the Bill, it shall be sent, together with the Objections, to the other House, by which it shall likewise be reconsidered, and if approved by two thirds of that House, it shall become a Law. But in all such Cases the Votes of both Houses shall be determined by yeas and Nays, and the Names of the Persons voting for and against the Bill shall be entered on the Journal of each House respectively. If any Bill shall not be returned by the President within ten Days (Sundays excepted) after it shall have been presented to him, the Same shall be a Law, in like Manner as if he had signed it, unless the Congress by their Adjournment prevent its Return, in which Case it shall not be a Law.

3: Every Order, Resolution, or Vote to which the Concurrence of the Senate and House of Representatives may be necessary (except on a question of Adjournment) shall be presented to the President of the United States; and before the Same shall take Effect, shall be approved by him, or being disapproved by him, shall be repassed by two thirds of the Senate and House of Representatives, according to the Rules and Limitations prescribed in the Case of a Bill.

Section 8

1: The Congress shall have Power To lay and collect Taxes, Duties, Imposts and Excises, to pay the Debts and provide for the common Defense and general Welfare of the United States; but all Duties, Imposts and Excises shall be uniform throughout the United States;

2: To borrow Money on the credit of the United States;

3: To regulate Commerce with foreign Nations, and among the several States, and with the Indian Tribes;

4: To establish an uniform Rule of Naturalization, and uniform Laws on the subject of Bankruptcies throughout the United States;

5: To coin Money, regulate the Value thereof, and of foreign Coin, and fix the Standard of Weights and Measures;

6: To provide for the Punishment of counterfeiting the Securities and current Coin of the United States;

7: To establish Post Offices and post Roads;

8: To promote the Progress of Science and useful Arts, by securing for limited Times to Authors and Inventors the exclusive Right to their respective Writings and Discoveries;

9: To constitute Tribunals inferior to the supreme Court;

10: To define and punish Piracies and Felonies committed on the high Seas, and Offences against the Law of Nations;

11: To declare War, grant Letters of Marque and Reprisal, and make Rules concerning Captures on Land and Water;

12: To raise and support Armies, but no Appropriation of Money to that Use shall be for a longer Term than two Years;

13: To provide and maintain a Navy;

14: To make Rules for the Government and Regulation of the land and naval Forces;

15: To provide for calling forth the Militia to execute the Laws of the Union, suppress Insurrections and repel Invasions;

16: To provide for organizing, arming, and disciplining, the Militia, and for governing such Part of them as may be employed in the Service of the United States, reserving to the States respectively, the Appointment of the Officers, and the Authority of training the Militia according to the discipline prescribed by Congress;

17: To exercise exclusive Legislation in all Cases whatsoever, over such District (not exceeding ten Miles square) as may, by Cession of particular States, and the Acceptance of Congress, become the Seat of the Government of the United States, and to exercise like Authority over all Places purchased by the Consent of the Legislature of the State in which the Same shall be, for the

Erection of Forts, Magazines, Arsenals, dock-Yards, and other needful Buildings;—And

18: To make all Laws which shall be necessary and proper for carrying into Execution the foregoing Powers, and all other Powers vested by this Constitution in the Government of the United States, or in any Department or Officer thereof.

Section 9

1: The Migration or Importation of such Persons as any of the States now existing shall think proper to admit, shall not be prohibited by the Congress prior to the Year one thousand eight hundred and eight, but a Tax or duty may be imposed on such Importation, not exceeding ten dollars for each Person.

2: The Privilege of the Writ of Habeas Corpus shall not be suspended, unless when in Cases of Rebellion or Invasion the public Safety may require it.

3: No Bill of Attainder or ex post facto Law shall be passed.

4: No Capitation, or other direct, Tax shall be laid, unless in Proportion to the Census or Enumeration herein before directed to be taken.[Z]

5: No Tax or Duty shall be laid on Articles exported from any State.

6: No Preference shall be given by any Regulation of Commerce or Revenue to the Ports of one State over those of another: nor shall Vessels bound to, or from, one State, be obliged to enter, clear, or pay Duties in another.

7: No Money shall be drawn from the Treasury, but in Consequence of Appropriations made by Law; and a regular Statement and Account of the Receipts and Expenditures of all public Money shall be published from time to time.

8: No Title of Nobility shall be granted by the United States: And no Person holding any Office of Profit or Trust under them, shall, without the Consent of the Congress, accept of any present, Emolument, Office, or Title, of any kind whatever, from any King, Prince, or foreign State.

Section 10

1: No State shall enter into any Treaty, Alliance, or Confederation; grant Letters of Marque and Reprisal; coin Money; emit Bills of Credit; make any Thing but gold and silver Coin a Tender in Payment of Debts; pass any Bill of Attainder, ex post facto Law, or Law impairing the Obligation of Contracts, or grant any Title of Nobility.

2: No State shall, without the Consent of the Congress, lay any Imposts or Duties on Imports or Exports, except what may be absolutely necessary for executing it's inspection Laws: and the net Produce of all Duties and Imposts, laid by any State on Imports or Exports, shall be for the Use of the Treasury of the United States; and all such Laws shall be subject to the Revision and Control of the Congress.

3: No State shall, without the Consent of Congress, lay any Duty of Tonnage, keep Troops, or Ships of War in time of Peace, enter into any Agreement or Compact with another State, or with a foreign Power, or engage in War, unless actually invaded, or in such imminent Danger as will not admit of delay.

Article II (Article 2 - Executive)

Section 1

1: The executive Power shall be vested in a President of the United States of America. He shall hold his Office during the Term of four Years, and, together with the Vice President, chosen for the same Term, be elected, as follows

2: Each State shall appoint, in such Manner as the Legislature thereof may direct, a Number of Electors, equal to the whole Number of Senators and Representatives to which the State may be entitled in the Congress: but no Senator or Representative, or Person holding an Office of Trust or Profit under the United States, shall be appointed an Elector.

3: The Electors shall meet in their respective States, and vote by Ballot for two Persons, of whom one at least shall not be an Inhabitant of the same State with themselves. And they shall make a List of all the Persons voted for, and of the Number of Votes for each; which List they shall sign and certify, and transmit sealed to the Seat of the Government of the United States, directed to the President of the Senate. The President of the Senate shall, in the Presence of the Senate and House of Representatives, open all the Certificates, and the Votes shall then be counted. The Person having the greatest Number of Votes shall be the President, if such Number be a Majority of the whole Number of Electors appointed; and if there be more than one who have such Majority, and have an equal Number of Votes, then the House of Representatives shall immediately chuse by Ballot one of them for President; and if no Person have a Majority, then from the five highest on the List the said House shall in like Manner chuse the President. But in chasing the President, the Votes shall be taken by States, the Representation from each State having one Vote; A quorum for this Purpose shall consist of a Member or Members from two thirds of the States, and a Majority of all the States shall be necessary to a Choice. In every Case, after the Choice of the President, the Person having the greatest Number of Votes of the Electors shall be the Vice President. But if there should remain two or more who have equal Votes, the Senate shall chuse from them by Ballot the Vice President.[8]

4: The Congress may determine the Time of choosing the Electors, and the Day on which they shall give their Votes; which Day shall be the same throughout the United States.

5: No Person except a natural born Citizen, or a Citizen of the United States, at the time of the Adoption of this Constitution, shall be eligible to the Office of President; neither shall any Person be eligible to that Office who shall not have attained to the Age of thirty five Years, and been fourteen Years a Resident within the United States.

6: In Case of the Removal of the President from Office, or of his Death, Resignation, or Inability to discharge the Powers and Duties of the said Office,[9] the Same shall devolve on the Vice-president, and the Congress may by Law provide for the Case of Removal, Death, Resignation or Inability, both of the President and Vice President, declaring what Officer shall then act as President, and such Officer shall act accordingly, until the Disability be removed, or a President shall be elected.

7: The President shall, at stated Times, receive for his Services, a Compensation, which shall neither be increased nor diminished during the Period for which he shall have been elected, and he shall not receive within that Period any other Emolument from the United States, or any of them.

8: Before he enter on the Execution of his Office, he shall take the following Oath or Affirmation:—"I do solemnly swear (or affirm) that I will faithfully execute the Office of President of the United States, and will to the best of my Ability, preserve, protect and defend the Constitution of the United States."

Section 2

1: The President shall be Commander in Chief of the Army and Navy of the United States, and of the Militia of the several States, when called into the actual Service of the United States; he may require the Opinion, in writing, of the principal Officer in each of the executive Departments, upon any Subject relating to the Duties of their respective Offices, and he shall have Power to grant Reprieves and Pardons for Offences against the United States, except in Cases of Impeachment.

2: He shall have Power, by and with the Advice and Consent of the Senate, to make Treaties, provided two thirds of the Senators present concur; and he shall nominate, and by and with the Advice and Consent of the Senate, shall appoint Ambassadors, other public Ministers and Consuls, Judges of the supreme Court, and all other Officers of the United States, whose Appointments are not herein otherwise provided for, and which shall be established by Law: but the Congress may by Law vest the Appointment of such inferior Officers, as they think proper, in the President alone, in the Courts of Law, or in the Heads of Departments.

3: The President shall have Power to fill up all Vacancies that may happen during the Recess of the Senate, by granting Commissions which shall expire at the End of their next Session.

Section 3

He shall from time to time give to the Congress Information of the State of the Union, and recommend to their Consideration such Measures as he shall judge necessary and expedient; he may, on extraordinary Occasions, convene both Houses, or either of them, and in Case of Disagreement between them, with Respect to the Time of Adjournment, he may adjourn them to such Time as he shall think proper; he shall receive Ambassadors and other public Ministers; he shall take Care that the Laws be faithfully executed, and shall Commission all the Officers of the United States.

Section 4

The President, Vice President and all civil Officers of the United States, shall be removed from Office on Impeachment for, and Conviction of, Treason, Bribery, or other high Crimes and Misdemeanors.

Article III (Article 3 - Judicial)

Section 1

The judicial Power of the United States, shall be vested in one supreme Court, and in such inferior Courts as the Congress may from time to time ordain and establish. The Judges, both of the supreme and inferior Courts, shall hold their Offices during good Behaviour, and shall, at stated Times, receive for their Services, a Compensation, which shall not be diminished during their Continuance in Office.

Section 2

1: The judicial Power shall extend to all Cases, in Law and Equity, arising under this Constitution, the Laws of the United States, and Treaties made, or which shall be made, under their Authority;—to all Cases affecting Ambassadors, other public Ministers and Consuls;—to all Cases of admiralty and maritime Jurisdiction;—to Controversies to which the United States shall be a Party;—to Controversies between two or more States;—between a State and Citizens of another State;[10]—between Citizens of different States, —between Citizens of the same State claiming Lands under Grants of different States, and between a State, or the Citizens thereof, and foreign States, Citizens or Subjects.

2: In all Cases affecting Ambassadors, other public Ministers and Consuls, and those in which a State shall be Party, the supreme Court shall have original Jurisdiction. In all the other Cases before mentioned, the supreme Court shall have appellate Jurisdiction, both as to Law and Fact, with such Exceptions, and under such Regulations as the Congress shall make.

3: The Trial of all Crimes, except in Cases of Impeachment, shall be by Jury; and such Trial shall be held in the State where the said Crimes shall have been committed; but when not committed within any State, the Trial shall be at such Place or Places as the Congress may by Law have directed.

Section 3

1: Treason against the United States, shall consist only in levying War against them, or in adhering to their Enemies, giving them Aid and Comfort. No Person shall be convicted of Treason unless on the Testimony of two Witnesses to the same overt Act, or on Confession in open Court.

2: The Congress shall have Power to declare the Punishment of Treason, but no Attainder of Treason shall work Corruption of Blood, or Forfeiture except during the Life of the Person attainted.

Article IV (Article 4 - States' Relations)

Section 1

Full Faith and Credit shall be given in each State to the public Acts, Records, and judicial Proceedings of every other State. And the Congress may by general Laws prescribe the Manner in which such Acts, Records and Proceedings shall be proved, and the Effect thereof.

Section 2

1: The Citizens of each State shall be entitled to all Privileges and Immunities of Citizens in the several States.

2: A Person charged in any State with Treason, Felony, or other Crime, who shall flee from Justice, and be found in another State, shall on Demand of the executive Authority of the State from which he fled, be delivered up, to be removed to the State having Jurisdiction of the Crime.

3: No Person held to Service or Labour in one State, under the Laws thereof, escaping into another, shall, in Consequence of any Law or Regulation therein, be discharged from such Service or Labour, but shall be delivered up on Claim of the Party to whom such Service or Labour may be due.

Section 3

1: New States may be admitted by the Congress into this Union; but no new State shall be formed or erected within the Jurisdiction of any other State; nor any State be formed by the Junction of two or more States, or Parts of States, without the Consent of the Legislatures of the States concerned as well as of the Congress.

2: The Congress shall have Power to dispose of and make all needful Rules and Regulations respecting the

Territory or other Property belonging to the United States; and nothing in this Constitution shall be so construed as to Prejudice any Claims of the United States, or of any particular State.

Section 4

The United States shall guarantee to every State in this Union a Republican Form of Government, and shall protect each of them against Invasion; and on Application of the Legislature, or of the Executive (when the Legislature cannot be convened) against domestic Violence.

Article V (Article 5 - Mode of Amendment)

The Congress, whenever two thirds of both Houses shall deem it necessary, shall propose Amendments to this Constitution, or, on the Application of the Legislatures of two thirds of the several States, shall call a Convention for proposing Amendments, which, in either Case, shall be valid to all Intents and Purposes, as Part of this Constitution, when ratified by the Legislatures of three fourths of the several States, or by Conventions in three fourths thereof, as the one or the other Mode of Ratification may be proposed by the Congress; Provided that no Amendment which may be made prior to the

Year One thousand eight hundred and eight shall in any Manner affect the first and fourth Clauses in the Ninth Section of the first Article; and that no State, without its Consent, shall be deprived of its equal Suffrage in the Senate.

Article VI (Article 6 - Prior Debts, National Supremacy, Oaths of Office)

1: All Debts contracted and Engagements entered into, before the Adoption of this Constitution, shall be as valid against the United States under this Constitution, as under the Confederation.

2: This Constitution, and the Laws of the United States which shall be made in Pursuance thereof; and all Treaties made, or which shall be made, under the Authority of the United States, shall be the supreme Law of the Land; and the Judges in every State shall be bound thereby, any Thing in the Constitution or Laws of any State to the Contrary notwithstanding.

3: The Senators and Representatives before mentioned, and the Members of the several State Legislatures, and all executive and judicial Officers, both of the United States and of the several States, shall be bound by Oath or Affirmation, to support this Constitution; but no religious Test shall ever be required as a Qualification to any Office or public Trust under the United States.

Article VII (Article 7 - Ratification)

The Ratification of the Conventions of nine States, shall be sufficient for the Establishment of this Constitution between the States so ratifying the Same.

The Word "the", being interlined between the seventh and eight Lines of the first Page, The Word "Thirty" being partly written on an Erasure in the fifteenth Line of the first Page. The Words "is tried" being interlined between the thirty second and thirty third Lines of the first Page and the Word "the" being interlined between the forty third and forty fourth Lines of the second Page.

Amendments to the Constitution

Congress OF THE United States

begun and held at the City of New-York, on Wednesday the fourth of March, one thousand seven hundred and eighty nine.

THE Conventions of a number of the States, having at the time of their adopting the Constitution, expressed a desire, in order to prevent misconstruction or abuse of its powers, that further declaratory and restrictive clauses should be added: And as extending the ground of public confidence in the Government, will best ensure the beneficent ends of its institution.

RESOLVED by the Senate and House of Representatives of the United States of America, in Congress assembled, two thirds of both Houses concurring, that the following Articles be proposed to the Legislatures of the several States, as amendments to the Constitution of the United States, all, or any of which Articles, when ratified by three fourths of the said Legislatures, to be valid to all intents and purposes, as part of the said Constitution; viz.

ARTICLES in addition to, and Amendment of the Constitution of the United States of America, proposed by Congress, and ratified by the Legislatures of the several States, pursuant to the fifth Article of the original Constitution.[12]

(Articles I through X are known as the Bill of Rights) *ratified*

-

Article the first. .... After the first enumeration required by the first Article of the Constitution, there shall be one Representative for every thirty thousand, until the number shall amount to one hundred, after which, the proportion shall be so regulated by Congress, that there shall be not less than one hundred Representatives, nor less than one Representative for every forty thousand persons, until the number of Representatives shall amount to two hundred, after which the proportion shall be so regulated by Congress, that there shall not be less than two hundred Representatives, nor more than one Representative for every fifty thousand persons.

-

Article the second. .... No law, varying the compensation for the services of the Senators and Representatives, shall take effect, until an election of Representatives shall have intervened. see Amendment XXVII

Article [I] (Amendment 1 - Freedom of expression and religion) [13]

Congress shall make no law respecting an establishment of religion, or prohibiting the free exercise thereof; or abridging the freedom of speech, or of the press; or the right of the people peaceably to assemble, and to petition the Government for a redress of grievances.

Article [II] (Amendment 2 - Bearing Arms)

A well-regulated Militia, being necessary to the security of a free State, the right of the people to keep and bear Arms, shall not be infringed.

Article [III] (Amendment 3 - Quartering Soldiers)

No Soldier shall, in time of peace be quartered in any house, without the consent of the Owner, nor in time of war, but in a manner to be prescribed by law.

Article [IV] (Amendment 4 - Search and Seizure)

The right of the people to be secure in their persons, houses, papers, and effects, against unreasonable searches and seizures, shall not be violated, and no Warrants shall issue, but upon probable cause, supported by Oath or affirmation, and particularly describing the place to be searched, and the persons or things to be seized.

Article [V] (Amendment 5 - Rights of Persons)

No person shall be held to answer for a capital, or otherwise infamous crime, unless on a presentment or indictment of a Grand Jury, except in cases arising in the land or naval forces, or in the Militia, when in actual service in time of War or public danger; nor shall any person be subject for the same offence to be twice put in jeopardy of life or limb; nor shall be compelled in any criminal case to be a witness against himself, nor be deprived of life, liberty, or property, without due process of law; nor shall private property be taken for public use, without just compensation.

Article [VI] (Amendment 6 - Rights of Accused in Criminal Prosecutions)

In all criminal prosecutions, the accused shall enjoy the right to a speedy and public trial, by an impartial jury of the State and district wherein the crime shall have been committed, which district shall have been previously ascertained by law, and to be informed of the nature and cause of the accusation; to be confronted with the witnesses against him; to have compulsory process for obtaining witnesses in his favor, and to have the Assistance of Counsel for his defense.

Article [VII] (Amendment 7 - Civil Trials)

In Suits at common law, where the value in controversy shall exceed twenty dollars, the right of trial by jury shall be preserved, and no fact tried by a jury, shall be otherwise re-examined in any Court of the United States, than according to the rules of the common law.

Article [VIII] (Amendment 8 - Further Guarantees in Criminal Cases)

Excessive bail shall not be required, nor excessive fines imposed, nor cruel and unusual punishments inflicted.

Article [IX] (Amendment 9 – Un enumerated Rights)

The enumeration in the <u>Constitution</u>, of certain rights, shall not be construed to deny or disparage others retained by the people.

Article [X] (Amendment 10 - Reserved Powers)

The powers not delegated to the United States by the Constitution, nor prohibited by it to the States, are reserved to the States respectively, or to the people.

Attest, Frederick Augustus John Beckley, Clerk of Muhlenberg Speaker of the the House of House of Representatives. Representatives. John Adams, Vice-President of Sam. A. Otis Secretary the United States, and President of the Senate. of the Senate.

(end of the Bill of Rights)

[Article XI] (Amendment 11 - Suits Against States)

The Judicial power of the United States shall not be construed to extend to any suit in law or equity, commenced or prosecuted against one of the United States by Citizens of another State, or by Citizens or Subjects of any Foreign State. *ratified #11   affects 10*

[Article XII] (Amendment 12 - Election of President)

The Electors shall meet in their respective states, and vote by ballot for President and Vice-President, one of whom, at least, shall not be an inhabitant of the same state with themselves; they shall name in their ballots the person voted for as President, and in distinct ballots the person voted for as Vice-President, and they shall make distinct lists of all persons voted for as President, and of all persons voted for as Vice-President, and of the number of votes for each, which lists they shall sign and certify, and transmit sealed to the seat of the government of the United States, directed to the President of the Senate;—The President of the Senate shall, in the presence of the Senate and House of

Representatives, open all the certificates and the votes shall then be counted;—The person having the greatest number of votes for President, shall be the President, if such number be a majority of the whole number of Electors appointed; and if no person have such majority, then from the persons having the highest numbers not exceeding three on the list of those voted for as President, the House of Representatives shall choose immediately, by ballot, the President. But in choosing the President, the votes shall be taken by states, the representation from each state having one vote; a quorum for this purpose shall consist of a member or members from two-thirds of the states, and a majority of all the states shall be necessary to a choice. And if the House of Representatives shall not choose a President whenever the right of choice shall devolve upon them, before the fourth day of March next following, then the Vice-President shall act as President, as in the case of the death or other constitutional disability of the President.[14] —The person having the greatest number of votes as Vice-President, shall be the Vice-President, if such number be a majority of the whole number of Electors appointed, and if no person have a majority, then from the two highest numbers on the list, the Senate shall choose the Vice-President; a quorum for the purpose shall consist of two-thirds of the whole number of Senators, and a majority of the whole number shall be necessary to a choice. But no person constitutionally ineligible to the office of President shall be eligible to that of Vice-President of the United States. *ratified #12* *affects 8*

Article XIII (Amendment 13 - Slavery and Involuntary Servitude)

Neither slavery nor involuntary servitude, except as a punishment for crime whereof the party shall have been duly convicted, shall exist within the United States, or any place subject to their jurisdiction. *affects 11*

Congress shall have power to enforce this article by appropriate legislation. *ratified #13*

Article XIV (Amendment 14 - Rights Guaranteed: Privileges and Immunities of Citizenship, Due Process, and Equal Protection)

1: All persons born or naturalized in the United States, and subject to the jurisdiction thereof, are citizens of the United States and of the State wherein they reside. No State shall make or enforce any law which shall abridge the privileges or immunities of citizens of the United States; nor shall any State deprive any person of life, liberty, or property, without due process of law; nor deny to any person within its jurisdiction the equal protection of the laws.

2: Representatives shall be apportioned among the several States according to their respective numbers, counting the whole number of persons in each State, excluding Indians not taxed. But when the right to vote at any election for the choice of electors for President and Vice President of the United States, Representatives in Congress, the Executive and Judicial officers of a State, or the members of the Legislature thereof, is denied to any of the male inhabitants of such State, being twenty-one years of age,[15] and citizens of the United States, or in any way abridged, except for participation in rebellion, or other crime, the basis of representation therein shall be reduced in the proportion which the number of such male citizens shall bear to the whole number of male citizens twenty-one years of age in such State. *affects 2*

3: No person shall be a Senator or Representative in Congress, or elector of President and Vice President, or hold any office, civil or military, under the United States, or under any State, who, having previously taken an oath, as a member of Congress, or as an officer of the United

States, or as a member of any State legislature, or as an executive or judicial officer of any State, to support the Constitution of the United States, shall have engaged in insurrection or rebellion against the same, or given aid or comfort to the enemies thereof. But Congress may by a vote of two-thirds of each House, remove such disability.

4: The validity of the public debt of the United States, authorized by law, including debts incurred for payment of pensions and bounties for services in suppressing insurrection or rebellion, shall not be questioned. But neither the United States nor any State shall assume or pay any debt or obligation incurred in aid of insurrection or rebellion against the United States, or any claim for the loss or emancipation of any slave; but all such debts, obligations and claims shall be held illegal and void.

5: The Congress shall have power to enforce, by appropriate legislation, the provisions of this article. *ratified #14*

Article XV (Amendment 15 - Rights of Citizens to Vote)

The right of citizens of the United States to vote shall not be denied or abridged by the United States or by any

State on account of race, color, or previous condition of servitude.

The Congress shall have power to enforce this article by appropriate legislation. *ratified #15*

Article XVI (Amendment 16 - Income Tax)

The Congress shall have power to lay and collect taxes on incomes, from whatever source derived, without apportionment among the several States, and without regard to any census or enumeration. *ratified #16*   *affects 2*

[Article XVII] (Amendment 17 - Popular Election of Senators)

1: The Senate of the United States shall be composed of two Senators from each State, elected by the people thereof, for six years; and each Senator shall have one vote. The electors in each State shall have the qualifications requisite for electors of the most numerous branch of the State legislatures. *affects 3*

2: When vacancies happen in the representation of any State in the Senate, the executive authority of such State shall issue writs of election to fill such vacancies: Provided, That the legislature of any State may empower the executive thereof to make temporary appointments until the people fill the vacancies by election as the legislature may direct. *affects 4*

3: This amendment shall not be so construed as to affect the election or term of any Senator chosen before it becomes valid as part of the Constitution. *ratified #17*

Article [XVIII] (Amendment 18 - Prohibition of Intoxicating Liquors)*16*

1: After one year from the ratification of this article the manufacture, sale, or transportation of intoxicating liquors within, the importation thereof into, or the exportation thereof from the United States and all territory subject to the jurisdiction thereof for beverage purposes is hereby prohibited.

2: The Congress and the several States shall have concurrent power to enforce this article by appropriate legislation.

3: This article shall be inoperative unless it shall have been ratified as an amendment to the Constitution by the legislatures of the several States, as provided in the Constitution, within seven years from the date of the submission hereof to the States by the Congress. *ratified #18*

Article [XIX] (Amendment 19 - Women's Suffrage Rights)

The right of citizens of the United States to vote shall not be denied or abridged by the United States or by any State on account of sex. *affects 15*

Congress shall have power to enforce this article by appropriate legislation. *ratified #19*

Article [XX] (Amendment 20 - Terms of President, Vice President, Members of Congress: Presidential Vacancy)

1: The terms of the President and Vice President shall end at noon on the 20th day of January, and the terms of Senators and Representatives at noon on the 3d day of January, of the years in which such terms would have ended if this article had not been ratified; and the terms of their successors shall then begin. *affects 5*

2: The Congress shall assemble at least once in every year, and such meeting shall begin at noon on the 3d day of January, unless they shall by law appoint a different day. *affects 5*

3: If, at the time fixed for the beginning of the term of the President, the President elect shall have died, the Vice President elect shall become President. If a President shall not have been chosen before the time fixed for the beginning of his term, or if the President elect shall have failed to qualify, then the Vice President elect shall act as President until a President shall have qualified; and the Congress may by law provide for the case wherein neither a President elect nor a Vice President elect shall have qualified, declaring who shall then act as President, or the manner in which one who is to act shall be selected, and such person shall act accordingly until a President or Vice President shall have qualified. *affects 9*   *affects 14*

4: The Congress may by law provide for the case of the death of any of the persons from whom the House of Representatives may choose a President whenever the right of choice shall have devolved upon them, and for the case of the death of any of the persons from whom the Senate may choose a Vice President whenever the right of choice shall have devolved upon them. *affects 9*

5: Sections 1 and 2 shall take effect on the 15th day of October following the ratification of this article.

6: This article shall be inoperative unless it shall have been ratified as an amendment to the Constitution by the legislatures of three-fourths of the several States within seven years from the date of its submission. *ratified #20*

Article **[XXI]** (Amendment 21 - Repeal of Eighteenth Amendment)

1: The eighteenth article of amendment to the Constitution of the United States is hereby repealed. *affects 16*

2: The transportation or importation into any State, Territory, or possession of the United States for delivery or use therein of intoxicating liquors, in violation of the laws thereof, is hereby prohibited.

3: This article shall be inoperative unless it shall have been ratified as an amendment to the Constitution by conventions in the several States, as provided in the Constitution, within seven years from the date of the submission hereof to the States by the Congress. *ratified #21*

Amendment XXII (Amendment 22 - Presidential Tenure)

1: No person shall be elected to the office of the President more than twice, and no person who has held the office of President, or acted as President, for more than two years of a term to which some other person was elected President shall be elected to the office of the President more than once. But this article shall not apply to any person holding the office of President when this article was proposed by the Congress, and shall not prevent any person who may be holding the office of President, or acting as President, during the term within which this article becomes operative from holding the office of President or acting as President during the remainder of such term.

2: This article shall be inoperative unless it shall have been ratified as an amendment to the Constitution by the legislatures of three-fourths of the several states within seven years from the date of its submission to the states by the Congress. *ratified #22*

Amendment XXIII (Amendment 23 - Presidential Electors for the District of Columbia)

1: The District constituting the seat of government of the United States shall appoint in such manner as the Congress may direct: A number of electors of President and Vice President equal to the whole number of Senators and Representatives in Congress to which the District would be entitled if it were a state, but in no event more than the least populous state; they shall be in addition to those appointed by the states, but they shall be considered, for the purposes of the election of President and Vice President, to be electors appointed by a state; and they shall meet in the

District and perform such duties as provided by the twelfth article of amendment.

2: The Congress shall have power to enforce this article by appropriate legislation. *ratified #23*

Amendment XXIV (Amendment 24 - Abolition of the Poll Tax Qualification in Federal Elections)

1. The right of citizens of the United States to vote in any primary or other election for President or Vice President, for electors for President or Vice President, or for Senator or Representative in Congress, shall not be denied or abridged by the United States or any state by reason of failure to pay any poll tax or other tax.

2. The Congress shall have power to enforce this article by appropriate legislation. *ratified #24*

Amendment XXV *affects 9* (Amendment 25 - Presidential Vacancy, Disability, and Inability)

1: In case of the removal of the President from office or of his death or resignation, the Vice President shall become President.

2: Whenever there is a vacancy in the office of the Vice President, the President shall nominate a Vice President who shall take office upon confirmation by a majority vote of both Houses of Congress.

3: Whenever the President transmits to the President pro tempore of the Senate and the Speaker of the House of Representatives his written declaration that he is unable to discharge the powers and duties of his office, and until he transmits to them a written declaration to the contrary, such powers and duties shall be discharged by the Vice President as Acting President.

4: Whenever the Vice President and a majority of either the principal officers of the executive departments or of such other body as Congress may by law provide, transmit to the President pro tempore of the Senate and the Speaker of the House of Representatives their written declaration that the President is unable to discharge the powers and duties of his office, the Vice President shall immediately assume the powers and duties of the office as Acting President.

Thereafter, when the President transmits to the President pro tempore of the Senate and the Speaker of the House of Representatives his written declaration that no inability exists, he shall resume the powers and duties of his office unless the Vice President and a majority of either the principal officers of the executive department or of such other body as Congress may by law provide, transmit within four days to the President pro tempore of the Senate and the Speaker of the House of Representatives their written declaration that the President is unable to discharge the powers and duties of his office. Thereupon Congress shall decide the issue, assembling within forty-eight hours for that purpose if not in session. If the Congress, within twenty-one days after receipt of the latter written declaration, or, if Congress is not in session, within twenty-one days after Congress is required to assemble, determines by two-thirds vote of both Houses that the President is unable to discharge the powers and duties of his office, the Vice President shall continue to discharge the same as Acting President; otherwise, the President shall resume the powers and duties of his office. *ratified #25*

Amendment XXVI (Amendment 26 - Reduction of Voting Age Qualification)

1: The right of citizens of the United States, who are 18 years of age or older, to vote, shall not be denied or abridged by the United States or any state on account of age. *affects 15*

2: The Congress shall have the power to enforce this article by appropriate legislation. *ratified #26*

Amendment XXVII (Amendment 27 - Congressional Pay Limitation)

No law varying the compensation for the services of the Senators and Representatives shall take effect until an election of Representatives shall have intervened. *ratified #27*

REFERENCES

o Seymour M. Hersh, The Dark Side of Camelot Back Bay Books; Reprint edition (September 1, 1998).

o Carmon, Irin (October 13, 2016). "The Allegations Women Have Made Against Donald Trump" (http://www.nbcnews.com/politics/2016-election/allegations-women-have-made-against-donald-trump-n66573.1 N) BC News. Retrieved October 15, 2016.

o "Donald Trump Aide Apologizes for Saying, 'You Can't Rape Your Spouse' " (https://www.nytimes.com/politics/first-draft/2015/07/28/donald-trump-aide-apologizes-for-saying-you-cant-rape-your-spouse. /T) he New York Times. July 28,2015. Retrieved October 16, 2016.

o Kurtzleben, Danielle (October 13, 2016)." A List Of The Accusations About Trump's Alleged Inappropriate Sexual Conduct" (https://www.npr.org/2016/10/13/497799354/a-list-of-donald-trumps-accusers-of-inapprorpiate-sexual-conduct). NPR. Retrieved October 13, 2016.

o Rindler, Danielle; Sadof, Karly Domb (2017-01-13). "An unusual first family" (https://www.washingtonpost.com/politics/an-unusual-first-family/2017/01/13/26a95bb4-d9f4-11e6-9a3 1d296534b31e_sto.rhytml). Washington Post. ISSN 0190-8286 (https://www.worldcat.org/issn/0190-8286). Retrieved 2018-03-18.

o "Summer Zervos Suing Donald Trump for Defamation" (http://www.thedailybeast.com/articles/2017/01/17/apprenticecontestant-summer-zervos-slaps-donald-trump-with-defamation-lawsuit.htm. l)17 January 2017. Retrieved January 17, 2017.

o Ford, Matt. "The 19 Women Who Accused President Trump of Sexual Misconduct (https://www.theatlantic.com/politics/archive/2017/12/what-about-the-19-women-who-accused-trump/547724"/.) The Atlantic. Published December 7, 2017. Retrieved January 11, 2018.

o Bump, Philip (October 16, 2016). "Trump blames a media conspiracy for women opposing him. He should blame himself"

(https://www.washingtonpost.com/news/the-
fix/wp/2016/10/16/trump-blames-a-media-
conspiracy-for-women-opposing-him-he-should-
blame-himself/.) The Washington Post. Retrieved
October 17, 2016.

o Epstein, Reid J. (October 14, 2016)." Donald Trump
Fends Off New Sexual Misconduct Claims, Calling
Allegations a Conspiracy"
(https://www.wsj.com/articles/donald-trump-denies-
new-sexual-misconduct-claims-calling-allegations-
aconspiracy-1476478799). The Wall Street Journal.
Retrieved October 18, 2016.

o Diamond, Jeremy; Diaz, Daniella (October 15,
2016)". Trump on sex assault allegations: 'I am a
victim' "
(http://www.cnn.com/2016/10/14/politics/donald-
trump-sexual-assault-allegations/index.htm. l)CNN.
Retrieved October 18, 2016.

o Korasick, John. "Watergate scandal." In Critchlow,
Donald T., and Gary B. Nash, eds. Encyclopedia of
American History: Contemporary United States,
1969 to the Present, Revised Edition (Volume X).

New York: Facts on File, Inc., 2010. American History Online. Facts on File, Inc.

o Perry, James M. (chief political correspondent,Wall Street Journal), "Watergate Case Study," (http://www.columbia.e du/itc/journalism/j6075/edit/readings/watergate.htm,l)from Class Syllabus for "Critical Issues in Journalism."(http://w ww.columbia.edu/itc/journalism/j6075/)Columbia School of Journalism, Columbia University, retrieved July 27, 2018

o "A burglary turns into a constitutional crisis"(http://www.cnn.com/2004/US/06/11/watergat e/index.html?_s=PM:US.(CNN. June 16, 2004. Retrieved May 13, 2014.

o   Ervin, Sam, U.S. Senator, et. al., Final Report of the Watergate Committee.

o   Manheim, Karl; Solum, Lawrence B. (Spring 1999)".Nixon   Articles   of Impeachment"(https://web.archive.org/web/20 170303075538/http://classes.lls.edu/archive/manhei mk/371d1/nixonarticles.htm.1I)mpeachment Seminar.   Archived   from   the   original (http://classes.lls.edu/archive/manheimk/371d1/nixo narticles.htmlo) n March 3, 2017.

- o   Bill Marsh (October 30, 2005)."Ideas & Trends – When Criminal Charges Reach the White House"(https://query.nytimes.com/gst/fullpage.html?res=9904E7DF1F3FF933A05753C1A9639C8B63.)The New York Times. Retrieved September 30, 2014.

- o   Dickinson, William B.; Mercer Cross; Barry Polsky (1973)W.   atergate: chronology of a crisis(http://worldcat.org/oclc/   20974031).   1. Washington D. C.: Congressional QuarterlyInc. pp. 8 133 140 180 188.ISBN 0-87187-059-2. OCLC 20974031 (https://www.worldcat.org/oclc/20974031).   This book is volume one of a two-volume set. Both volumes share the same ISBN and Library of Congress call numbe, rE859 .C62 1973.

- o "The   Smoking   Gun   Tape" (http://www.watergate.info/tapes/72-06-23_smoking gun.shtml)(Transcript of the recording of a meeting between   President   Nixon   and   H.   R.

Haldeman.)Watergate.info website. June 23, 1972. Retrieved January 17, 2007.

o narrative by R.W. Apple, jr. ; chronology by Linda Amster ; general ed.: Gerald Gold. (1937). The Watergate hearings: break-in and cover-up; proceedings (http://www.worldcat.org/oclc/865966&referer=brief _results). New York: Viking Press. ISBN 0-670-75152-9.

o Nixon, Richard (1974).The White House Transcripts (http://www.worldcat.org/oclc/1095702). New York: Viking Press. ISBN 0-670-76324-1. OCLC 1095702 (https://www.worldcat.org/oclc/1095702).

o The evidence was quite simple: the voice of the President on June 23, 1972 directed thCeentral Intelligence Agency (CIA) to halt an FBI investigation that would be politically embarrassing to his re-election. This direction was an obstruction of justice.White, Theodore Harold (1975).Breach of Faith: The Fall of Richard Nixon(http://www.worldca t.org/oclc/1370091&referer=brief_results.) New

York: Atheneum Publishers. p. 7.ISBN 0-689-10658-0.

o White (1975), Breach of Faith, p. 29. "And the most punishing blow of all was to come in late afternoon when the President received, in his Oval Office, the Congressional leaders of his party --Barry Goldwater, Hugh Scott and John Rhodes. The accounts of all three coincide. Goldwater averred that there were not more than fifteen votes left in his support in the Senate".

o "Soon Alexander Haig and James St. Clairlearned of the existence of this tape and they were convinced that it would guarantee Nixon's impeachment in the House of Representatives and conviction in the SenateD."ash, Samuel (1976). Chief Counsel: Inside the Ervin Committee – The Untold Story of Watergate (http://www.worldcat.or g/oclc/2388043). New York: Random House. pp. 259–260.ISBN 0-394-40853-5.

o Trahair, R.C.S From Aristotelian to Reaganomics: A Dictionary of Eponyms With Biographies in the Social Sciences. Santa Barbara, Calif.: Greenwood Publishing Group, 1994I.SBN 0-313-27961-6.

o Smith, Ronald D. and Richte,r William Lee. Fascinating People and Astounding Events From American History. Santa Barbara, Calif.: ABC-CLIO, 1993.ISBN 0-87436-693-3

o Lull, James and Hinerman, Stephen.Media Scandals: Morality and Desire in the Popular Culture MarketplaceN. ew York: Columbia University Press, 1997.ISBN 0-231-11165-7

o Hamilton, Dagmar S. "The Nixon Impeachment and the Abuse of Presidential Pow,e"rIn Watergate and Afterward: The Legacy of Richard M. Nixon.Leon Friedman and William F. Levantrosser, eds. Santa Barbara, Calif.: Greenwood Publishing Group, 1992.ISBN 0-313-27781-8

o "El 'valijagate' sigue dando disgustos a Cristina Fernández |
Internacional("http://internacional.elpais.com/interna cio
nal/2008/11/04/actualidad/1225753214_850215.htm. l)EL PAÍS. November 4, 2008. Retrieved July 28, 2014.

o Dean, John W. (2014). The Nixon Defense: What He Knew and When He Knew .ItViking. p. xvii. ISBN 978-0-670- 02536-7.

o "Watergate Retrospective: The Decline and Fall" (http://www.time.com/time/magazine/article/0,9171, 942983-1,00.ht ml), Time, August 19, 1974

o Meyer, Lawrence (November 10, 1988)."John N. Mitchell, Principal in Watergate, Dies at 75" (https://www.washingto npost.com/wpsrv/national/longterm/watergate/stories /mitchobit.htm.)The Washington Post.

o Rugaber, Walter (January 18, 1973)."Watergate Trial in Closed Session"(https://www.nytimes.com/1973/01/18/archi ves/watergate-trial-in-closed-session-judge-clears-court-to-hea.hrtml). The New York Times. Retrieved April 21, 2018.

o G Gordon Liddy, Will, p. 195, St. Martin's Press (January 1, 1980)ISBN 978-0312880149

o G Gordon Liddy, Will, p. 226, St. Martin's Press (January 1, 1980)ISBN 978-0312880149

o G Gordon Liddy, Will, p. 232, St. Martin's Press (January 1, 1980)ISBN 978-0312880149 o Pear, Robert (June 14, 1992)."Watergate, Then and Now – 2 Decades After a Political Burglary, the Questions Still Linger" (https://www.nytimes.com/1992/06/15/us/watergate-then-now-2-decades-after-political-burglary-questions-stil l-linger.html). The New York Times. Retrieved May 18, 2015.

o Shirley, Craig (2012-06-20)."The Bartender's Tale: How the Watergate Burglars Got Caught | Washingtonian" (http s://www.washingtonian.com/2012/06/20/the-bartenders-tale-how-the-watergate-burglars-got-caught/.) Washingtonian. Retrieved 2018-10-29.

o Lewis, Alfred E. (June 18, 1972)."5 Held in Plot to Bug Democrats' Office Here" (https://www.washingtonpost.com/w pdyn/content/article/2002/05/31/AR2005111001227. htm.l)The Washington Post. Retrieved 28 December 2017.

o Genovese, Michael A. (1999).The Watergate Crisis. Westport, Conn.: Greenwood Press.ISBN 9780313298783.

o Dickinson, William B.; Mercer Cross; Barry Polsky (1973)".Watergate: Chronology of a Crisis"(http://worldcat.org/ocl c/20974031). 1. Washington D. C.: Congressional QuarterlyInc.: 4. ISBN 0-87187-059-2. OCLC 20974031 (https://w ww.worldcat.org/oclc/20974031). Retrieved 1 May 2014.

o Sirica, John J. (1979).To Set the Record Straight: The Break-in, theTapes, the Conspirators, the Pardon. New York: Norton. p. 44. ISBN 0-393-01234-4.

o "Transcript Of A Recording Of A Meeting Bewt een The President And H.R. Haldeman In The Oval Ofifce On June 23, 1972 From 10:04 To 11:39 AM" (https://www.nixonlibrary.gov/sites/default/files/forr esearchers/find/tapes/watergat e/trial/exhibit_01.pdf)(PDF). Richard Nixon Presidential Library and Museum.

o "Brief Timeline of Events"(http://watergate.info/chronology/brief-timeline-of-events.)Malcolm Farnsworth. Retrieved May 24, 2012.

o Times, Special To The New York (1988-11-10). "John N. Mitchell Dies at 75; Major Figure in Watergate" (https://www.nytimes.com/1988/11/10/obituaries/john-nm-itchell-dies-at-75-major-figure-in-watergate.html.)The New York Times. ISSN 0362-4331 (https://www.worldcat.org/issn/0362-4331). Retrieved 2017-01-25.

o Meyer, Lawrence (November 10, 1988)."John N. Mitchell, Principal in Watergate, Dies at 75" (https://www.washingtonpost.com/wpsrv/national/longterm/watergate/stories/mitchobit.htm.)The Washington Post.

o Quote: "There were still simply too many unanswered questions in the case. By that time, thinking about the break-i and reading about it, I'd have had to be some kind of moron to believe that no other people were involved. No political campaign committee would turn over so much money to a man like Gordon Liddy without someone higher up in the organization approving the transaction. How could I not see that? These questions about the case were on my mind during a pretrial session in my courtroom

December 4.S" irica, John J. (1979).To Set the Record Straight: The Break-in, the Tapes, the Conspirators, the Pardon (http://worldcat.org/isbn/0393012344.) New York: Norton. p. 56. ISBN 0-393-01234-4.

- o "Woodward Downplays Deep Throat"(http://www.politico.com/blogs/media/2012/06/woodward-and-bernstein-downpl ay-deep-throat-125950.html), Politico.com blog, June 2012. Retrieved February 8, 2015
- o "The profound lies of Deep Throat"(http://www.pressherald.com/2012/02/19/the-profound-lies-of-deep-throat_2012-0 2-19/), The Miami Herald, republished in Portland Press Herald, February 14, 2012
- o "Covering Watergate: Success and Backlash" (http://www.time.com/time/magazine/article/0,9171, 943934-1,00.html.(Time. July 8, 1974. Retrieved July 24, 2011.
- o Crouse, Timothy, The Boys on the Bus, Random House, 1973, pg. 298

o "The Nation: More Evidence: Huge Case for Judgment"(http://www.time.com/time/magazine/artic le/0,9171,911434- 3,00.html). Time. July 29, 1974. Retrieved July 24, 2011.

o "The Nixon Years: Down from the Mountaintop" (http://www.time.com/time/magazine/article/0,9171, 942981-11,00.ht ml). Time. August 19, 1974. Retrieved July 24, 2011.

o Dean, John W. The Nixon Defense, p.344, Penguin Group, 2014ISBN 978-0-670-02536-7

o Dean, John W. The Nixon Defense: What He Knew and When He Knew ,Itpp. 415–416, Penguin Group, 2014 ISBN 978-0-670-02536-7

o "Watergate Scandal, 1973 In Review"(http://www.upi.com/Audio/Year_in_Revie w/Events-of-1973/Watergate-Scanda l/12305770297723-4/). United Press International. September 8, 1973. Retrieved June 17, 2010.

o "When Judge Sirica finished reading the lette,rthe courtroom exploded with excitement and reporters ran to the rear entrance to phone their newspapers. The bailfifkept banging for silence. It was a stunning development, exactly what I had been waiting fo.r

Perjury at the trial. The involvement of others. It looked as if Watergate was about to break wide open."Dash, Samuel (1976).Chief Counsel: Inside the Ervin Committee–The Untold Story of Watergate (http://www.worldcat.org/oclc/2388043). New York: Random House. p. 30.ISBN 0-394-40853-5.

o Dean, John W. The Nixon Defense: What He Knew and When He Knew ,Itpp. 610–620, Penguin Group, 2014 ISBN 978-0-670-02536-7

o "Sequels: Nixon: Once More, with Feeling"(http://www.time.com/time/magazine/article/0,9171,918947-2,00.html,Time, May 16, 1977

o "Watergate Scandal, 1973 in Review"(http://www.upi.com/Audio/Year_in_Revie w/Events-of-1973/Watergate-Scanda l/12305770297723-4/). United Press International. September 8, 1973. Retrieved June 17, 2010.

o Garay, Ronald. "Watergate" (http://www.museum.tv/eotv/watergate.htm.) The Museum of Broadcast Communication. Retrieved January 17, 2007.

o Kranish, Michael (July 4, 2007)."Select Chronology for Donald G.

Sanders"(http://www.boston.com/news/nation/wa
shington/articles/2007/07/04/not_all_would_put_a_h
eroic_sheen_on_thompsons_watergate_role/?page=.
2B)oston Globe.

o "Watergate Scandal, 1973 In
Review"(http://www.upi.com/Audio/Year_in_Revie
w/Events-of-1973/Watergate-Scanda
l/12305770297723-4/). United Press International.
September 8, 1973. Retrieved June 17, 2010.

o Noble, Kenneth (July 2, 1987)."Bork Irked by
Emphasis on His Role in Watergate"
(https://www.nytimes.com/1987/0   7/02/us/bork-
irked-by-emphasis-on-his-role-in-
watergate.htm.l)The New York Times. Retrieved
May 26, 2009.

o Pope, Rich. "Nixon, Watergate and Walt Disney
World? There is a
connection"(http://www.orlandosentinel.com/trave
l/attractions/the-daily-disney/os-nixon-watergate-
and-walt-disney-world-20161028-sto.rhytml).
OrlandoSentinel.com.

o Apple, Jr., R.W. "Nixon Declares He Didn't Profit
From

o PublicLife"(https://www.nytimes.com/learning/gener al/onthis day/big/1117.html#article). New York Times.

o Richard Nixon: Question-and-Answer Session at the Annual Convention of the Associated Press Managing Editors Association, Orlando, Florida(http://www.presidency.ucsb.edu/mediaplay.p hp?id=4046&admin=37), The American Presidency Project.

o Kilpatrick, Carroll (November 18, 1973)."Nixon Tells Editors, 'I'm Not a Crook"(https://www.washingtonpost.com/wp- srv/national/longterm/watergate/articles/111873- 1.htm.)The Washington Post.

o "The Legal Aftermath Citizen Nixon and the Law"(http://www.time.com/time/magazine/article/0, 9171,942980,00.htm l). Time. August 19, 1974. Retrieved July 24, 2011.

o Theodore White. Breach of Faith: The Fall of Richard Nixon(http://www.worldcat.org/oclc/1370091&refee r r=brief_res ults). Readers Digest Press, Athineum Publishers, 1975, pp. 296–298.

o Bernstein, C. and Woodward, B: The Final Days, p. 252. New York: Simon & Schuster, 1976.

o "Obituary: Hugh Scott, A Dedicated Public Servant"(http://articles.mcall.com/19940726/news/29 94945_1_mr-scott-   white-house-hugh-scott).   The Morning Call. July 26, 1994. Retrieved December 8, 2015.

o "GOP   Leaders   Favour Stepdown"(http://stanforddailyarchive.com/cgi-bin/stanford?a=d&d=stanford19740510-01.2.4   3#). The Stanford Daily. Associated Press. May 10, 1974. Retrieved December 8, 2015.

o Patricia Sullivan (June 24, 2004)."Obituary: Clayton Kirkpatrick,   89;   Chicago   Tribune   Editor" (https://www.washingto   npost.com/wp-dyn/articles/A1123-2004Jun23.htm.l)The Washington Post. Retrieved December 8, 2015.

o "Time Magazine – U.S. Edition – May 20, 1974 Vol. 103   No.   20" (http://www.time.com/time/magazine/0,92637, 60174 0520,00.html).   Time.   May   20,   1974. Retrieved July 24, 2011.

- "Time Magazine – U.S. Edition – May 13, 1974 Vol. 103 No. 19" (http://www.time.com/time/magazine/0,92637, 60174 0513,00.html). Time. May 13, 1974. Retrieved July 24, 2011.

- Kutler, S: Abuse of Power, page 247. Simon & Schuste,r 1997.

- "Transcript Prepared by the Impeachment Inquiry Staff for the House Judiciary Committee of a Recording of a Meeting Among the President, John Dean and H.R. Haldeman on March 21, 1973 from 10:12 to 11:55 am(h"ttp://www.nixonlibrary.gov/forresearchers/find/tapes/watergate/wspf/886-008.pdf()PDF). Retrieved July 24, 2011.

- Kutler, S: Abuse of Power, page 111. Simon & Schuste,r 1997. Transcribed conversation between President Nixon and Haldeman.

- Clymer, Adam (May 9, 2003)."National Archives Has Given Up on Filling the Nixon aTpe Gap" (https://www.webcitati on.org/5sPqUFNJO?url=http://www.nytimes.com/2003/05/09/us/national-archives-has-given-up-on-filling-the-nixon-t ape-gap.html). The New York Times. Archived from the original (https://www.nytimes.com/2003/05/09/us/naitonal-arc hives-has-given-up-on-filling-the-nixon-tape-gap.html)on September 1, 2010. Retrieved January 17, 2007.

o Congressional Record, Vol. 120, Page H2349 (https://www.gpo.gov/fdsys/delivery/getpage.action?dbname=19 74_record&position=all&page=H2349)-50

o Congressional Record, Vol. 120, Page H2362 (https://www.gpo.gov/fdsys/delivery/getpage.action?dbname=19 74_record&position=all&page=H2362)-63

o Congressional Record, Vol. 120, Page H29219 (https://www.gpo.gov/fdsys/delivery/getpage.action?dbname=1 974_record&position=all&page=H29219(

o Bazan, Elizabeth B (December 9, 2010), "Impeachment: An Overview of Constitutional Provisions, Procedure, and Practice", Congressional Research Service reports

o " "Transcript of a Recording of a Meeting Betwen the President and H.R. Haldeman in the Oval Ofifce on June 23, 1972 from 10:04 to 11:39 am" Watergate Special Prosecution Force"(http://www.nixonlibrary.gov/forresearchers/fi n d/tapes/watergate/wspf/741-002.pdf)(PDF). Retrieved June 17, 2010.

o "Audio: Recording of a Meeting Between the President and H.R. Haldeman in the Oval Oficfe on June 23, 1972 from 10:04 to 11:39 am" Watergate Special Prosecution Force"(https://www.youtube.com/watch?v=_oe3Og U8W0s.(

o Statement Announcing Availability of Additional Transcripts of Presidential Tape Recordings (http://www.presidency.u csb.edu/ws/index.php?pid=4320&st=&st1=)August 5, 1974

o Bernstein and Woodward (1976): The Final Days, p. 309

o "The Administration: The Fallout from Ford's Rush to Pardon("http://www.time.com/time/magazine/article/ 0,9171,90 8732-8,00.html). Time. September 23, 1974. Retrieved July 24, 2011.

- Lucas, Dean."Famous Pictures Magazine – Nixon's V sign"(https://web.archive.org/web/20070926235546/http://www.famouspictures.org/mag/index.php?title=Nixon%27s_V_sign). Archived from the original (http://www.famouspictures.org/mag/index.php?title=Nixon%27s_V_sign)on September 26, 2007. Retrieved June 1, 2007.

- Katharine Graham,Personal History (New York: Alfred A. Knopf, 1997), p. 495.

- Schmidt, Steffen W. (2013), American Government and Politics Today, 2013–2014 Edition, Wadsworth Publishing,

- p. 181, ISBN 978-1133602132, "In 1974, President Richard Nixon resigned in the wake of a scandal when it was obvious that public opinion no longer supported him."

- "President Nixon's Resignation Speech"(https://www.pbs.org/newshour/character/links/nixon_speech.html). PBS. Retrieved August 29, 2009.

o Brokaw, Tom (August 6, 2004)."Politicians come and go, but rule of law endures"(http://www.msnbc.msn.com/id/55 93631/ns/us_news-nixon_anniversary/.) MSNBC. Retrieved August 29, 2009.

o "Gerald Ford's Proclamation Granting a Pardon to Richard Nixon("http://www.ford.utexas.edu/LIBRARY/speec hes/7 40061.htm). Ford.utexas.edu. Retrieved June 17, 2010.

o Ford, Gerald (September 8, 1974)."Gerald R. Ford Pardoning Richard Nixon"(http://www.historyplace.com/speeche s/ford.htm). Great Speeches Collection. The History Place. Retrieved December 30, 2006.

o Fulton, Mary Lou (July 17, 1990)."Nixon Library : Nixon Timeline – Page 2"(http://articles.latimes.com/1990-07-17/n ews/ss-339_1_richard-nixon/2.) Los Angeles Times. Retrieved July 28, 2014.

o Shane, Scott (December 29, 2006). "For Ford, Pardon Decision Was Always Clear-Cut".The New York Times. p. A1.

o Gettlin, Robert; Colodny, Len (1991). Silent Coup: The Removal of a President(http://www.worldcat.org/oclc/224931 43). New York: St. Martin's Press. p. 420.ISBN 0-312-05156-5. OCLC 22493143 (https://www.worldcat.org/oclc/224 93143.(

o Ford, Gerald R. (1979).A Time to Heal: The Autobiography of Gerald R. Ford(http://www.worldcat.org/oclc/483521 3). San Francisco: Harper & Row. pp. 196–199. ISBN 0-06-011297-2.Ford (1979), 4.

o Anita L. Allen, The New Ethics: A Tour of the 21st Century Landscape (New York: Miramax Books, 2004), 101.

o Thomas L. Shaffer & Mary M. Shafer, American Lawyers and Their Communities: Ethics in the Legal Profession

o)Notre Dame: University of Notre Dame Press, 1991), 1.

o Jerold Auerbach,Unequal Justice: Lawyers and Social Change in Modern America(New York: Oxford University Press, 1976), 301.

o Time, June 24, 1977, "The Law: Watergate Bargains: Were They Necessary"?

o Time, March 11, 1974, "The Nation: The Other Nixon Men"

o "Washington Post profile of Haldeman"(https://www.washingtonpost.com/wp-srv/onpolitics/watergate/haldeman.htm 1). The Washington Post. Retrieved July 28, 2014.

o Stout, David (February 16, 1999)."John D. Ehrlichman, Nixon Aide Jailed for Watergate, Dies at 73"(https://www.nytimes.com/1999/02/16/us/john-d-ehrlichman-nixon-aide-jailed-for-watergate-dies-at-73.html?pagewanted=a. lTl)he New York Times.

o David Rohde (1998-04-15)."Maurice Stans Dies at 90; Led Nixon Commerce Dept"(https://www.nytimes.com/1998/04/15/us/maurice-stans-dies-at-90-led-nixon-commerce-dept.htm.l)The New York Times. Retrieved 2017-12-05.

o "March 23, 1973: Watergate Burglars Sentenced; McCord Letter Revealed"(http://www.historycommons.org/context.jsp?item=a032373wgsentences&scale=0#a032373wgsentences.)History Commons. Retrieved September 30, 2014.

o Jennie Cohen (June 15, 2012)."Watergate: Where Are They Now?"(http://www.history.com/news/watergate-where- are-they-now). History. Retrieved September 30, 2014.

o "E. Howard Hunt Biography Writer, Spy (1918–2007)"(http://www.biography.com/people/e-howard-hunt-262375#syn opsis). Bio. Retrieved September 30, 2014.

o Albin Krebs & Robert McG. Thomas J.r(January 28, 1982). "Notes on People – Bernard Barker to Retire From Miami Job Early" (https://www.nytimes.com/1982/01/28/nyregoi n/notes-on-people-bernard-barker-to-retire-from-mia mi-job-early.html). The New York Times. Retrieved September 30, 2014.

- Jilian Fama & Meghan Kiesel (June 17, 2012)."Watergate Burglars: Where Are They Now?"(http://abcnews.go.com/ Politics/watergate-burglars-now/story?id=16567157#4.)ABC. Retrieved September 30, 2014.

- Theodore Schneyer, "Professionalism as Poiltics: The Making of a Modern Legal Ethics Code", inLawyers' Ideals/Lawyers' Practices: Transformations inthe American Legal Profession, eds. Robert L. Nelson, David M. Trubek, & Rayman L. Solomon, 95–143 (Ithaca: Cornell University Press, 1992), 104.

- American Bar Association (2015). "Standard 303, Curriculum"A. BA Standards and Rules of Procedure for Approval of Law Schools 2015–2016(http://www.americanbar.org/content/dam/aba/publications/misc/legal_education/Standards/2015_2016_aba_standards_for_approval_of_law_schools_final.authcheckdam.pd(fP) DF). Chicago: American Bar Association. p. 16.ISBN 978-1-63425-352-9. Retrieved 15 December 2016.

- "Historian's work gives a glimpse of Nixon "unplugge"d" (http://www.news.wisc.edu/20004).

University of Wisconsin- Madison. November 8, 2011. Retrieved September 30, 2014.

o "Nixon's secret Watergate testimony orderedreleased" (https://www.reuters.com/article/2011/07/29u/ s-nixon-waterg ate-idUSTRE76S4ZH20110729,) Reuters, July 29, 2011.

o Kim Geiger (November 10, 2011)."Nixon's long-secret grand jury testimony released"(http://www.latimes.com/news/ politics/la-pn-nixon-testimony-20111110,0,6436502.story.)Los Angeles Times. Retrieved November 10, 2011.

o "Long-sealed Watergate documents may bereleased Associated Press reprinted by Fox News June 2, 2012("http:// www.foxnews.com/politics/2012/06/02/long-sealed-watergate-documents-may-be-released/.)Fox News Channel. June 2, 2012. Retrieved July 28, 2014.

o "Fed'l Judge Unseals Watergate Trial Records for G. Gordon Liddy and James McCord ABA Journal November 2, 2012" (http://www.abajournal.com/news/article/fed_l

judge_unseals_watergate_trial_records_for_g._gordo
n_liddy_an   d_james_mc/).   Abajournal.com.
November 2, 2012. Retrieved July 28, 2014.

o Thomas J. Johnson,Watergate and the Resignation of
Richard Nxion: Impact of a Constitutional Crisis,
"The Rehabilitation of Richard Nixon", eds. P.
Jeffrey and Thomas Maxwell-Long: Washington,
D.C., CO. Press, 2004, pp. 148–149.

o "The   Nation: David   Can   Be   a
Goliath"(http://content.time.com/time/subscriber/arti
cle/0,33009,947901-2,00.htm.l(Time. May 9, 1977.

o Stelter, Brian (September 1, 2013)."David Frost,
Interviewer Who Got Nixon to Apologize for
Watergate,   Dies   at   74"
(https://www.nytimes.com/2013/09/02/world/europe/
david-frost-known-for-nixon-interview-dead-at-
74.html?pagewant ed=all). The New York Times.
Retrieved November 25, 2014.

o "Follow The Money: On The Trail Of Watergate
Lore," NPR, June 16, 2012

o "Historical Marker Installed Outside 'Deep Throat'
Garage("https://www.arlnow.com/2011/08/17/histori

cal-marker-ins   talled-outside-deep-throat-garage/.)
17 August 2011. Retrieved 23 January 2018.

o "Watergate   Investigation   Historical
Marker"(https://www.hmdb.org/marker.asp?marker=
55498). Retrieved 23 January 2018.

o Lewis, Danny. "The Parking Garage Where Deep
Throat Spilled the Beans on Watergate Is Being Torn
Down" (http s://www.smithsonianmag.com/smart-
news/parking-garage-where-deep-throat-spilled-
beans-watergate-being-torn-do wn-180961733/?q=).
Retrieved 23 January 2018.

o Maher, Kris (20 June 2014)."Watergate Parking
Garage   to   Be   Torn   Down"
(https://www.wsj.com/articles/watergate-p   arking-
garage-to-be-torn-down-1402874716.)Retrieved   23
January 2018 – via www.wsj.com.

o Jessica Gresko, Associated Press (July 16,
2013)".Watergate Records Released 40 Years After
Being   Filed   Under   Seal"
(http://www.huffingtonpost.com/2013/07/16/waterga
te-records_n_3606339.htm.l)The Huffington Post.
Retrieved September 6, 2014.

o Greenberg, David (June 5, 2005)."The Unsolved Mysteries of Watergate" (https://www.nytimes.com/2005/06/05/wee kinreview/05green.html). The New York Times.

o Senior Judge Royce Lamberth (June 11, 2013)."In Re: Petition of Luke Nitcher"(https://web.archive.org/web/20140 910195819/http://www.dcd.uscourts.gov/dcd/sites/dc d/files/12-mc-74_memorandum_opinion.pdf)(PDF). United States District Court for the District of Columbia. Archived from the original (http://www.dcd.uscourts.gov/dcd/sites/dc d/files/12-mc-74_memorandum_opinion.pdf)(PDF) on September 10, 2014. Retrieved September 9, 2014.

o Donald L. Bartlett,Howard Hughes, p. 410, W. W. Norton & Co., 2004ISBN 978-0-393-32602-4

o Charles Higham Howard Hughes, p. 244, Macmillan, 2004ISBN 978-0-312-32997-6.

o DuBois, Larry, and Laurence Gonzales (Sepet mber 1976). "Hughes, Nixon and the C.I.A.: The Watergate Conspiracy Woodward and Bernstein Missed," Playboy o Fred Emery Watergate, p. 30, Simon & Schuste,r 1995 ISBN 978-0-684-81323-3

o "The Nation: It Goes Back to the Big Man Time Magazine January 13, 1975 issue"(http://www.time.com/time/magazi ne/article/0,9171,917056,00.html.) Time. January 13, 1975. Retrieved July 28, 2014.

o "Unholy Fury review"(http://www.smh.com.au/entertainment/book s/unholy-fury-review-insightful-account-of-whitlamn ixon-spat-20150525-gh2mr9.html.) Sydney Morning Herald. May 15, 2015. Retrieved August 7, 2017.

o Sulzberger, C. L. (October 30, 1973)."The Thoughts of Premier Chou"(https://news.google.com/newspapers?id=6v dRAAAAIBAJ&sjid=IXMDAAAAIBAJ&pg=7052 %2C5281708.)St. Petersburg Times. The New York Times Service.p. 4-A. Retrieved November 21, 2016 – via Google News.

o "Mao Tse-tung Said to Hold Former Opinion of Nixon" (https://news.google.com/newspapers?id=GppKAA AAIBAJ&sji

d=iZQMAAAAIBAJ&pg=1961%2C3810476.)Nash ua Telegraph. Associated Press. July 10, 1975. p. 25. Retrieved November 22, 2014.

o Chamberlain, John (November 9, 1976)."Another Look at Mao Tse-tung" (https://news.google.com/newspapers?id= RvdOAAAAIBAJ&sjid=40sDAAAAIBAJ&pg=329 3%2C3013773.)Ludington Daily News. p. 4. Retrieved

o November 23, 2014 – via Google News Archive.

o Freed, Kenneth J. (August 15, 1973)."Watergate and Its Effects on Foreign Afairs Discussed" (https://news.google. com/newspapers?id=vp8rAAAAIBAJ&sjid=VfwFA AAAIBAJ&pg=6874%2C2181142.) Nashua Telegraph. Associated Press. p. 21. Retrieved November 25, 2014.

o Halloran, Richard (March 20, 1975)."Watergate Effects Abroad Are Slight"(https://news.google.com/newspapers?id

o =Xx8qAAAAIBAJ&sjid=9ygEAAAAIBAJ&pg=72 53%2C5576885.)The New York Times. p. 13.

Retrieved November 25, 2014 – via Google News Archive.

o "Watergate Comes Out into Open at ForeignParley" (https://news.google.com/newspapers?id=XoQsAAA AIBAJ&sjidds0EAAAAIBAJ&pg=7342%2C834424 .) Spartanburg Herald-Journa.l Associated Press. August 5, 1973. p.A8. Retrieved November 23, 2014.

o "Watergate may sap U.S. power"(https://news.google.com/newspapers?id=A5 EjAAAAIBAJ&sjid=6qEAFAAAAIBAJ&p g=3593%2C1690124). The Gazette. Montreal. August 8, 1973. p. 2. Retrieved November 23, 2014 – via Google News Archive.

o Moseley, Ray (June 16, 1973)."Brezhnev to ignore Watergate in talks" (https://news.google.com/newspapers?id=cK JUAAAAIBAJ&sjid=r48DAAAAIBAJ&pg=7240% 2C4226076.)Daily Record. 72 (142). Ellensburg, Washington. United Press Internationa.l p. 1. Retrieved November 23, 2014.

o "Brezhnev to Shun Talk of Watergate" (https://news.google.com/newspapers?id=XTkoAAA

AIBAJ&sjid=yigEAAAAIB
AJ&pg=7434%2C4352706). The Milwaukee
Journa.l June 15, 1973. Part 1, page 3. Retrieved
November 23, 2014 – via Google News Archive.

o Gavshon, Arthur L.(July 18, 1973). "Britain's Leader
Shows Restraint Over
Bugging"(https://news.google.com/news
papers?id=yHsgAAAAIBAJ&sjid=sWcFAAAAIBA
J&pg=1093%2C2199417). The Lewiston Daily Sun.
Retrieved November 25, 2014 – via Google News
Archive.

o "Fidel says Watergate least of exiles'
crimes"(https://news.google.com/newspapers?id=HY
c1AAAAIBAJ&sjid=nesAF
AAAIBAJ&pg=4339%2C455617.) The Miami
News. Reuters. December 2, 1974. p. 2A. Retrieved
November 23, 2014 – via Google News Archive.

o "The name-calling in the wake of
defeat"(https://news.google.com/newspapers?id=so
MuAAAAIBAJ&sjid=e30AFAA
AIBAJ&pg=1077%2C746828). New Straits Times.
Malaysia. May 6, 1975. Retrieved November 23,
2014 – via Google News Archive.

- "Scandal Hurt Policy—Kissinger"(https://news.google.com/newspapers?id=kFwqAAAAIBAJ&sjid=AlcEAAAAIBAJ&pg=1509%2C3522410). The Pittsburgh Press. United Press International. January 11, 1977. pA. -4. Retrieved November 21, 2016 – via Google News.
- "Publisher criticizes the media"(https://news.google.com/newspapers?id=75Q1AAAAIBAJ&sjid=JTIHAAAAIBAJ&pg
- Lodi News-Sentinel. United Press International. January 30, 1975. Retrieved October 24, 2015.

- The Watergate Files, at the Gerald R. Ford Presidential Library, National Archives. Official and unoffical documents on the Watergate scandal from the Presidenital collection of President Nixon's successo,rVice President Gerald R. Ford.
- Hersh, S, 1983, The Price of Power: Kissinger in the Nixon White HouseF,aber & Faber, London"FBI Records: Watergate". The Vault. Federal Bureau of Investigation. Retrieved November 7, 2014.
- "Working Draft: A CIA Watergate History". CIA's Office of the Inspector Genera.l Retrieved September

5, 2016. "Nixon Grand Jury Records". United States National Archives. 1972–1979. Retrieved January 13, 2012.

o "Records of the Watergate Special Prosccutoi n Force". United States National Archives. 1971–1977. Retrieved January 13, 2012.

o Campbell, W. Joseph (June 16, 2012)."Five media myths of Watergate". BBC. Retrieved November 7, 2014.

o Doyle, James (1977).Not Above the Law: the battles of Watergate prosecutors Cox and Jaworsk.i New York: William Morrow and Company. ISBN 0-688-03192-7.

o Hougan, Jim (1984). Watergate, Deep Throat and the CIA. New York: Random House, Inc.ISBN 0-394-51428-9. This was the first book to question the orthodox narrative oTf he Washington Post.[1[

o Schudson, Michael(1992). Watergate in American memory: how we remember, forget, and reconstruct the past.New York: BasicBooks. ISBN 0-465-09084-2.

- Holland, Max (2012). Leak: Why Mark Felt Became Deep Throa.t Lawrence, KN: University Press of Kansas. ISBN 978-0-7006-1829-3.

- White, Theodore Harold(1975). Breach of faith: the fall of Richard Nixon. New York: Atheneum Publishers.ISBN 0- 689-10658-0. A comprehensive history of the Watergate Scandal by Teddy White, a respected journalist and author of The Making of the President series.

- Woodward, Bob and Bernstein, Carlwrote a best-selling book based on their experiences covering the Watergate Scandal for The Washington Post titled All the President's Men, published in 1974.A film adaptation, starring Robert Redford and Dustin Hoffman as Woodward and Bernstein respectively, was released in 1976.

- Woodward, Bob; Bernstein, Carl (2005).The Final Days. New York: Simon & Schuster. ISBN 0-7432-7406-7. – contains further details from March 1973 through September 1974.

- U.S. News Staff (2014-08-08). "Watergate and the White House: The 'ThirdR- ate Burglary' That Toppled a President. Summarized key Watergate dates and detailsand its impact on President Richard Nixon by U.S. News."U.S. News & World Report. Archived from the original on2016-10-24. Retrieved 2017-01-07 – via The Internet Archive, but originally published in U.S. News & World Report on Aug. 19, 1974.

o Rawson, Hugh (2013-01-13)."Words of Watergate: A work about political vocabulary which ofef rs lessons about the dangers of using deceptive language that remain relevant today by Hugh Rawson, director of Penguin USA's reference books operation". dictionaryblog.cambridge.org – A blog from Cambridge Dictionar.yArchived from the original on 2017-08-05. Retrieved 2017-08-05 – via The Internet Archive.

o Rawson, Hugh (2013-01-28)."Words of Watergate: Part 2; A work about political vocabulary which ofef rs lessons about the dangers of using deceptive language that remain relevant today by Hugh Rawson, director of Penguin USA's reference books operation." dictionaryblog.cambridge.org – A blog from Cambridge Dictionar.yArchived from the original on 2017-08-05. Retrieved 2017-08-05 – via The Internet Archive.

o Waldron, Lamar (2012).The Hidden History. Berkeley, California: Counterpoint publishesr . ISBN 1-582-43813-7.

o Watergate Trial Conversations– Richard Nixon Presidential Library and Museum FBI Records: The Vault – Watergate at vault.fbi.gov

o "A New Explanation of Watergate," by J. Anthony Lukas, The New York Times, January 11, 1984. Retrieved from "https://en.wikipedia.org/w/index.php?title=Watergate_scandal&oldid=868939351"

o Understanding the Iran-Contra Affair. Brown University. http://www.brown.edu/Research/Understanding_the_Iran_Contra_Affair/index.php

o 1 Draper, Theodore. A Very Thin Line: the Iran-Contra Affairs. New York: Hill and Wang, 1991, p. 4

o Perry, Robert, and Peter Kornbluh. "Iran-Contra's Untold Story." Foreign Policy 72 (1988). Web. 14 Nov. 2010.

o Draper, Theodore. A Very Thin Line: the Iran-Contra Affairs. New York: Hill and Wang, 1991 Affairs. New York: Hill and Wang, 1991.

o Johnson, Loch K. America's Secret Power: the CIA in a Democratic Society. New York: Oxford UP, 1989.

o Strong, Robert A. Decisions and Dilemmas: Case Studies in Presidential Foreign Policy Making since 1945. M.E. Sharpe, M.E. Sharpe.

o 36 Busby, Robert. Reagan and the Iran-Contra Affair: the Politics of Presidential Recovery. New York: St. Martin's, 1999.

o Williams, Robert. Political Scandals in the USA. Chicago, IL: Fitzroy Dearborn Pub., 2000,

o 38 Gutmann, Amy, and Dennis F. Thompson. Ethics and Politics: Cases and Comments. 3rd ed. Belmont, CA: Thomson/Wadsworth, 2006,

o Shane, Scott; Mazzetti, Mark (16 February 2018)." Inside a 3-Year Russian Campaign to Influence U.S. Voters"
(https://www.nytimes.com/2018/02/16/us/politics/russia-mueller-election.html). The New York Times. ISSN 0362-4331

(https://www.worldcat.org/issn/0362-4331).
Retrieved 17 February 2018.

- o Feldman, Brian (January 6, 2017)." DNI Report:
  High Confidence Russia Interfered With U.S.
  Election
  ("http://nymag.com/selectall/2017/01/report-high-
  confidence-russia-interfered-with-u-s-election.htm.
  ln) ymag.com. Retrieved October 6, 2017.

- o "Assessing Russian Activities and Intentions in
  Recent   US
  Elections("https://www.dni.gov/files/documents/ICA
  _2017_01.pdf) (PDF). Office of the Director of
  National Intelligence. January 6, 2017. Retrieved
  June 24, 2017.

- o "Joint Statement from the Department Of Homeland
  Security and Ofifce of the Director of National
  Intelligence on

- o Election   Security"
  (https://www.dhs.gov/news/2016/10/07/joints- tatement-
  department-homeland-security-and-office-d

- o irector-national). Department of Homeland Security.
  October 7, 2016. Retrieved April 10, 2017.

o   Ackerman, Spencer; Thielman, Sam. "US officially accuses Russia of hacking DNC and interfering with election" (https://www.theguardian.com/technology/2016/oct/07/ us-russia-dnc-hack-interfering-presidential-election.)The Guardian. Retrieved October 7, 2016.

o   Franceschi-Bicchierai, Lorenzo (October 20, 2016)". New evidence proves Russian hackers were behind the hack on Podesta, connecting the dots on different parts of the complex hacking campaign "(https://motherboard.vice.com/ en_us/article/mg7xjb/how-hackers-broke-into-john-podesta-and-colin-powells-gmail-account.s   v)ice.com. Retrieved July 9, 2017.

o   "Cyber researchers confirm Russian government hack of Democratic National Committe e(h" ttps://www.washingtonp   ost.com/world/national-security/cyber-researchers-confirm-russian-government-hack-of-democratic-national-committee/2016/06/20/e7375bc0-3719-11e6-9ccd d6005beac8b3_stor.yhtml).   The   Washington   Post. Retrieved July 26, 2016.

- o "Moscow denies Russian involvement in U.S. DNC hacking ("https://www.reuters.com/article/us-usa-eleciton-hack-russia-idUSKCN0Z02EK). Reuters. June 14, 2016.
- o Mills, Curt (December 15, 2016)." Kremlin Denies Putin's Involvement in Election Hacking "(https://www.usnews.com/news/world/articles/2016-12-15/russian-officials-deny-vladimir-putins-involvement-in-election-hacking.)U.S. News& World Report. Retrieved December 16, 2016.
- o Doroshev, Anton; Arkhipov, Ilya (October 27, 2016)." Putin Says U.S. Isn't Banana Republic, Must Get Over Itsel f("h
  - o ttps://www.bloomberg.com/news/articles/2016-10-27/putin-says-u-s-isn-t-banana-republic-should-get-over-itsel.f) Bloomberg News. Retrieved February 2, 2017.
- o Rid, Thomas (July 24, 2016)." All Signs Point to Russia Being Behind the DNC Hack "(https://motherboard.vice.com/en_us/article/4xa5g9/all-signs-point-to-russia-being-behind-the-dnc-hack.)Motherboard. Retrieved December 23, 2017.

o "Top U.S. intelligence oficial: Russia meddled in election by hacking, spreading of propaganda ("https://www.washingtonpost.com/world/national-security/top-us-cyber-ofifcials-russia-poses-a-major-threat-to-the-countrys-infrastructure-and-networks/2017/01/05/36a60b42-d34c-11e6-9cb0-54ab630851e8_sto.rhytml). The Washington Post. January 5,2017.

o Russians indicted in Mueller investigation (https://www.cnn.com/2018/07/13/politics/russia-investigation-indictments/index.html). CNN.com, July 13, 2018

o Arkin, William M.; Dilanian, Ken; McFadden, Cynthia (December 19, 2016). "What Obama Said to Putin on the Red Phone About the Election Hack" (http://www.nbcnews.com/news/us-news/what-obama-said-putin-red-phone-about-election-hack-n697116). NBC News. Retrieved December 22, 2016.

o Kopan, Tal; Liptak, Kevin; Sciutto, Jim (December 9, 2016). "Obama orders review of Russian election-related hacking" (http://www.cnn.com/2016/12/09/politics/obama-orders-review-into-russian-hacking-of-2016-election/index.html). CNN. Retrieved December 10, 2016.

o Levine, Sam (December 10, 2016). "Chuck Schumer Calls For Investigation Into Russian Interference In The Election" (http://www.huffingtonpost.com/entry/chuck-schumer-russiainvestigation_us_584c1f4de4b0e05aded4329f.) The Huffington Post. Retrieved December 10, 2016.

o Montanaro, Domenico; Seipel, Arnie (December 12, 2016)".M cConnell, Differing With Trump, Says He Has 'Highest Confidence' In Intel Agencies" (https://www.npr.org/2016/12/12/505260062/mcconnell-differing-with-trump-says-he-has-highest-confidence-in-intel-agencies) . NPR. Retrieved December 12, 2016.

o Fandos, Nicholas (December 11, 2016)." Trump Links C.I.A. Reports on Russia to Democrats' Shame Over Election" (https://www.nytimes.com/2016/12/11/us/poltiics/trump-russia-democrats.html.) The New York Times.

o Strohm, Chris (December 10, 2016)." Team Trump Mocks Suggestion of Russian Meddling in Election "(https://www.bloomberg.com/politics/articles/2016-12-10/trump-s-team-mocks-probe-of-foreign-intervention-in-electio.n) Bloomberg News. Retrieved December 10, 2016.

- Liptak, Kevin (15 March 2018). "Trump administration finally announces Rusia sanctions over election meddling" (https://www.cnn.com/2018/03/15/politics/russia-sanctions-trump-yevgeniy-viktorovich-prigozhin/index.htm.l)CNN.

- Lee, Carol E.; Sonne, Paul (December 30, 2016)." U.S. Sanctions Russia Over Election Hacking; Moscow Threatens to Retaliate" (https://www.wsj.com/articles/u-s-punishes-ur   ssia-over-election-hacking-with-sanctions-1483039178.) The Wall Street Journal.

- "Trump Administration Imposes New Sanctions on Putin Cronies" (https://www.nytimes.com/2018/04/06/us/poiltics/trump-sanctions-russia-putin-oligarchs.html.) New York Times. 6 April 2018. Retrieved 6 April 2018.

- "US imposes sanctions against Russian oligarchs and government ofifcials" (https://www.cnn.com/2018/04/06/politics/russia-sanctions-oligarchs/index.html). CNN. 6 April 2018. Retrieved 6 April 2018.

- "US unveils new Russia sanctions over cyberattacks "(https://www.cnn.com/2018/06/11/politics/us-russia-cyber-sanctions/index.html). CNN. 11 June 2018.

- o "Ukraine, three other countries align with EU Council's sanctions decision following Putin's "elections" in occupied Crimea" (https://www.unian.info/politics/10150460-ukraine-three-other-countries-align-with-eu-council-s-sanctions-decision-following-putin-s-elections-in-occupied-crimea.htm.l)Unian. 12 June 2018.

- o Collinson, Stephen (March 20, 2017)." Comey confirms FBI investigating Russia, Trump ties" (http://www.cnn.com/2017/03/20/politics/comey-hearing-russia-wiretapping/index.htm.l)CNN.

- o Carney, Jordain (January 24, 2017)." Senate committee moving forward with Russia hacking probe ("http://thehill.com/blogs/floor-action/senate/315987-senate-committee-moving-forward-with-russia-hacking-probe)The Hill. Retrieved March 4, 2017.

- o Wright, Austin (January 25, 2017). "Second Hill panel to probe possible ties between Russia, Trump campaign" (http://www.politico.com/story/2017/01/house-inet lligence-committee-russia-trump-234168.) Politico. Retrieved February 28, 2017.

- o Stone, Peter; Gordon, Greg (January 18, 2017)." FBI, 5 other agencies probe possible covert Kremlin aid to Trump"

- o (http://www.mcclatchydc.com/news/politicsgovernment
  /article127231799.html). McClatchy.
- o Aleem, Zeesham (January 21, 2017)." 6 different agencies
  have come together to nivestigate Trump's possible Russia
  ties" (https://www.vox.com/policy-and
  politics/2017/1/21/14335112/trump-russia-intelligence-fbi.)
  Vox. Retrieved March 15, 2017.
- o Roberts, Rachel (May 11, 2017). "Donald Trump fired
  James Comey because 'he refused to end Russia
  investigation', say multiple FBI insiders"
  (https://www.independent.co.uk/news/donald-trump-james-
  comey-firing-russia-investigation-refuse-end-fbi-insiders-
  director-hillary-a7729691.htm.l)The Independent.
  Retrieved May 11, 2017.
- o Murray, Mark. "James Comey, Donald Trump and the
  Russia Investigation: A Timeline of Events"
  (https://www.nbcnews.com/politics/politics-
  news/amp/james-comey-donald-trump-russia-investigation-
  timeline-events-n76949, 6N)BC News (June 7, 2017):
  "When I decided to [fire Comey], I said to myself, I said
  you kno, wthis Russia thing with Trump and Russia is a
  made up story."

o Smith, Allan (June 7, 2017). "Comey told Trump 3 times that he wasn't under investigation, but his refusal to publicly say so infuriated Trump" (http://www.businessinsider.com/comey-told-trump-he-wasnt-under-investigation-2017-6.) Business Insider. Retrieved June 10, 2017.

o Levine, Mike; Kelsey, Adam (May 17, 2017). "Robert Mueller appointed special counsel to oversee probe into Russia's interference in 2016 election" (http://abcnews.go.com/Politics/robert-mueller-appointed-special-counsel-oversee-probe-russias/story?id=47472673). ABC News. Retrieved May 17, 2017.

o Sara Murray and Jeremy Herb. "Trump still unconvinced Russia meddled in 2016 election" (https://www.cnn.com/2018/02/13/politics/trump-unconvinced-russia-meddled-election/index.htm.1)CNN. Retrieved February 28, 2018.

o Thomsen, Jacqueline (June 17, 2018)." Roger Stone: Russian wanted Trump to pay $2M for dirt on Clinton during the campaign" (http://thehill.com/homenews/administration/392662-roger-stone-russian-wanted-trump-to-pay-2m-fordirt-on-clinton-during). thehill.com. Retrieved June 19, 2018.

- Popper, Nathaniel (13 July 2018)." How Russian Spies Hid Behind Bitcoin in Hacking Campaign ("https://www.nytimes.com/2018/07/13/technology/bitcoin-russian-hacking.html?hp&action=click&pgtype=Homepage&clickSource=story-heading&module=b-lede-package-region®ion=top-news&W.Tnav=top-news).   NYT. Retrieved 14 July 2018.
- "Putin turned Russia election hacks in Trump's favor: U.S. officials"   (https://www.reuters.com/article/us-usa-trump-cyber-idUSKBN1441RS).   Reuters.   December   15,   2016. Retrieved December 16, 2016.
- Ross,   Brian;   Schwartz,   Rhonda;   Meek,   James   Gordon (December   15,   2016)".O fficials: Master Spy Vladimir Putin   Now   Directly   Linked   to   US   Hacking "(http://abcnews.go.com/International/officials-master-spy-vladimir-putin-now-directly-linked/story?id=44210901). ABC News. Retrieved December 15, 2016.
- Pegues, Jeff (December 14, 2016). More details on U.S. probe   of   Russian   hacking   of   DNC (https://www.youtube.com/watch?v=psEGXYu4yoo). CBS News. Retrieved December 15, 2016 – via YouTube.
- Arkin, William M.; Dilanian, Ken; McFadden, Cynthia (December 14, 2016). "U.S. Officials: Putin Personally

Involved in U.S. Election Hack" (http://www.nbcnews.com/news/us-news/u-s-officials-putin-personally-involved-u-s-election-hack-n696146). NBC News. Retrieved December 14, 2016.

o Barbara Starr; Pamela Brown; Evan Perez; Jim Sciutto; Elise Labott (December 15, 2016)." Intel analysis shows

o Putin approved election hacking" (http://edition.cnn.com/2016/12/15/politics/russian-hacking-vladimir-putin-donald-trump/). CNN. Retrieved December 15, 2016.

o "White House suggests Putin involved in hacking, ups Trump criticism" (http://www.foxnews.com/politics/2016/12/15/white-house-says-trump-obviously-knew-about-russian-hacking-suggets-putin-was-involved.htm. lF)ox News.Associated Press. December 15, 2016. Retrieved December 15, 2016.

o "ODNI Statement on Declassified Intelligence Community Assessment of Russian Activities and Intentions in Recent U.S. Elections"(https://web.archive.org/web/20170413224426/https://www.dni.gov/index.php/newsroom/press-releases/224-press-releases-2017/1466-odni-statement-on-declassified-intelligence-community-assessment-of-

russian-activities-and-intentions-in-recent-u-s-elections
)(Press release). Ofice of the Director of National Intelligence. January 6, 2017. Archived from the original (https://www.dni.gov/index.php/newsroom/press-releases/224-press-rele

o Andrew Higgins, Putin Hints at U.S. Election Meddling by 'Patriotically Minded' Russian s(https://www.nytimes.com/2
  o 017/06/01/world/europe/vladimir-putin-donald-trump-hacking.htm,l)The New York Times (June 1, 2017).

o Scott, Eugene (July 16, 2018). "Trump dismissed the idea that Putin wanted him to win. Putin just admitted that hedid" (https://www.washingtonpost.com/news/thefix/wp/2018/07/16/trump-dismissed-the-idea-that-putin-wanted-him-to-win-putin-just-admitted-that-he-did/). The Washington Post. Retrieved August 16, 2018.

o Tal Kopan, FBI director: Hackers 'poking around' voter system s(http://www.cnn.com/2016/09/28/politics/fbi-ajmes-comey-election-cyberattacks/), CNN (September 28, 2016).

o U.S. official: Hackers targeted voter registratoi n systems of 20 states (http://www.chicagotribune.com/news/nationworld/ct-hackers-target-election-systems-20160930-stor.yhtml), Associated Press (September 30, 2016).

o Robert Windrem, William M. Arkin, and Ken DilanianR, ussians Hacked Two U.S. Voter Databases, Officials Say (http://www.nbcnews.com/news/us-news/russians-hacked-two-u-s-voter-databases-say-officials-n639551), NBC News August 30, 2016).

o Mike Levine & Pierre Thomas, Russian Hackers Targeted Nearly Half of States' Voter Registration Systems, Successfully Infiltrated 4 (http://abcnews.go.com/US/russian-hackers-targeted-half-states-voter-registration-systems/story?id=42435822), ABC News (September 29, 2016).

o Fessler, Pam (September 20, 2017). "10 Months After Election Day, Feds Tell States More About Russian Hacking" (https://www.npr.org/2017/09/22/552956517/ten-months-after-election-day-feds-tell-state-smore-about-russian-hacking). NPR. Retrieved September 22, 2017.

o Mulvihill, Geoff (September 22, 2017). "The federal government is telling election officials in 21 states that hackers targeted their systems last year, although in most cases the systems were not breached"(http://hosted.ap.org/dynamic/stories/U/US_RUS SIAN_HACKING_STATES_DCOL?SITE=OKPON&SE CTION=HOME&TEMPLATE=DEFAULT). Associated Press. Retrieved September 22, 2017.

o Mulvihill, Geoff. "Hackers targeted election voting systems in 21 states, US government reveal s("https://www.independent.co.uk/news/world/americas/us-politics/us-election-hacking-voting-systems-breach-states-revealed-a7962542.html). The Independent. The Independent. Retrieved 2 October 2017.

o "Russia did not hack our voting systems, says California "(https://www.independent.co.uk/news/worlda/ mericas/us-politics/russia-hacking-us-election-voting-systems-did-not-happen-california-a7970976.htm. lT) he Independent. Retrieved 30 September 2017.

o Karoun Demirjian, Senate Intelligence Committee releases interim report on election securi t(yhttps://www.washingto npost.com/powerpost/senate-intelligence-committee-releases-interim-report-on-election-security/2018/05/08/4b33d992-531e-11e8-9c91-7dab596e8252_story.html), Washington Post (May 8, 2018).

o Russian Targeting of Election Infrastructure During the 2016 Election: Summary of Initial Findings and Recommendations (https://www.burr.senate.gov/imo/media/doc/RussRptInstl mt1-%20ElecSec%20Findings,Recs2.pdf), Senate Intelligence Committee, May 8, 2018.

o Parker, Ned; Landay, Jonathan; Walcott, John (April 20, 2017). "Exclusive: Putin-linked think tank drew up plan to sway 2016 U.S. election – documents" (https://www.reuters.com/article/us-usa-russia-election-exclusive-idUSKBN17 L2N3). Reuters. Retrieved April 20, 2017.

o Lagunina, Irina; Maternaya, Elizabeth (April 20, 2017)". Trump and secret documents of the Kremlin" Трамп итайные документы Кремля (http://www.svoboda.org/a/28440991.html) (in Russian). Radio Svoboda. Retrieved April 22, 2017.

o Stubbs, Jack; Pinchuk, Denis (April 21, 2017).K ing, Larry, ed. "Russia denies Reuters report think tank drew up plan to sway U.S. election" (https://www.reuters.com/article/us-usa-russia-election-denial-idUSKBN17M191). Reuters. Retrieved April 21, 2017.

o Howard, Philip N.; Gorwa, Robert (May 20, 2017)." Facebook could tell us how Russia interfered in our elections. Why won't it?" (https://www.washingtonpost.com/opinions/facebook-could-tell-us-how-russia-interfered-in-our-elections-why-wont-it/2017/05/19/c061a606-3b21-11e7-8854-21f359183e8c_sto.rhytml). The Washington Post.

o Salzman, Ari (June 7, 2017). "Facebook's Fake Accountability" (http://www.barrons.com/articles/facebooks-fake-accountability-1496861464). Barron's. Retrieved June 10, 2017.

o Salzman, Ari (May 5, 2017). "Facebook, Tesla Realize Technology Can't Solve Everything" (http://www.barrons.com/articles/facebook-tesla-realize-technology-cant-solve-everything1494018925.)Barron's. Retrieved June 10, 2017.

o Weisburd, Andrew; Watts, Clint (August 6, 2016). "Trolls for Trump – How Russia Dominates Your Twitter Feed to Promote Lies (And, Trump, Too)" (http://www.thedailybeast.com/articles/2016/08/06/how-russia-dominates-your-twitter-feed-to-promote-lies-and-o trump-too.html.) The Daily Beast. Retrieved November 24, 2016.

o Ali Watkins; Sheera Frenkel (November 30, 2016). "Intel Officials Believe Russia Spreads FakeN ews" (https://www.buzzfeed.com/alimwatkins/intel-of ficials-believe-russia-spreads-fake-news). BuzzFeed News. Retrieved December 1, 2016.

o Benedictus, Leo (November 6, 2016)." Invasion of the troll armies: from Russian Trump supporters to Turkish state stooges" (https://www.theguardian.com/media/2016/nov/06/troll-armies-social-media-trump-russian.) The Guardian. Retrieved December 2, 2016.

o "Probe reveals stunning stats about fake election headlines on Facebook ("https://www.cbsnews.com/news/facebook-fake-election-news-more-popular-than-real-news-buzzfeed-investigation./)CBS News: CBS Interactive. November 17, 2016. Retrieved August 27, 2018.

o Andrew Weisburd; Clint Watts; JM Berger (November 6, 2016). "Trolling for Trump: How Russia is Trying to Destroy Our Democracy" (http://warontherocks.com/2016/11/trolling-for-trump-how-o russia-is-trying-to-destroy-our-democracy/). War on the Rocks. Retrieved December 6, 2016.

o "U.S. officials defend integrity of vote, despite hacking fears" (http://www.witn.com/content/news/-US-officials-defendintegrity-of-vote-despite-hacking-fears--403109766.htm.l)WITN-TV. November 26, 2016. Retrieved December 2, 2016.

o Dougherty, Jill (December 2, 2016). "The reality behind Russia's fake news" (http://edition.cnn.com/2016/12/02/politics/russia-fake-news-reality/). CNN. Retrieved December 2, 2016.

o Goel, Vindu; Shane, Scott (2017-09-06)." Fake Russian Facebook Accounts Bought $100,000 in Political Ads ("https://www.nytimes.com/2017/09/06/technology/facebook-russian-political-ads.html). The New York Times. ISSN 0362-4331 (https://www.worldcat.org/issn/0362-4331). Retrieved 2017-09-06.

o Leonnig, Carol; Hamburger, Tom; Helderman, and Rosalind. "Facebook says it sold political ads to Russiancompany during 2016 election" (https://www.washingtonpost.com/politics/facebook-says-it-sold-political-ads-to-russian-company-during-2016-election/2017/09/06/32f01fd2-931e-11e7-89fa bb822a46da5b_sto.rhytml). WashingtonPost. Retrieved 2017-09-06.Julian Borger (4 October 2017).

o "Top Senate intelligence duo: Russia did interfere in 2016 election" (https://www.theguardian.com/world/2017/oct/04/senate-intelligence-committee-russia-election-interferenc.e T) heGuardian.com. Retrieved 18 October 2017.

o "Facebook gives election ad data to U.S. special counsel: source ("https://www.reuters.com/article/us-facebook-propaganda-mueller/facebook-gives-election-ad-data-to-u-s-special-counsel source-idUSKCN1BI03.V R) euters. September 7, 2017. Retrieved 2017-09-07.

o Gambino, Lauren (October 3, 2017)." Facebook says up to 10 m people saw ads bought by Russian agency ("https://www.theguardian.com/technology/2017/oct/02/facebook-says-up-to-10m-people-saw-ads-bought-by-russian-agency) – via www.theguardian.com.

o "Facebook says 126 million Americans may have seen Russia-linked political post s("https://www.reuters.com/article/us-usa-trump-russia-socialmedia/facebook-says-126-million-americans-may-have-seen-russia-linked-political-posts-idUSKBN1CZ2OI). Reuters. October 31, 2017.

o Samuelsohn, Darren (September 7, 2017)." Facebook faces backlash over Russian meddling "(http://www.politico.com/story/2017/09/07/facebook-backlash-russian-meddling-242463.)Politico. Retrieved 7 September 2017.

o "These Are the Ads Russia Bought on Facebook in 2016 "(https://www.nytimes.com/2017/11/01/us/poiltics/russia-2016-election-facebook.html). The New York Times. ISSN 0362-4331 (https://www.worldcat.org/issn/0362-4331).Retrieved 2017-11-03.

o Clayton, Mark (June 17, 2014)." Ukraine election narrowly avoided 'wanton destruction' from hackers ("https://www.csmonitor.com/World/Passcode/2014/0617/Ukraine-election-narrowly-avoided-wanton-destruction-from-hacker.s T)he
Christian Science Monitor. Retrieved August 16, 2017.

o Watkins, Ali (August 14, 2017)." Obama team was warned in 2014 about Russian interference ("http://www.politico.com/story/2017/08/14/obama-russia-election-interference-241547.)Politico. Retrieved August 16, 2017.

o Kramer, Andrew E.; Higgins, Andrew (Augus t16, 2017). "In Ukraine, a Malware Expert Who Could Blow the

Whistle on Russian Hacking"(https://www.nytimes.com/2017/08/16/world/euro pe/russia-ukraine-malware-hacking-witness.html). The New York Times. Retrieved August 16, 2017.

o "Key quotes from Congress' hearing on Russia and the U.S. election ("https://www.reuters.com/article/us-usa-trumprussia-factbox-idUSKBN16R229). Reuters. March 20, 2017.

o Englund, Will (July 28, 2016)." The roots of the hostility between Putin and Clinton "(https://www.washingtonpost.com/world/europe/the-roots-of-the-hostility-between-putin-and-clinton/2016/07/28/85ca74ca-5402-11e6-b652-315ae5d4d4dd_story.html). The Washington Post. Retrieved July 29, 2016.

o "The top four reasons Vladimir Putin might have a grudge against Hillary Clinton ("http://news.nationalpost.com/news/world/the-top-four-reasons-vladimir-putin-might-have-a-grudge-against-hillary-clinto.n N) ational Post. December 16, 2016.

o "Why Putin hates Hillary" (http://www.politico.com/story/2016/07/clinton-putin-226153). Politico. July 26, 2016.

o " 'Pro-Kremlin youth groups' could be behind DNC hack "(http://www.dw.com/en/pro-kremlin-youth-groups-could-be-behind-dnc-hack/a-19430216). Deutsche Welle. July 27, 2016.

o Sciutto, Jim (June 28, 2017). "How one typo let Russian hackers in" (http://edition.cnn.com/2017/06/27/politics/russia-dnc-hacking-csr/index.html). Retrieved November 3, 2017.

o Harding, Luke (December 14, 2016)." Top Democrat's emails hacked by Russia atfer aide made typo, investigationfinds" (https://www.theguardian.com/us-news/2016/dec/14/dnc-hillary-clinton-emails-hacked-russia-aide-typo-investigation-finds). Retrieved November 3, 2017.

o Sharockman, Aaron (December 18, 2016)." It's True: WikiLeaks dumped Podesta emails hour after Trump video surfaced" (http://www.politifact.com/truth-o-meter/statements/2016/dec/18/john-podesta/its-true-wikileaks-dumped-podesta-emails-hour-afte/). Retrieved November 3, 2017.

o Smith, David (October 8, 2016). "WikiLeaks releases what appear to be Clinton's paid Wall Street speeches" (https://www.theguardian.com/us-news/2016/oct/07/wikileaks-hillary-clinton-paid-wall-street-speeches.) Retrieved November 3, 2017.

o "18 revelations from Wikileaks' hacked Clinton emails "(https://www.bbc.com/news/world-us-canada-37639370). Reuters. October 27, 2017. Retrieved November 3, 2017.

o Cohen, Marshall (October 7, 2017)." Access Hollywood, Russian hacking and the Podesta emails: One year later("http://edition.cnn.com/2017/10/07/politics/one-year-accesshollywood-russia-podesta-email/index.htm. lR)etrieved November 3, 2017.

o "Joint Statement from the Department Of Homeland Security and Ofifce of the Director of National Intelligence on Election Security" (https://www.dhs.gov/news/2016/10/07/joints- tatement-department-homeland-security-and-office-director-national). Department of Homeland Security. October 7, 2016. Retrieved November 3, 2017.

o "Assessing Russian Activities and Intentions in Recent US Elections ("https://www.dni.gov/files/documents/ICA_2017_01.pdf) (PDF). Office of the Director of National Intelligence. January 6, 2017. Retrieved November 3, 2017.

- o Johnstone, Liz (December 18, 2017)." John Podesta: FBI Spoke to Me Only Once About My Hacked Emails ("https://www.nbcnews.com/politics/politics-news/john-podesta-fbi-spoke-me-only-once-about-my-hacked-n697511.) Retrieved November 3, 2017.

- o Siddiqui, Sabrina; Gambino, Lauren; Roberts, Dan (July 25, 2016)".D NC apologizes to Bernie Sanders amid convention chaos in wake of email leak" (https://www.theguardian.com/us-news/2016/jul/25/debbie-wasserman-schultz-booed-dnc-fbi-email-hack) – via The Guardian." 'Lone Hacker' Claims Responsibility for Cyber Attack on Democrats ("http://www.nbcnews.com/tech/tech-news/lone-hacker-claims-responsibility-cyber-attack-democrats-n593491.)NBC News. Reuters. June 16, 2016.

- o " "Guccifer" leak of DNC Trump research has a Russian's fingerprints on it" (https://arstechnica.com/security/2016/06/guccifer-leak-of-dnc-trump-research-has-a-russians-fingerprints-on-it./)Retrieved July 26, 2016.

- o "The 4 Most Damaging Emails From the DNC WikiLeaks Dump ("http://abcnews.go.com/Politics/damaging-emails-dnc-wikileaks-dump/story?id=40852448). ABC News. July 25, 2016.

- o "Leaked DNC emails reveal details of anti-Sanders sentimen t("https://www.theguardian.com/us-news/2016/jul/23/dnc-emails-wikileaks-hillary-bernie-sanders.) The Guardian. July 24, 2016.

- o Ashley Parker; David E. Sanger (July 27, 2016). "Donald Trump Calls on Russia to Find Hillary Clinton's Missing Emails" (https://www.nytimes.com/2016/07/28/us/poiltics/donald-trump-russia-clinton-emails.html?_r=0.) The New York Times. Retrieved February 21, 2017.

- o Donald Trump [@realDonaldTrump] (July 27, 2016). "If Russia or any other country or person has Hillary Clinton's 33,000 illegally deleted emails, perhaps they should share them with the FBI !("https://twitter.com/realDonaldTrump/status/75833514718 3788032) (Tweet) – via Twitter.

- o Toosi, Nahal; Kim, Seung Min (July 27, 2016.) " 'Treason'? Critics savage Trump over Russia hack comments "(http://www.politico.com/story/2016/07/trump-russia-clinton-emails-treason-226303). Politico. Retrieved February 26, 2017.

o "Trump: Russia remarks on Clinton emails were sarcasm" (https://www.bbc.com/news/election-us-2016-36917349). BBC News. July 28, 2016.

o Lesniewski, Niels (July 28, 2016). "Reid Says Trump Should Get Fake Intel Briefings" (http://www.rollcall.com/news/politics/harry-reid-says-trump-should-get-fake-intel-briefings.)Roll Call. United States. Retrieved February 12, 2017.

o Noble, Jason (July 28, 2016). "Trump's Russia comments could be a felony, Vilsack charges" (http://www.desmoinesregister.com/story/news/politics/2016/07/28/donald-trump-email-hack-russia-comments-could-be-felony-tom-vilsackcharges/87655860/). The Des Moines Register. Retrieved February 12, 2017.

o Kelly, Caroline (July 28, 2016). "Former Obama mentor: Trump's Russian hack 'jokes' could 'constitute treason' " (http://www.politico.com/story/2016/07/laurence-tribe-trump-russia-226371). Politico. Retrieved February 12, 2017.

o "18 revelations from Wikileaks' hacked Clinton emails "(https://www.bbc.com/news/world-us-canada-37639370).BBC News. October 27, 2016.

o Desiderio, Andrew; Woodruff, Betsy (December 18, 2016). "Clinton Chairman Continues to Blame Russia for Loss"(http://www.thedailybeast.com/articles/2016/12/18/clinton-chairman-continues-to-blame-russia-for-loss.htm.l)The Daily Beast.

o Kathryn Watson (April 13, 2017). "CIA director calls WikiLeaks Russia-aided "non-state hostile intelligence servic"e" (http://www.cbsnews.com/news/cia-director-calls-wikileaks-a-nonstate-hostile-intelligence-service/.) CBS News.

o "U.S. intel report identifies Russians who gave emails to WikiLeaks -oficf ials" (https://www.reuters.com/article/us-usa-russia-cyber-celebrate-idUSKBN14P2NI.) Reuters. January 6, 2017. Retrieved February 12, 2017.

o Porter, Tom (November 28, 2016). "How US and EU failings allowed Kremlin propaganda and fake news to spread through the West" (http://www.ibtimes.co.uk/how-us-eu-failings-allowed-kremlin-propaganda-fake-news-spread-through-west-1593071). International Business Times. Retrieved November 29, 2016.

o Schindler, John R. (November 5, 2015)." Obama Fails to Fight Putin's Propaganda Machine "(http://observer.com/2015/11/obama-fails-to-fight-putinspropaganda-machine./)New York Observer. Retrieved November 28, 2016.

o Stengel, Richard (April 29, 2014). "Russia Today's Disinformation Campaign"(https://web.archive.org/web/20140502031846/ http://blogs.state.gov/stories/2014/04/29/russia-today-s-disinformation-campaig.n U) nited States Departmentof State. Archived from the original (http://blogs.state.gov/stories/2014/04/29/russia-today-s-disinformation-campaign) on May 2, 2014. Retrieved November 28, 2016.

o Alperovitch, Dmitri (June 15, 2016)." Bears in the Midst: Intrusion into the Democratic National Committee ("https://www.crowdstrike.com/blog/bears-midst-intrusion-democratic-national-committee/). CrowdStrike. RetrievedDecember 24, 2016.

o Poulsen, Kevin (January 6, 2017). "How the U.S. Hobbled Its Hacking Case Against Russia and Enabled rTuthers"

    o (http://www.thedailybeast.com/articles/2017/01/06/how-the-u-s-enabled-russian-hack-truthers.htm.l) The Daily Beast.

    o Retrieved January 8, 2017.

- "Threat Group 4127 Targets Hillary Clinton Presidential Campaign" (https://www.secureworks.com/research/threat-group-4127-targets-hillary-clinton-presidential-campaign.) SecureWorks. Retrieved July 26, 2016.

- Thielman, Sam (July 26, 2016)." DNC email leak: Russian hackers Cozy Bear and Fancy Bear behind breach ("https://www.theguardian.com/technology/2016/jul/26/dnc-email-leak-russian-hack-guccifer-2.) The Guardian.

- Lipton, Eric; Sanger, David E.; Shane, Scott (December 13, 2016). "The Perfect Weapon: How Russian Cyberpower Invaded the U.S" (https://www.nytimes.com/2016/12/13/us/poiltics/russia-hack-election-dnc.html)– via NYTimes.com.

- "The Dukes Whitepaper" (https://www.f-secure.com/documents/996508/1030745/dukes_whitepaper.pdf) (PDF).

- U.S. Department of Homeland Security and Federal Bureau of Investigation (December 29, 2016")G. RIZZLY STEPPE – Russian Malicious Cyber Activity "(https://www.us-cert.gov/sites/default/files/publications/JAR_16-20296A_GRIZZLY%20STEPPE-2016-1229.pdf)   (PDF).

United States Computer Emergency Readiness Team. Retrieved January 2, 2017.

o "Does a BEAR Leak in the Woods?" (https://www.threatconnect.com/blog/does-a-bear-leak-in-the-woods/).ThreatConnect. August 12, 2016.

o "Threat Group-4127 Targets Hillary Clinton Presidential Campaign" (https://www.secureworks.com/research/threat-group-4127-targets-hillary-clinton-presidential-campaign.) SecureWorks. June 16, 2016. Retrieved January 23, 2017.

o Gallagher, Sean. "Recapping the facts—Did the Russians 'hack' the election? A look at the established fact s(h" ttps://arstechnica.com/security/2016/12/the-public-evidence-behind-claims-russia-hacked-for-trump.   /A) rsTechnica. Retrieved December 31, 2016.

o "Dutch agencies provide crucial intel about Russia's interference   in   US-election s("https://www.volkskrant.nl/wetenschap/dutch-agencies-provide-crucial-intel-about-russia-s-interference-in-us-elections~b4f8111b. /R) etrieved July 30, 2018.

o "Russia Hacker Indictments Should Make the Kremlin Squirm ("https://www.bloomberg.com/view/articles/2018-07-16/russia-hacker-indictments-should-make-the-kremlin-squirm.)Retrieved July 30, 2018.

o "From the Start, Trump Has Muddied a Clear Message: Putin Interfered"(https://www.nytimes.com/2018/07/18/world/europe/trump-intelligence-russian-election-meddling-.htm.l)Retrieved July 30, 2018.

o Harding, Luke; Kirchgaessner, Stephanie; Hopkins, Nick (April 13, 2017). "British spies were first to spot Trumpteam's links with Russia" (https://www.theguardian.com/uk-news/2017/apr/13/british-spies-first-to-spot-trump-team-links-russia). The Guardian. Retrieved April 13, 2017.

o Lichtblau, Eric (April 6, 2017). "C.I.A. Had Evidence of Russian Effort to Help Trump Earlier Than Believed" (https://www.nytimes.com/2017/04/06/us/trump-russia-cia-john-brennan.html). The New York Times. Retrieved April 13, 2017.

o Miller, Greg (June 23, 2017). "Putin denied meddling in the U.S. election. The CIA caught him doing just that("https://www.washingtonpost.com/news/postpoliitcs/wp/2017/06/23/putin-denied-meddling-in-the-u-s-election-the-cia-caught-him-doing-just-that/). The Washington Post. Retrieved June 24, 2017.

- o Rosenberg, Matthew; Goldman, Adam; Apuzzo, Matt (May 24, 2017). "Top Russian Officials Discussed How to Influence Trump Aides Last Summer" (https://www.nytimes.com/2017/05/24/us/poiltics/russia-trump-manafort-flynn.html). The New York Times. Retrieved May 30, 2017.

- o LoBianco, Tom (May 23, 2017). "Ex-CIA chief John Brennan: Russians contacted Trump campaign" (http://edition.cnn.com/2017/05/23/politics/john-brennan-house-intelligence-committee/index.htm. lC) NN.

- o "Vladimir Putin Wins the Election No Matter Who The Next President Is ("http://www.thedailybeast.com/articles/2016/11/04/vladimir-putin-wins-the-election-no-matter-who-the-next-president-is.htm. l)The Daily Beast. November 4,2016. Retrieved December 2, 2016.

- o "Spy Agency Consensus Grows That Russia Hacked D.N.C .("https://www.nytimes.com/2016/07/27/us/poiltics/spy-agency-consensus-grows-that-russia-hacked-dnc.htm l)The New York Times. Retrieved July 26, 2016.

- o Sciutto, Jim; Raju, Manu (December 2, 2016)." Democrats want Russian hacking intelligence declassified ("http://www.cnn.com/2016/12/02/politics/democrats-rusian-hacking-intelligence/). CNN.

o Entous, Adam; Nakashima, Ellen; Mille,r Greg (December 9, 2016). "Secret CIA assessment says Russia was trying to help Trump win White House" (https://www.washingtonpost.com/world/national-security/obama-orders-review-of-russian-hacking-during-presidential-campaign/2016/12/09/31d6b300-be2a-11e6-94ac-3d324840106c_sto.hrytml). The Washington Post. Retrieved December 10, 2016.

o Sanger, David E.; Shane, Scott (December 9, 2016)." Russian Hackers Acted to Aid Trump in Election, U.S. Says" (https://www.nytimes.com/2016/12/09/us/obama-russia-election-hack.html). The New York Times. Retrieved December 10, 2016.

o Mazzetti, Mark; Lichtblau, Eric (December 11, 2016). "C.I.A. Judgment on Russia Built on Swell of Evidence "(https://www.nytimes.com/2016/12/11/us/politics/ciaj-udgment-intelligence-russia-hacking-evidence.htm.l) The New York Times. Retrieved December 12, 2016.

o LaFraniere, Sharon; Mazzetti, Mark; Apuzzo, Matt (2017-12-30)".H ow the Russia Inquiry Began: A Campaign Aide, Drinks and Talk of Political

Dirt"(https://www.nytimes.com/2017/12/30/us/poiltics/how
-fbi-russia-investigation-begangeorge-papadopoulos.html).
The New York Times. ISSN 0362-4331
(https://www.worldcat.org/issn/0362-4331). Retrieved
2017-12-30.

o Pearson, Rick. "FBI told state GOP in June its emails
had been hacked
"(http://www.chicagotribune.com/news/local/politics/ct-
illinois-republican-party-email-hack-met-1212-
20161211-sto.rhytml). Chicago Tribune.

o Rossoll, Nicki (December 11, 2016)." Reince Priebus:
'RNC Was Not Hacked' "
(http://abcnews.go.com/Politics/reince-priebus-rnc-
hacked/story?id=44110357.) ABC News. Retrieved
December 12, 2016.

o Moscow Spy Scandal Snowballs: What We Know
(https://www.rferl.org/a/russia-fsb-arrests-spy-scandal-
snowballs/28270682.html) Radio Free Europe/Radio
Liberty, January 31, 2017.

o "FBI Investigating DNC Hack Some Democrats Blame
on Russia
("https://www.bloomberg.com/politics/articles2/ 016-
07-25/fbi-investigating-dnc-cyber-hack-some-

o democrats-blame-on-russia.)Bloomberg Politics. July 25, 2016.

o "Bears in the Midst: Intrusion into the Democratic National Committee ("https://www.crowdstrike.com/blog/bears-midst-intrusion-democratic-national-committee/.) June 15, 2016. Retrieved July 26, 2016.

o Lichtblau, Eric; Myers, Steven Lee (October 31, 2016)." Investigating Donald Trump, F.B.I. Sees No Clear Link to Russia" (https://www.nytimes.com/2016/11/01/us/poiltics/fbi-russia-election-donald-trump.html.) The New York Times. Retrieved December 11, 2016.

o Nakashima, Ellen; Entous, Adam (December 10, 2016)". FBI and CIA give difering accounts to lawmakers on Russia's motives in 2016hacks"(https://www.washingtonpost.com/amphtml/world/national-security/fbi-and-cia-givediffering-accounts-to-lawmakers-on-russias-motives-in-2016-hacks/2016/12/10/c6dfadfa-bef0-11e6-94ac-3d324840106c_story.html). The Washington Post. Retrieved March 4, 2017.

o Lederman, Josh; Klapper, Bradley (December 16, 2016). "Official: FBI Backs CIA Conclusion on Russain Hacking Motive"(https://web.archive.org/web/20161217014318/ http://abcnews.go.com/Politics/wireStory/white-house-suggests-putin-involved-us-hacking-44231311) . ABC News. Associated Press. Archived from the original (http://abcnews.go.com/Politics/wireStory/white-house-suggests-putin-involved-us-hacking-4423131   1o)n December 17, 2016. Retrieved December 16, 2016.

o Strohm, Chris (December 30, 2016)." Russia 'Grizzly Steppe' Hacking Started Simpl,y U.S. Says" (https://www.bloom   berg.com/news/articles/2016-12-30/russia-s-grizzly-steppe-cyberattacks-started-simply-u-s-say.s B) loomberg News. Retrieved January 4, 2017.

o "Joint DHS, ODNI, FBI Statement on Russian Malicious   Cyber   Activity ("https://www.fbi.gov/news/pressrel/press-releases/joint-dhs-odni-fbi-statement-on-russian-malicious-cyber-activity,)FBI National Press Ofice (December 29, 2016).

o Sanger, David E. (December 29, 2016). "Obama Strikes Back at Russia for Election Hacking "(https://www.nytimes.com/2016/12/29/us/politics/russi a-election-hacking-sanctions.html?_r=0.   )The   New York Times. Retrieved December 29, 2016.

o   Brühl, Jannis; Tanriverdi, Hakan (December 30, 2016). "Viele Indizien gegen Russland, aber kaum Beweise" (http://www.sueddeutsche.de/digital/hacking-vorwuerfe-gegen-russland-viele-indizien-gegen-russland-aber-kaum-beweise-1.3316005).   Süddeutsche Zeitung. Retrieved January 1, 2017.

o   Harding, Luke (May 10, 2017). "What do we know about alleged links between Trump and Russia?" (https://www.theguardian.com/us-news/2017/may/10/qa-what-we-know-about-alleged-links-between-trump-and-russ.ia   t)he   Guardian. Retrieved October 25, 2017.

o   Wilber, Del Quentin; Cloud, Davis S. (March 20, 2017)." Comey says FBI began investigation into Russia meddling   in   July" (http://www.latimes.com/politics/washington/la-na-essential-washington-updates-comey-fbi-launched-investigation-into-1490023083-htmlstory.html).   Los Angeles Times. Retrieved March 21, 2017.

- Rosenberg, Matthew (March 20, 2017)." Comey Confirms FBI Investigation"(https://www.nytimes.com/2017/03/20/us/ politics/intelligence-committee-russia-donald- trump.htm.l)The New York Times. Retrieved March 20, 2017.

- "Joint Statement from the Department Of Homeland Security and Ofifce of the Director of National Intelligence onElection Security" (https://www.dhs.gov/news/2016/10/07/joints- tatement- department-homeland-security-and-office-director- national). Department of Homeland Security. October 7, 2016. This article incorporates text from this source, which is in the public domain.

- Carroll, Lauren. "17 intelligence organizations or 4? Either way, Russia conclusion still valid" (http://www.politifact.com/truth-o- meter/article/2017/jul/06/17-intelligence-organizations- or-four-either-way-r. /P) olitifact. Retrieved July 11,2017.

- Miller, Greg; Entous, Adam (January 6, 2017). "Declassified report says Putin 'ordered' effort to undermine faith in U.S. election and help Trump" (https://www.washingtonpost.com/world/nationalsecurity/intelligence-chiefs-expectedin-new-york-to-brief-trump-on-russian-hacking/2017/01/06/5f591416-d41a-11e6-9cb0-54ab630851e8_sto.hrytml). The Washington Post.

o Sanger, David E. (January 6, 2017)." Putin Ordered 'Influence Campaign' Aimed at U.S. Election, Report Says ("https://www.nytimes.com/2017/01/06/us/politics/russia-hack-report.html). The New York Times. Retrieved May 30, 2017.

o "Top intelligence officials stop short of providing evidence of Russian hacking at Senate hearing ("https://www.pbs.org/newshour/bb/top-intelligence-officials-stop-short-providing-evidence-russian-hacking-senate-hearing./)PBS News Hour. January 10, 2017. Retrieved May 30, 2017.

o Hess, Peter (January 6, 2017)." RT America Is Put in the Spotlight on Damnnig Intelligence Report" (https://www.inverse.com/article/26079-rt-america-intelligence-report.) Inverse."Meet The Press 03-05-17" (http://www.nbcnews.com/meet-the-press/meet-press-

03-05-17-n729271). NBC. March 5, 2017. Retrieved June 1, 2017.

o " 'This Week' Transcript 5-14-17: The Firing of Director Comey "(http://abcnews.go.com/Politics/week-transcript-14-17-firing-director-comey/story). ABC News. May 14, 2017. Retrieved May 14, 2017.

o Lardner, Richard; Riechmann, Deb (June 21 ,2017). "Intel officials detail how Russian cyberattacks sought to interfere with U.S. elections" (https://www.pbs.org/newshour/politics/intel-officials-detail-russian-cyberattacks-soughtinterfere-u-s-elections). PBS Newshour. Retrieved February 4, 2018.

o "James Clapper: I didn't know about Papadopoulos, Trump Tower meetings when I said there was no Trump-Russia collusion" (http://www.businessinsider.com/trump-russia-collusion-james-clapper-papadopoulos-2071-11).

o Michael S. Schmidt; Matthew Rosenberg; Adam Goldman; Matt Apuzzo (January 19, 2017). "Intercepted Russian Communications Part of Inquiry Into Trump Associates" (https://www.nytimes.com/2017/01/19/us/poiltics/trump

-russi a-associates-investigation.html). The New York Times. Retrieved January 20, 2017.

o Comey, James (June 7, 2017). "Statement for the Record – Senate Select Committee on Intelligence ("https://www.intelligence.senate.gov/sites/default/files/documents/os-jcomey-060817.pd f()PDF). Retrieved July 8, 2017.

o Schofield, Matthew (June 8, 2017)." Did Russia interfere in the 2016 elections? No doubt, Comey says ("http://www.mcclatchydc.com/news/politics-government/congress/article155129289.htm. l)McClatchy DC Bureau. Retrieved July 7, 2017.

o Politico Staff (June 8, 2017). "Full text: James Comey testimony transcript on Trump and Russia" (http://www.politico.com/story/2017/06/08/full-text-james-comey-trump-russia-testimony-239295.)Politico. Retrieved June 9, 2017.

o Stone, Peter; Gordon, Greg (January 18, 2018)." FBI investigating whether Russian money went to NRA to help Trump" (http://www.mcclatchydc.com/news/nation-world/national/article195231139.html). McClatchy DC. Retrieved 19 January 2018.

o Savransky, Rebecca (January 18, 2018). "FBI looking into whether Russian banker gave money to NRA to support Trump: report" (http://thehill.com/homenews/campaign/369488-fbi-looking-into-whether-russian-banker-gave-moneyto-nra-to-support-trump). The Hill. Retrieved 19 January 2018.

o Spies, Mike (November 9, 2016). "The NRA Placed Big Bets on the 2016 Election, and Won Almost All of Them" (https://www.opensecrets.org/news/2016/11/then-ra-placed-big-bets-on-the-2016-election-and-won-almost-all-of-them./) Open Secrets. Retrieved 19 January 2018.

o Sheth, Sonam (May 26, 2018)." The FBI has obtained wiretaps of a Putin ally tied to the NRA who met with Trump Jr. during the campaign" (http://www.businessinsider.com/fbi-obtains-alexander-torshin-wiretaps-from-spanish-poclie-2018-5). Business Insider. Retrieved May 29, 2018.

o Delk, Josh (May 26, 2018)." FBI obtained wiretap conversations of Kremlin-linked banker who met with Trump Jr: report" (http://thehill.com/blogs/blog-briefing-room/389499-fbi-obtained-wiretap-conversations-of-kremlin-linked-banker-who-met). The Hill. Retrieved May 29, 2018.

o Porter, Tom (May 26, 2018). "Trump Jr. Should Be 'concerned': Putin Ally's Wiretapped Calls Sent to FBI, Says Spanish Prosecutor" (http://www.newsweek.com/trump-jr-should-be-concerned-over-putin-allys-wiretapped-calls-spanish-945753). Newsweek. Retrieved May 29, 2018.

o Mak, Tim (February 23, 2017). "The Kremlin and GOP Have a New Friend—and Bo,y Does She Love Guns" (https://www.thedailybeast.com/the-kremlin-and-goph-ave-a-new-friendand-boy-does-she-love-guns.) The Daily Beast. Retrieved 19 January 2018.

o Pavlich, Katie (May 6, 2014). "Part 1: Meet the Woman Working With the NRA and Fighting For Gun Rights in Russia"(https://townhall.com/columnists/katiepavlich/2014/05/06/meet-the-woman-fighting-for-gun-rights-in-russia-n1830491). Townhall. Archived (https://web.archive.org/web/20180222161815/https://townhall.com/columnists/katiepavlich/2014/05/06/meet-the-woman-fighting-for-gun-rights-in-russian1830491 f)rom the original on 2018-02-22. Retrieved April 8, 2018.

o Mak, Tim (March 1, 2018). "Depth Of Russian Politician's Cultivation Of NRA Ties Revealed" (https://www.npr.org/2018/03/01/590076949/depth-ofrussian-politicians-cultivation-of-nra-ties-revealed. N) PR. Archived (https://web.archive.org/web/20180715200921/https://www.npr.org/2018/03/01/590076949/depth-of-russianp-oliticians-cultivation-of-nra-ties-revealed) from the original on 2018-07-15. Fandos, Nicholas (December 3, 2017)."

o Operative Offered Trump Campaign 'Kremlin Connection' Using N.R.A. iTes" (https://www.nytimes.com/2017/12/03/us/poltiics/trump-putin-russia-nra-campaign.html.) The New York Times. Retrieved 19 January 2018.

o "Russian National Charged in Conspiracy to Act as an Agent of the Russian Federation Within the United States (https://www.justice.gov/opa/pr/russian-nationalchargedconspiracy-act-agent-russian-federation-within-united-states.) www.justice.gov.

16 July 2018. Archived(https://web.archive.org/web/20180717034454/http://www.justice.gov/opa/pr/russian-national-charged-conspiracy-act-agent-russian-federation-within-united-state sfr)om the original on 17 July 2018. Retrieved 16 July 2018.

o Miller, Kevin (December 1, 2016). "Angus King: Russian involvement in U.S. election 'an arrow aimed at the heart of democracy' " (http://www.pressherald.com/2016/12/01/sen-king-russian-involvement-in-u-s-election-an-arrow-aimedat-the-heart-of-democracy/). Portland Press Herald. Retrieved December 2, 2016.

o Jim Sciutto; Manu Raju (December 3, 2016)." Democrats want Russian hacking intelligence declassified ("http://edition.cnn.com/2016/12/02/politics/democrats-russian-hacking-intelligence./)CNN. Retrieved December 3, 2016.

o "Angus King among senators asking president to declassify information about Russia and electio n(h"ttp://www.pressherald.com/2016/11/30/angus-king-among-senators-asking-president-to-declassify-information-about-russia-and-election/).   Portland Press Herald. November 30, 2016. Retrieved December 2, 2016.

o Timberg, Craig (November 30, 2016)." Effort to combat foreign propaganda advances in Congress" (https://www.washingtonpost.com/business/economy /effort-to-combat-foreign-propaganda advancesincongress/2016/11/30/9147e1ac-e221-47be-ab92-9f2f7e69d452_story.html).   The Washington Post. Retrieved December 1, 2016.

o Porter, Tom (December 1, 2016). "US House of representatives backs proposal to counter global Russian subversion" (http://www.ibtimes.co.uk/us-house-representatives-backs-proposal-counter-global-russian-subversion-1594342).   International Business Times UK edition. Retrieved December 1, 2016.

o Demirjian, Karoun (December 8, 2016). "Republicans ready to launch wide-ranging probe of Russia,   despite   Trump's stance"(http://www.chicagotribune.com/news/nation world/politics/ct-senate-probe-russia-trump-

20161208-stor.yhtml). Chicago Tribune. The Washington Post. Retrieved December 10, 2016.

o "Senate Republicans join Democrats in calling for probe of Russian electioneering hack s(h" ttp://www.cbsnews.com/news/senate-republicans-join-democrats-probe-russian-electioneering-hacks./)CBS News. Associated Press.December 11, 2016. Retrieved December 11, 2016.

o Peralta, Eyder (December 11, 2016)." As Trump Dismisses CIA, Congress Looks To Confront Russian Cyberattacks" (https://www.npr.org/sections/thetwo-way/2016/12/11/505178242/as-trump-dismisses-ciac-ongress-looks-to-confront-russian-cyberattacks). NPR. Retrieved December 11, 2016.

o John McCain, Lindsey Graham, Chuck Schumer, Jack Reed (December 11, 2016). "McCain, Graham, Schumer, Reed Joint Statement on Reports That Russia Interfered with the 2016 Election ("http://www.armed-services.senate.gov/press-releases/mccain-graham-schumer-reed-joint-statement-on-reports-that-russia-interfered-with-the-

2016-election). United States Senate Committee on Armed Services. Retrieved December 11, 2016.

o "McCain to Trump on Russian hacking: 'The facts are there' – CBS" (https://www.reuters.com/article/us-usa-trump-mccain-idUSKBN1400UX). Reuters. December 11, 2016. Retrieved December 11, 2016.

o Meyer, Theodoric (December 11, 2016)." McCain wants select committee to investigate Russian hacking ("https://www.politico.com/story/2016/12/john-mccain-rusian-hacking-232481). Politico. Retrieved September 7, 2018.

o Theodore Schleifer; Deirdre Walsh. "McCain: Russian cyberintrusions an 'act of wa'r" (http://www.cnn.com/2016/12/30/politics/mccain-cyber-hearing/index.html.) CNN. Retrieved January 14, 2017.

o Brown, Greg (December 11, 2016). "Lankford joins in call for bipartisan investigation into Russian electioninterference" (http://www.fox23.com/news/trump-team-fires-back-after-cia-determines-russian-interference-in-the-republicans-favor/475055309). KOKI-TV. Retrieved December 11, 2016.

o Elise Viebeck; Karoun Demirjian (December 11, 2016). "Key GOP senators join call for bipartisan Russia election probe, even as their leaders remain mum" (https://www.washingtonpost.com/news/powerpost/ wp/2016/12/11/key-gop-senators-join-call-for-bipartisan-russia-election-probe-even-as-their-leaders-remain-mum. T) he Washington Post. Retrieved December 12, 2016.

o David Smith, "FBI covered up Russian influence on Trump's election win, Harry Reid claims" (https://www.theguardian.com/us-news/2016/dec/10/fbi-russia-trump-election-harry-reid-james-comey-wikileak,s T) he Guardian (December 10, 2016).

o Nicholas Fandos, "Bipartisan Letter Seeks Single Inquiry Into Russian Hacking Claim ("https://www.nytimes.com/2016/12/18/us/politics/d onald-trump-transition.html?_r=0,) The New York Times (December 18, 2016).

o Diaz, Daniella (December 14, 2016)." Graham: Russians hacked my campaign email account "(http://edition.cnn.com/2016/12/14/politics/lindsey-graham-hacking-russia-donald-trump./)CNN. Retrieved December 15, 2016.

o Blitzer, Wolf (December 14, 2016). "Graham: Russians hacked my campaign" (https://www.youtube.com/watch?v=EzrIdmHaMZE) (video). CNN. Retrieved December 15, 2016 – via YouTube.

o Williams, Katie Bo (December 15, 2016)." Graham: Tillerson must say Russia hacked US to earn his confirmationvote" (http://thehill.com/policy/national-security/310549-graham-tillerson-must-say-russia-hacked-us-to-earn-his-confirmation). The Hill. Retrieved December 16, 2016.

o Keith, Tamara (December 16, 2016)." In Leaked Remarks, Hillary Clinton Explains Putin's 'Beef' With He r("https://www.npr.org/2016/12/16/505858615/in-leaked-remarks-hillary-clinton-explains-putins-beewf-ith-her). NPR. Retrieved December 17, 2016.

o "Senate Intelligence Committee votes to give leaders solo subpoena powe r("https://www.washingtonpost.com/powerpost/senate-intelligence-committee-votes-to-give-leaders-solo-subpoena-power/2017/05/25/8ecb655a-4189-11e7-adba-394ee67a7582_story.html). The Washington Post. Retrieved May 27, 2017.

o U.S. Senator Richard Burr of North Carolina." Notification: Senate Intel Committee Grants Chairman and iVceChairman Authority to Issue Subpoenas" (https://www.burr.senate.gov/press/releases/notification-senate-intel-committee-grants-chairman-and-vice-chairman-authority-to-issue-subpoenas -()Press release). Retrieved May 27, 2017.

o Demirjian, Karoun (2017-12-18). "Senate intel committee investigating Jill Stein campaign for 'collusion with the Russians'(https://www.washingtonpost.com/powerpost/senate-intel-committee-investigating-jill-stein-campaign-forcollusion-with-the-russians/2017/12/18/ea7f3f1a-e44b-11e7-833f-15503155f84f_story.html). Washington Post.ISSN o 0190-8286 (https://www.worldcat.org/issn/0190-8286). Retrieved 2017-12-19.

o "Senate Intelligence Committee requests Trump campaign documents"(https://www.washingtonpost.com/news/powerpost/wp/2017/05/26/senate-intelligence-committee-requests-trump-campaign-documents. /T)he Washington Post. Retrieved May 27, 2017.

o Karoun Demirjian, Russia favored Trump in 2016, Senate panel says, breaking with House GOP (https://www.washingtonpost.com/powerpost/russia-favored-trump-in-2016-senate-panel-says-breaking-with-house-gop/2018/05/16/6cf95a6a-58f6-11e8-8836-a4a123c359ab_story.html), Washington Post (May 16, 2018).

o Jarrett, Laura. "Justice Dept.: 'Reckless' to release Nunes memo without review ("https://www.cnn.com/2018/01/24/politics/nunes-memo-fbi/index.html). CNN. Retrieved 2018-01-25.

o "U.S. Senator Ben Cardin Releases Report Detailing Two Decades of Putin's Attacks on Democracy, Calling for Policy Changes to Counter Kremlin Threat Ahead of 2018, 2020 Elections | U.S. Senator

Ben Cardin of Marylan (https://www.cardin.senate.gov/newsroom/press/rele ase/us-senator-ben-cardin-releases-report-detailing-two-decadesof-putins-attacks-on-democracy-calling-for-policy-changes-to-counter-kremlin-threat-ahead-of-2018-2020-election. s)www.cardin.senate.gov. Retrieved 2018-01-17.

o "Democratic report warns of Russian meddling in Europe, US ("https://www.nytimes.com/aponline/2018/011/0/us/politics/ap-us-trump-russia-probe-congress.html.) New York Times.

o Harris, Shane (December 11, 2016)." Donald Trump Fuels Rift With CIA Over Russian Hack" (https://www.wsj.com/articles/trump-blames-democrats-for-reports-of-russia-hacking-1481467907.)The Wall Street Journal. Retrieved December 12, 2016.

o Rachael Bade, "Ryan stops short of call for Russia probe "(http://www.politico.com/story/2016/12/paul-yran-russia-hacking-probe-232484), Politico (December 12, 2016).

o Steinhauer, Jennifer (December 12, 2016). "McConnell and Ryan Back Russia Inquiries, Raising Potential Clash With Trump"(https://www.nytimes.com/2016/12/12/us/poi ltics/mcconnell-supports-inquiry-of-russian-hacking-duringelection.html). The New York Times. Retrieved December 12, 2016.

o Ellen Nakashima; Adam Entous (December 10, 2016)". FBI and CIA give difering accounts to lawmakers on Russia's motives in 2016 hacks" (https://www.washingtonpost.com/world/nationalsec urity/fbi-and-cia-give-differing-accounts-to-lawmakers-on-russias-motives-in-2016-hacks/2016/12/10/c6dfadfa-bef0-11e6-94ac-3d324840106c_story.html). The Washington Post. Retrieved December 12, 2016.

o Jones, Susan (December 15, 2016)." Intelligence Agencies Refuse to Brief House Intelligence Committee on Russian Hacking" (http://www.cnsnews.com/news/article/susan-jones/intelligence-agencies-refuse-brief-house-intelligence-committee-russian). The Christian Science Monitor. Retrieved December 16, 2016. cf.

Kelly, Erin (December 14, 2016). "Intelligence officials refuse to brief House panel on Russian hacking"(https://www.usatoday.com/story/news/polit ics/onpolitics/2016/12/14/intelligence-officials-refuse-brief-house-panel-russian-hacking/95453412./)USA Today. Retrieved December 16, 2016. cf. "Intelligence Community Statement on Review of Foreign Influence on U.S. Elections" (https://web.archive.org/web/20161215133205/https: //www.dni.gov/index.php/newsroom/press-releases/215-press-releases-2016/1456-intelligence-community-statement-on-review-of-foreign-influence-on-u-s-elections). Office of the Director of National Intelligence. December 14, 2016.

o Ghitis, Frida (February 13, 2017)." Flynn's talks with Russian ambassador point to larger problem ("http://www.cnn.com/2017/02/10/opinions/trump-flynn-russia-relations-ghitis./)CNN. Retrieved February 28, 2017.

o Wang, Amy (February 25, 2017). "Top Republican says special prosecutor should investigate Russian meddling in Trump's election" (https://www.washingtonpost.com/news/the

fix/wp/2017/02/25/top-republican-says-special-prosecutor-should-investigate-russian-meddling-in-trumps-election./)The Washington Post. Retrieved February 27, 2017.

o "GOP Congressman: Special Prosecutor Needed for Russia Probe ("https://www.nytimes.com/aponline/2017/022/5/us/politics/ap-us-trump-russia-investigation.html?_r=0.) The New York Times. Associated Press. February 25, 2017. Retrieved February 27, 2017.

o "Top intel Democrat: "Circumstantial evidence of collusion" between Trump and Russia" (http://www.nbcnews.com/politics/politics-news/schif-defends-committee-examining-russia-trump-connections-n735391.) NBC News. RetrievedMarch 19, 2017.

o Kailani Koenig, "Schiff: 'More Than Circumstantial Evidence'T rump Associates Colluded With Russia "(http://www.nbcnews.com/politics/politics-news/schiff-more-circumstantial-evidence-trump-associates-colluded-russia-n737446,) NBC News (March 22, 2017).

- Demirjian, Karoun (April 6, 2017). "House Intelligence Chairman Devin Nunes recuses himself from Russia probe ("https://www.washingtonpost.com/powerpost/house-intelligence-chairman-devin-nunes-recuses-himself-from-russia-probe/2017/04/06/8122b5bc-1ad2-11e7-855e-4824bbb5d748_stor.hytml). The Washington Post. Retrieved April 6, 2017.
- "Rep. Devin Nunes cleared of accusations of disclosing classified inte l("https://www.nbcnews.com/politics/congress/nunes-cleared-accusations-he-disclosed-secrets-related-russia-investigation-n82764.6).
- Zengerle, Patricia (March 12, 2018)." Republicans shut down House Russia probe over Democratic objections ("https://www.reuters.com/article/us-usa-trump-russia-congress/house-republicans-say-probe-found-no-evidence-of-collusion-between-trump-russia-idUSKCN1GO2S1.) Reuters. Retrieved 12 March 2018.
- Ewing, Philip (March 15, 2018). "House Intel Republicans Have Cleared Trump. So Are The Russia Investigations Over?"

(https://www.npr.org/2018/03/15/593576455/house-intel-republicans-have-cleared-trumps-o-are-the-russia-investigations-over). NPR. Retrieved 15 March 2018.

o Nicholas Fandos (March 12, 2018). "Despite Mueller's Push, House Republicans Declare No Evidence of Collusion" (https://www.nytimes.com/2018/03/12/us/poltiics/house-intelligence-trump-russia.html.) New York Times.

o Memoli, Mike (March 12, 2018)." House Republicans say investigation found no evidence of Russia-rTump collusion" (https://www.nbcnews.com/politics/congress/house-republicans-say-investigation-found-no-evidence-russia-trump-collusion-n855986). NBC News. Retrieved 13 March 2018.

o Collinson, Stephen (March 13, 2018)." From the GOP with love -- Trump gets gift from Russia panel" (https://www.cnn.com/2018/03/13/politics/russiainvestigation-trump/index.htm.l)CNN. Retrieved 15 March 2018.

o Karoun Demirjian, Intel panel Republicans seem to back away from finding that Russia was not trying to helpr Trmp (https://www.washingtonpost.com/powerpost/intel-panel-republicans-seem-to-back-away-from-finding-that-russia-was-not-trying-to-help-trump/2018/03/13/7b4c9594-2716-11e8-874b-d517e912f125_sto.rhytml), Washington Post (March 13, 2018).

o "House intelligence Democrats outline how to keep their Russia investigation alive ("https://www.cnn.com/2018/03/14/politics/adam-schif-house-intelligence-democrats/index.html). CNN. March 15, 2018. Retrieved 15 March 2018.

o Fandos, Nicholas; LaFraniere, Sharon (April 27, 2018)". Republicans on House Intelligence Panel Absolve Trump Campaign in Russian Meddling" (https://www.nytimes.com/2018/04/27/us/poiltics/house-intelligence-committee-russia-investigation-report.html). Retrieved April 30, 2018 – via NYTimes.com.

o "Fox News Research on Twitter"
(https://twitter.com/FoxNewsResearch/status/989880
960534630400). Retrieved April 30, 2018.

o Detrow, Scott (December 15, 2016). "Obama On
Russian Hacking: 'We Need To Take Action. And
We Will' "
(https://www.npr.org/2016/12/15/505775550/obama-
on-russian-hacking-we-need-to-take-action-nad-we-
will). NPR. Retrieved December 16, 2016.

o "Obama says he told Putin to 'cut it out' on Russia
hacking
("http://www.politico.com/story/2016/12/obama-
putin-232754). Politico. December 16, 2016.

o Sanger, David E.; Shane, Scott (December 9, 2016)."
Russian Hackers Acted to Aid Trump in Election,
U.S. Says"
(https://www.nytimes.com/2016/12/09/us/obama-
russia-election-hack.html). The New York Times.
Retrieved April 10, 2017.

o Weise, Elizabeth; Korte, Gregory (Decembe r9,
2016). "Obama orders review of foreign attempts to
hack U.S.
election"(https://www.usatoday.com/story/tech/news

o /2016/12/09/obama-orders-review-election-hcaking/95204588/).USA Today. Retrieved December 10, 2016.

o Josh Gerstein; Jennifer Scholtes; Eric Geller; Martin Matishak (December 9, 2016")O. bama orders 'deep dive' of election-related hacking" (http://www.politico.com/story/2016/12/obama-orders-full-review-of-election-relate-hacking-232419). Politico. Retrieved December 10, 2016.

o Elise Labott, "Official: Probe 'solely about lessons learned' on foreign hacking" (http://www.cnn.com/2016/12/10/politics/russia-hacking-analysis/index.html), CNN (December 10, 2016).

o Griffiths, Brent (December 12, 2016). "White House rails against Trump for not accepting evidence of Russiahacking" (http://www.politico.com/story/2016/12/trump-russia-hacking-white-house-232516). Politico. Retrieved December 13, 2016.

o Shear, Michael D.; Landler, Mark (December 16, 2016). "Obama Says He Told Putin: 'Cut It Out' on Hacking"

o (https://www.nytimes.com/2016/12/16/us/politics/ob
ama-putin-hacking-news-conference.html) . The
New York Times. Retrieved December 16, 2016.

o Fabian, Jordan (December 16, 2016)." Obama turns
down temperature on Trump fight"
(http://thehill.com/homenews/administration/310788
-obama-seeks-to-tone-down-hacking-fight-with-
trump.)The Hill. Retrieved December 17, 2016.

o Rosenberg, Matthew; Goldman, Adam; Schmidt,
Michael S. (March 2, 2017). "Obama Administration
Rushed to Preserve Intelligence of Russian Election
Hacking
"(https://www.nytimes.com/2017/03/01/us/poiltics/o
bama-trump-russia-election-hacking.html). The New
York Times. p. A1.

o "Germany's Angela Merkel slams planned US
sanctions on
Russia(http://www.dw.com/en/germanys-angela-
merkelslams-planned-us-sanctions-on-russia/a-
39276878"). Deutsche Welle. June 16, 2017.

o Greenberg, Andy. "US Hits Russia With Biggest
Spying Retaliation "Since the Cold War" "

(https://www.wired.com/2016/12/obama-russia-hacking-sanctions-diplomats/.) Wired.

o "Obama Strikes Back at Russia for Election Hacking "(https://www.nytimes.com/2016/12/29/us/poiltics/russia-election-hacking-sanctions.html). The New York Times. December 29, 2016.

o Cowan, Richard (December 31, 2016)." Trump praises Putin for holding back in U.S-.Russia spy dispute" (https://www.reuters.com/article/us-usa-russia-cyber-idUSKBN14I1TY). Reuters. Retrieved February 7, 2017.

o "Russia retaliates against US 'spy' expulsions "(https://www.theguardian.com/world/2001/mar/22/russia.usa). The Guardian. March 22, 2001. Retrieved February 28, 2017.

o Mark Mazzetti & Michael S. Schmidt, "Two Russian Compounds, Caught Up in History's Echoes" (https://www.nytimes.com/2016/12/29/us/politics/russia-spy-compounds-maryland-long-island.htm, 1T)he New York Times (December29, 2016).

o Ian Duncan, "Shut down Russian Eastern Shore retreat offers glimpse at spy battles" (http://www.baltimoresun.com/news/maryland/bsmd-russian-retreat-maryland-spying-20161230-sto.rhytml), The Baltimore Sun (December 30,2016).

o "U.S. shuts Russian compounds in Maryland, New York over hacking" (http://www.cbsnews.com/news/us-shuts-russian-compounds-maryland-new-york-hacking/.) CBS News. Associated Press. December 30, 2016. Retrieved December 30, 2016.

o "U.S. imposes sanctions on Russia over election interference ("http://www.cbsnews.com/news/us-russia-sanctions-election-interference-2016/). CBS News. December 29, 2016. Retrieved December 29, 2016.

o "US expels 35 Russian diplomats, closes two compounds: repor t("http://www.dw.com/en/us-expels-35-russian-diplomats-closes-two-compounds-report/a-36947857.) Deutsche Welle. December 29, 2016. Retrieved December 29, 2016.

o Evan Perez and Daniella Diaz." Russia sanctions announced by White House "(http://www.cnn.com/2016/12/29/politics/russia-sanctions-announced-by-white-house/index.htm.l)CNN.

o "Obama authorises US sanctions against Russia "(http://www.rte.ie/news/2016/1229/841742-us-russia/). Raidió Teilifís Éireann. December 29, 2016.

o Russia, mulling expulsions, says too many U.S. spies work in Moscow (https://www.reuters.com/article/us-usa-russia-sanctions-retaliation-idUSKBN19Z0RV) Reuters, June 14, 2017.

o Senate overwhelmingly passes new Russia and Iran sanction s(https://www.washingtonpost.com/powerpost/senate overwhelmingly-passes-new-russia-and iransanctions/2017/06/15/df9afc2a-51d8-11e7-91eb9611861a988f_sto.hrytml) WP, June 15, 2017.

o Senate GOP, Dems agree on new sanctions on Russia (http://www.foxnews.com/politics/2017/06/13/senate -gop-dems-agree-on-new-sanctions-on-russia.html)AP, June 13, 2017.

o Democrats introduce new bill on Russia and Iran sanctions(https://www.reuters.com/article/us-usa-russiasanctions-idUSKBN19X1ZV) Reuters, July 12, 2017.

o Marcos, Cristina (July 25, 2017). "House passes Russia sanctions deal" (http://thehill.com/homenews/house/343700-house-passes-russia-sanctions-deal). The Hill. Retrieved July 25, 2017.

o Putin: Russia promises retaliation as Senate passes sanctions b il(lhttps://www.theguardian.com/world/2017/ju/l27/putin-russia-us-sanctions-bill) The Guardian, July 28, 2017.

o Facing veto override on Russia sanctions, Trump's signing statement raises constitutional issues (https://www.usatoday.com/story/news/politics/2017/08/02/trump-russia-sanctions-signing-statement-raises-constitutional-issues/534099001/) USA TODAY, August 2, 2017

o Statement by President Donald J. Trump on the Signing of H.R. 3364 (https://www.whitehouse.gov/the-press-office/2017/08/02/statement-president-donald-j-trump-signing-hr-3364 T) he White House, August 2, 2017.

o Baker, Peter. "Trump Signs Russian Sanctions Into Law, With Caveats" (https://www.nytimes.com/2017/08/02/world/europe/ trump-russia-sanctions.html). The New York Times. The New York Times Company. Retrieved August 2, 2017.

o Etehad, Melissa. "The Russia sanctions bill, explained: 'Putin is kind of giving up hop'e" (http://www.latimes.com/world/la-fg-russian-sanctions-20170731-htmlstory.html). Los Angeles Times. Los Angeles Times. Retrieved August 2, 2017.

o Statement by President Donald J. Trump on Signing the "Countering Americas' Adversaries Through Sanctions Act"(https://www.whitehouse.gov/the-press-office/2017/08/02/statement-president-donald-j-trump-signing-countering-americas) The White House, August 2, 2017.

o Europe 'stands ready to act' if US sanctions on Russia afef ct its oil and gas supplies (https://www.independent.co.uk/news/world/america s/us-politics/us-russia-sanctions-latest-europe-ready-to-act-jean-claude-juncker-energy-securityamericao first-a7861851.html) The Independent, July 26, 2017.

o "White House says there's no need for new Russia sanctions ("https://www.washingtonpost.com/world/national-security/rich-russians-still-waiting-toexhale/2018/01/29/7df459ca-052a-11e8-8777-2a059f168dd2_sto.hrytml).Washington Post. 2018-01-29. Retrieved 2018-01-30.

o MacFarquhar, Neil (December 30, 2016). "Vladimir Putin Won't Expel U.S. Diplomats as Russian Foreign Minister Urged" (https://www.nytimes.com/2016/12/30/worlde/urope/russia-diplomats-us-hacking.html.) The New York Times. Retrieved June 27, 2017.

o "Plane with Russian diplomats expelled from US lands in Moscow ("http://tass.com/world/923649.) Russian News Agency TASS. January 2, 2017.

o Crabtree, Justina (May 19, 2017). "There's a mad house, not a house of cards on Capitol Hill, says Russian bank CEO" (https://www.cnbc.com/2017/05/19/theres-a-mad-house-not-a-house-of-cards-on-capitol-hill-says-russian-ban k-ceo.html). CNBC. Retrieved May 30, 2017.

o Nechepurenko, Ivan (July 14, 2017)." Russia Warns U.S. It Could Expel Americans Over Diplomatic Dispute" (https://www.nytimes.com/2017/07/14/world/europe/russia-diplomats-foreign-ministry-spies-expel.htm.l) The New York Times. Retrieved July 18, 2017.

o Roth, Andrew (July 30, 2017)." Putin orders cut of 755 personnel at U.S. missions "(https://www.washingtonpost.com/world/putin-orders-cut-of-755-personnel-at-us-missions/2017/07/30/8a4b0044-7555-11e7-8c17-533c52b2f014_story.html). The Washington Post. Retrieved August 5, 2017.

o Putin confirms 755 US diplomatic staff must leave (https://www.bbc.com/news/world-europe-40769365) BBC, July 30, 2017.

o Michael D. Shear; Matt Apuzzo (May 10, 2017). "Trump Fires Comey amid Russia Inquiry—Clinton EmailInvestigation Cited—Democrats Seek Special Counse l"(https://www.nytimes.com/2017/05/09/us/poiltics/j

○ ames-comey-fired-fbi.html). The New York Times. p. A1. Retrieved May 10, 2017.

○ Levy, Pema (May 19, 2017). "Deputy AG Confirms That Decision to Fire Comey Came From rTump, Not Him" (https://www.motherjones.com/politics/2017/05/rose nstein-role-trump-sessions-comey-firing/.) Mother Jones.

○ Smith, David (May 9, 2017). "Donald Trump fires FBI director Comey over handling of Clinton investigation" (https://www.theguardian.com/us-news/2017/may/09/james-comey-fbi-fired-donald-trump). The Guardian. Retrieved May 9, 2017.

○ Sommer, Will (May 9, 2017). "Sessions was told to find reasons to fire Comey: reports "(http://thehill.com/homenews/administration/33265 1-sessions-was-told-to-find-reasons-to-fire-comey-report.s)The Hill. Retrieved May 10, 2017.

○ Pramuk, Jacob (May 9, 2017)." Justice Department was told to come up with reasons to fire Come, yreports say" (https://www.cnbc.com/2017/05/09/justice-depatrment-was-told-to-come-up-with-reasons-to-fire-comey-reports-sa.hytml). CNBC. Retrieved May 10, 2017.

o "President Trump just completely contradicted the official White House account of the Comey firing "(http://theweek.com/speedreads/698368/president-trump-just-completely-contradicted-oficf ial-white-house-account-comey-firing.) The Week. May 11, 2017. Retrieved May 11, 2017.

o Malloy, Allie (May 10, 2017). "Trump says he fired Comey because he wasn't "doing a good job" " (http://www.cnn.com/2017/05/10/politics/donald-trump-james-comey-firing./)CNN. Retrieved May 11, 2017.

o Kevin Liptak. "White House: Removing Comey will help bring Russia investigation to end ("http://www.cnn.com/2017/05/11/politics/comey-fbi-investigation-russia-sarah-huckabee-sanders/index.htm. lC) NN. Retrieved May 11, 2017.

o Lauter, David; Memoli, Michael A. (May 9, 2017). "Trump fires Comey as FBI director; Democrats call for a specialprosecutor in Russia investigation "(http://www.latimes.com/politics/la-na-pol-fbicomey-fired-20170509-story.html).Los Angeles Times. Retrieved May 11, 2017.

o Wilstein, Matt (May 9, 2017). "CNN's Jeffrey Toobin Goes Off on Trump for Firing Comey: 'What Kind of Country Is This?'(http://www.thedailybeast.com/articles/2017/05/09/white-house-fires-fbi-director-james-comey.html). The Daily Beast.

o Abbruzzese, Jason (May 9, 2017). "Everyone is comparing Donald Trump to Richard Nixon" (https://web.archive.org/web/20170730011516/http://thesilicontimes.com/everyone-is-comparing-donald-trump-to-richard-nixon. /T)he SiliconTimes. Archived from the original (http://thesilicontimes.com/everyone-is-comparing-donald-trump-to-richard-nixon/) on July 30, 2017.

o "Comey firing: Reaction from members of Congress on FBI director's dismissa (l"https://www.washingtonpost.com/news/powerpost/wp/2017/05/09/comey-firing-reaction-from-members-of-congress-on-fbi-directors-dismissa. lT/)he Washington Post.

o Tucker, Eric; Werner, Erica (June 9, 2017). "Comey says he was fired over Russia probe, blasts 'lie's" (https://apnews.com/091e046d17c4483fab14fa26d30 9afc3/Comey-says-he-was-fired-over-Russia-probe,- blasts-%27lies%2.7) Associated Press. Retrieved June 12, 2017.

o Matt Apuzzo; Maggie Haberman; Matthew Rosenberg (May 19, 2017). "Trump Told Russians That Firing 'Nut Job' Comey Eased Pressure From Investigation "(https://www.nytimes.com/2017/05/19/us/poiltics/tr ump-russia-comey.html). The New York Times. Retrieved May 19, 2017.

o Williams, Pete; Dilanian, Ken (May 17, 2017)." Special Counsel Will Take Over FBI Russia Campaign InterferenceInvestigation"(http://www.nbcnews.com/ politics/politics-news/special-counsel-will-take-over- fbi-russia-campaign-interference-investigation- n761271). NBC News. Retrieved May 17, 2017.

o "Order 3915-2017: Appointment of Special Counsel to Investigate Russian Interference With the 2016 Election and Related Matters"

(https://web.archive.org/web/20170517230612/https:
//assets.documentcloud.org/documents/3726381/Rob
ert-Mueller-Special-Counsel-Russia.pdf   )(PDF).
Office of the Deputy Attorney General, United States
Department of Justice. May 17, 2017. Archived
fromth   e   original
(https://assets.documentcloud.org/documents/372638
1/Robert-Mueller-Special-Counsel-Russia.pdf
)(PDF) on May 17, 2017.

o   Johnson, Kevin (May 17, 2017). "Justice Department
taps former FBI Director Robert Mueller as special
counsel   for   Russia   investigation"
(https://www.usatoday.com/story/news/politics/2017
/05/17/justice-department-taps-formre-fbi-director-
robert-mueller-special-counsel-russia-
investigation/101806472./)USA Today. Retrieved
July 18, 2017.

o   Tanfani, Joseph (May 17, 2017). "Former FBI
Director Robert Mueller named special prosecutor
for   Russia   investigation"
(http://www.latimes.com/politics/washington/la-na-
essential-washington-updates-former-fbi-director-

o robert-mueller-1495058507-htmlstory.html).   Los Angeles Times. Retrieved May 17, 2017.

o Karimi, Faith; Perez, Evan (June 16, 2017)." Robert Mueller expands special counsel office, hires 13 lawyers" (http://www.cnn.com/2017/06/16/politics/robert-mueller-special-counsel-lawyers/index.html).   CNN. Retrieved June 16, 2017.

o Demick, Barbara (May 24, 2017). "Marc Kasowitz helped Trump through bankruptcy and divorce. Now he's taking onthe biggest case of his career" (http://www.latimes.com/nation/la-na-kasowtiz-20170524-story.html). Los Angeles Times. Retrieved June 8, 2017.

o Jarrett, Laura; Perez, Evan (June 10, 2017)." Mueller staffing up Russia probe while Trump lawyer declares   victory" (http://www.cnn.com/2017/06/10/politics/robert-mueller-russia-investigation-team/index.html.) CNN. Retrieved June 10, 2017.

o Green, Miranda; de Vogue, Ariane (June 16, 2017). "Trump adds lawyer John Dowd to Russia legal team" (http://www.cnn.com/2017/06/16/politics/john-dowd-lawyer-donald-trump/index.html). CNN. Retrieved June 18, 2017.

o Manchester, Julia (2017-07-21). "Trump's personal lawyer resigns from top post amid legal team shakeup" (http://thehill.com/homenews/news/343069-trumps-personal-lawyer-resigns-from-top-post-amid-legal-team-shakeu. pT)heHill.Retrieved 2018-04-21.

o Diamond, Jeremy; Borger, Gloria. "Dowd resigns as Trump's lawyer amid disagreements on strategy" (https://www.cnn.com/2018/03/22/politics/john-dowd-white-house/index.htm.l)CNN. Retrieved 2018-04-21. "Source: Mueller Using D.C. Grand Jury In Russia Probe "(https://www.npr.org/2017/08/03/541432868/source-mueller-using-d-c-grand-jury-in-russia-probe). NPR.org.

o Entous, Adam; Nakashima, Ellen (May 22, 2017)." Trump asked intelligence chiefs to push back against FBI collusion probe after Comey revealed its existence "(https://www.washingtonpost.com/world/national-security/trumpasked-intelligence-chiefs-to-push-back-against-fbi-collusion-probe-after-comey-revealed-its-existence/2017/05/22/394933bc-3f10-11e7-9869-bac8b446820a_story.html). The Washington Post.

o Ensous, Adam (June 6, 2017). "Top intelligence official told associates Trump asked him if he could intervene with Comey on FBI Russia probe" (https://www.washingtonpost.com/world/national-security/top-intelligence-official-told-associates-trump-asked-him-if-he-could-intervene-with-comey-to-get-fbi-to-back-fo-flynn/2017/06/06/cc879f14-4ace-11e7-9669-250d0b15f83b_story.html). The Washington Post. Retrieved June 7, 2017.

o LoBianco, Tom (June 7, 2017). "Intelligence chiefs: No pressure from Trump administration on Russia probe" (http://www.cnn.com/2017/06/07/politics/russia-hearing-dan-coats/). CNN. Retrieved June 7, 2017.

o Wilber, Del Quentin; Viswanatha, Aruna (May 17, 2017). "Trump Asked Comey to Drop Flynn Investigation, According to Memo Written by Former FBI Director" (https://www.wsj.com/articles/trump-asked-comey-to-drop-flynn-investigation-according-to-memo-written-by-former-fbi-director-1494974774.   )The Wall Street Journal. Retrieved May 17, 2017.

o Barrett, Devlin; Nakashima, Ellen; Zapotosky, Matt. "Notes made by former FBI director Comey say Trump pressured him to end Flynn probe" (https://www.washingtonpost.com/world/nationasecurity/notes-made-by-former-fbi-directorcomey-say-trump-pressured-him-to-end-flynn-probe/2017/05/16/52351a38-3a80-11e7-9e48-c4f199710b69_sto.hrytml). The Washington Post. Retrieved May 17, 2017.

o Schmidt, Michael S. (May 16, 2017)." Comey Memo Says Trump Asked Him to End Flynn Investigation" (https://www.nytimes.com/2017/05/16/us/politics/jamesc-omey-trump-flynn-russia-investigation.html.) The New York Times. Retrieved May 16, 2017.

o Prokop, Andrew (June 8, 2017). "James Comey's troubling testimony about President Trump's conduct, explained" (https://www.vox.com/policy-anpolitics/2017/6/8/15761940/james-comeytestimonyobstruction-justice.)Vox. Retrieved June 8, 2017.

o Barrett, Devlin; Entous, Adam; Nakashima, Ellen; Horwitz, Sari (June 14, 2017)".S pecial counsel is investigating Trump for possible obstruction of justice, officials say" (https://www.washingtonpost.com/world/nationalsec urity/special-counsel-is-investigating-trump-for-possible-obstruction-of-justice/2017/06/14/9ce02506-5131-11e7-b064-828ba60fbb98_story.html). The Washington Post. Retrieved July 22, 2016.

o Roberts, Rachel (May 11, 2017). "Donald Trump fired James Comey because 'he refused to end Russia investigation', say multiple FBI insiders" (https://www.independent.co.uk/news/donald-trump-james-comey-firing-russia-investigation-refuse-end-fbi-insiders-director-hillary-a7729691.htm.l)The Independent. Retrieved May 11, 2017.

o Thomas, Pierre (June 19, 2017)." Where Things Stand with Special Counsel Mueller's Russia Probe ("http://abcnews.go.com/Politics/things-stand-special-counsel-muellers-russia-probe/story?id=4814230.4 A) BC News. "According to sources familiar with the process ... [a]n assessment of evidence and circumstances will be completed before a final decision is made to launch an investigation of the president of the United States regarding potential obstruction of justice."

- o "Trump's ex-campaign manager Manafort tot urn himself in to Mueller: reports "(http://www.abc.net.au/news/2017-10-30/paul-manafort-donald-trump-russia-inquiry/9101372.)ABC News. 2017-10-30. Retrieved 2017-10-30. https://www.justice.gov/file/1007271/download

- o Savage, Charlie (October 30, 2017)." What It Means: The Indictment of Manafort and Gates "(https://www.nytimes.com/2017/10/30/us/politics/special-counsel-indictments.html?_r=0.)The New York Times. Retrieved 30 October 2017.

- o William, David (February 18, 2018)." Former Trump aide Rick Gates to plead guitly; agrees to testify against Manafort, sources say" (http://www.latimes.com/politics/la-na-pol-rick-gates-plea-deal-20180218-story.html). Los Angeles Times. Retrieved February 18, 2018.

o CNN, Katelyn Polantz,. "Search warrant reveals Mueller's interest in Manafort's actions during rTump campaign" (https://www.cnn.com/2018/04/10/politics/paul-manafort-robert-mueller/index.html). cnn.com.

o Tillman, Zoe. "Paul Manafort Is Asking A Judge To Suppress Evidence That Agents Seized From His Home "(https://www.buzzfeed.com/zoetillman/paul-manafor-tis-asking-a-judge-to-suppress-evidence-that.) BuzzFeed.

o Bump, Phillip (30 October 2017)." Paul Manafort: A FAQ about Trump's indicted former campaign chairman "(https://www.washingtonpost.com/news/politics/wp/2017/10/30/paul-manafort-what-we-know-he-did-and-why-he-might-have-been-ensnared-by-the-investigation/). Washington Post. Retrieved 30 October 2017.

o "Ex-Trump Adviser George Papadopoulos Pelads Guilty in Mueller's Russia Probe "(https://www.nbcnews.com/news/us-news/trump-campaign-adviser-george-papadopoulos-pleads-guilty-lying-n81559.6 N) BC News. October 30, 2017. Retrieved 30 October 2017.

o Uchill, Joe. "Timeline: Campaign knew Russia had Clinton emails months before Trump 'joke' " (http://thehill.com/homenews/administration/357851 -timeline-campaign-knew-russia-had-clinton-emails- months-before-trum.p T)he Hill. Retrieved 19 November 2017.

o Polantz, Katelyn (March 27, 2018)." New Gates tie alleged in special counsel filing on van der Zwaan sentencing ("https://www.cnn.com/2018/03/27/politics/alex- van-der-zwaan-memorandum/index.html) . CNN. Retrieved April 6, 2018.

o Mayer, Jane. "How Russia Helped Swing the Election for Trump" (https://www.newyorker.com/magazine/2018/10/01/ how-russia-helped-to-swing-the-election-for- trump?mbid=social_facebook.)newyorker.com. The New Yorker.Retrieved 29 September 2018.

o "Special counsel issues indictment against 13 Russian nationals over 2016 election interferenc e(h" ttps://www.cnn.com/2018/02/16/politics/mueller-

russia-indictments-election-interference/index.htm.
lC) NN. February 16, 2018. Retrieved February 16, 2018.

o Indictment, United States v. Internet Research Agency LLC et al., docket entry 1, Feb. 16, 2018, case no. 18-cr-00032-DLF, U.S. District Court for the District of Columbia.

o Lafranier, Sharon (February 16, 2018). "13 Russians Indicted by Special Counsel in First Charges on 2016 Election   Interference" (https://www.nytimes.com/2018/02/16/us/poiltics/russians-indicted-mueller-election-interference.htm.l) The New York Times. Retrieved February 16, 2018.

o Horwitz,, Sari; Barrett, Devlin; Timberg, Craig (February 16, 2018). "Russian troll farm, 13 suspects indicted for interference in U.S. election" (https://www.washingtonpost.com/world/national-security/russian-troll-farm-13-suspects-indicted-for-interference-in-us-election/2018/02/16/2504de5e-1342-11e8-9570-29c9830535e5_sto.hrytml).   The Washington Post. Retrieved February 16, 2018.

o "Mueller Announces Guilty Plea of California Man in

Investigation("https://www.bloomberg.com/news/arti
cles/2018-02-16/mueller-announces-guilty-plea-of-
california-man-in-investigation.)February 16, 2018.
Retrieved February 16, 2018.

o   All of Robert Mueller's indictments and plea deals in
the Russia investigation so far that we know
o(fhttps://www.vox.com/policy-and-
politics/2018/2/20/17031772/mueller-indictments-
grand-jury)Vox, Andrew Prokopandrew, Jun 8,
2018. Retrieved July 2, 2018.

o   "Russian firm charged in election interference case
pleads   not   guilty
("https://www.usatoday.com/story/news/2018/05/09/
concord-management-arraignment-russia-
investigation/594454002./)May 9, 2018. Retrieved
May 13, 2018.

o   Wilkie, Christina (July 13, 2018)." 5 key takeaways
from the latest indictment in Mueller's Russia probe
("https://www.cnbc.com/2018/07/13/5-key-
takeaways-from-mueller-indictment-of-russian-
election-hackers.htm. lR) etrieved July 30, 2018.

o   "12 Russian Agents Indicted in Mueller Investigation
"(https://www.nytimes.com/2018/07/13/us/poiltics/m

ueller-indictment-russian-intelligence-hacking.html).
NY Times. July 13, 2018. Retrieved August 6, 2018.

o Paddock, Richard C. (March 5, 2018)." Escort Says
Audio Recordings Show Russian Meddling in U.S.
Election
("https://www.nytimes.com/2018/03/05/world/asia/n
astya-rybka-trump-putin.html). The New York
Times. Retrieved March 5, 2018.

o Paddock, Richard C. (August 31, 2018)." She
Gambled on Her Claim to Link Russians and Trump.
She   Is   Losing"
(https://www.nytimes.com/2018/08/31/world/asia/es
cort-anastasia-vashukevich-nastya-rybka-trump.htm.l
)The New York Times. Retrieved August 31, 2018.

o Kaewjinda, Kaweewit (August 20, 2018)."
Belarusian Escort Says She Made a Deal With an
Oligarch to Keep Quiet About Russian Meddling"
(http://time.com/5371527/thailand-russia-escort-
anastasia-vashukevich./)Time. Associated Press.
Retrieved August 31, 2018.

o Maza, Cristina (August 20, 2018). "Belarusian
Escort Says She Gave Evidence of Russian Election
Interference   to   Manafort-Linked   Oligarch"

(https://www.newsweek.com/belarusian-escort-says-she-gave-evidence-russian-election-interference-1081677). Newsweek. Retrieved August 31, 2018.

o John Bacon (July 4, 2018). "Lawsuit linking Trump to Russian Hackers, leak of Democratic emails tossed out" (https://www.usatoday.com/story/news/politics/2018/07/04/judge-tosses-suit-linking-trump-lea-kdemocratic-emails/757588002/). USAToday.

o Harris, Shane. "Russian Officials Overheard Discussing Trump Associates Before Campaign Began" (https://www.wsj.com/article_email/russian-officials-overheard-discussing-trump-associates-before-campaign-began-1499890354-lMyQjAxMTI3MjE5MjExMzI0Wj/). The Wall Street Journal. Retrieved July 12, 2017.

o Schmidt, Michael S.; Mazzetti, Mark; Apuzzo, Matt (February 14, 2017). "Trump Campaign Aides Had Repeated Contacts With Russian Intelligence "(https://www.nytimes.com/2017/02/14/us/poiltics/russia-intelligence-communications-trump.html). The New York Times. Retrieved March 2, 2017.

o "Trump team issued at least 20 denials of contacts with Russia" (https://www.usatoday.com/story/news/politics/2017/ 03/02/trump-teams-many-many-denials-contactsrussia/98625780./)USA Today. Retrieved March 13, 2017.

o "A Who's Who of the Trump Campaign's Russia Connections"(https://www.rollingstone.com/politics/ features/a-whos-who-of-the-trump-campaigns-russia-connections-w469977.)Rolling Stone. Retrieved March 13, 2017.

o Buzenberg, Bill (May 26, 2017). "How the Trump White House Has Tried to Interfere With the Russia Investigations" (https://www.motherjones.com/politics/2017/05/trump-white-house-interference-russia-investigations.) Mother Jones. Mother Jones and the Foundation for National Progress . Retrieved May 31, 2017.

o Miller, Greg, and Entous, Adam (February 24, 2017). "Trump administration sought to enlist intelligence officials, key lawmakers to counter Russia stories" (https://www.washingtonpost.com/world/national-security/trump-administrationsought-to-enlist-intelligence-officials-key-lawmakers-to-counter-russiastories/2017/02/24/c8487552-fa99-11e6-be05-1a3817ac21a5_story.html). The Washington Post. Retrieved March 2, 2017.

o Gloria Borger; Pamela Brown; Jim Sciutto; Marshall Cohen; Eric Lichtblau. "Sources: Russian oficials bragged they could use Flynn to influence Trump" (http://www.cnn.com/2017/05/19/politics/michael-flynn-donald-trump-russia-influ ence/index.html). CNN. Retrieved May 20, 2017.

o Logan, Bryan; Bertrand, Natasha (May 20, 2017)." Sources: Russian operatives reportedly bragged that they could use Mike Flynn to get to the White House" (http://www.businessinsider.de/russian-operatives-bragged-they-could-use-flynn-to-get-to-trump-2017-5?r=US&IR=T.) Business Insider. Retrieved July 26, 2017.

o Allen, Nick; Graham, Chris (May 20, 2017)." James Comey to testify before Senate panel after Donald rTump called fired FBI boss a 'nut job' " (https://www.telegraph.co.uk/news/2017/05/19/donald-trump-called-james-comey-nut-job-said-firing-eased-great/). The Telegraph. Retrieved July 26, 2017.

o Michael S. Schmidt; Matthew Rosenberg; Matt Apuzzo (March 2, 2017). "Kushner and Flynn Met With Russian Envoy in December, White House Says" (https://www.nytimes.com/2017/03/02/us/poiltics/ku shner-flynn-sessions-russia.html). The New York Times. Retrieved March 3, 2017.

o "Russian ambassador told Moscow that Kushner wanted secret communications channel with Kremlin(h"ttps://www.washingtonpost.com/world/na tional-security/russian-ambassador-told-moscow-that-kushner-wanted-secret-communications-channel-with-kremlin/2017/05/26/520a14b4-422d-11e7-9869-bac8b446820a_sto.rhytml).　　　The Washington Post. Retrieved May 27, 2017.

o Mazzetti, Mark; Apuzzo, Matt; Haberman, Maggie (May 26, 2017). "Kushner Is Said to Have Discussed a Secret Channel to Talk to Russia" (https://nyti.ms/2r7tYaC). The New York Times. Retrieved May 27, 2017.

o Prokop, Andrew (December 1, 2017)." What Michael Flynn has actually admitted to so fa, rexplained" (https://www.vox.com/policy-and-politics/2017/12/1/16724232/flynn-testify-against-trump.)Vox. Retrieved 12 January 2018.

o Dilanian, Ken (February 10, 2017). "Official: Flynn Discussed Sanctions With Russians Before Taking Office" (http://www.nbcnews.com/news/us-news/official-flynn-discussed-sanctions-russians-taking-ofifce-n719271). NBC News. Retrieved March 2, 2017.

o Murray, Sara; Borger, Gloria; Diamond, Jeremy (February 14, 2017)." Flynn resigns amid controversy over Russia contacts" (http://www.cnn.com/2017/02/13/politics/michael-flynn-white-house-national-security-adviser/.) CNN. Retrieved March 2, 2017.

o Johnson, Kevin (May 8, 2017). "Sally Yates warned White House that Michael Flynn was vulnerable to Russian blackmail"(https://www.usatoday.com/story/news/politics/2017/05/08/sally-yates-michael-flynn-rusasicontacts/101339968/). USA Today. Retrieved 12 January 2018.

o Herb, Jeremy (December 1, 2017)." Flynn charged with one count of making false statement "(http://www.cnn.com/2017/12/01/politics/michael-flynn-charged/index.htm.l) CNN.

o Cone, Allen (February 1, 2018). "Mueller seeks delay in Flynn sentencing" (https://www.upi.com/Mueller-seeks-delay-in-Flynn-sentencing/1681517517175/). UPI.

o SAMUELS, BRETT (May 1, 2018)." Mueller requests Flynn's sentencing be delayed at least two more months ("http://thehill.com/regulation/administration/385740 -mueller-requests-flynns-sentencing-be-delayed-at-least-two-mo.re) The Hill.

o Press, Associated (July 11, 2018). "Michael Flynn 'eager' to put case behind him while Mueller team requests delay" (http://www.theguardian.com/us-news/2018/jul/10/michael-flynn-mueller-case-delay-lobbying-firm.) the Guardian.

o Kutner, Max (October 31, 2017). "Who is Joseph Mifsud, the professor in the George Papadopoulos

investigation?" (http://www.newsweek.com/george-
papadopoulos-who-joseph-mifsud-professor-
697441.) Newsweek. Retrieved October 31, 2017.

o Herb, Jeremy; Cohen, Marshall. "Who is George
Papadopoulos?"
(http://www.cnn.com/2017/10/30/politics/who-is-
george-papadopoulos/index.html). CNN. Retrieved
October 31, 2017.

o LaFraniere, Sharon; Mazzetti, Mark; Apuzzo, Matt
(December 30, 2017)".H ow the Russia Inquiry
Began: A Campaign Aide, Drinks and Talk of
Political   Dirt"
(https://www.nytimes.com/2017/12/30/us/poiltics/ho
w-fbi-russia-investigation-began-george-
papadopoulos.html.) The New York Times. ISSN
0362-4331   (https://www.worldcat.org/issn/0362-
4331). Retrieved December 30, 2017.

o Wroe, David (January 2, 2018)." Joe Hockey
discussed Alexander Downer's Russia revelations
with   FB   I("http://www.smh.com.au/federal-
politics/political-news/oje-hockey-discussed-
downers-russia-revelations-with-fbi-20180101-

h0c58c.html). The Sydney Morning Herald. Retrieved January 2, 2018.

o Apuzzo, Matt; Goldman, Adam; Fandos, Nicholas (May 16, 2018)".C ode Name Crossfire Hurricane: The Secret Origins of the Trump Investigation" (https://www.nytimes.com/2018/05/16/us/poiltics/cr ossfire-hurricane-trump-russia-fbi-mueller-investigation.html). The New York Times. Retrieved 17 May 2018.

o "Code Name Crossfire Hurricane: The Secret Origins of the Trump Investigation" (https://www.nytimes.com/2018/05/16/us/politics/cr ossfire-hurricane-trump-russia-fbi-mueller-investigation.htm.l)Retrieved 2018-07-21.

o Hamburger, Tom; Leonnig, Carol D.; Helderman, Rosalind S. (August 14, 2017)." Trump campaign emails show aide's repeated efforts to set up Russia meetings" (https://www.washingtonpost.com/politics/trump-campaign-emailsshow-aides-repeated-eforts-to-set-up-russia-meetings/2017/08/14/54d08da6-7dc2-11e7-83c7-5bd5460f0d7e_sto.ryhtml). The Washington Post. Retrieved August 15, 2017.

o Glaser, April (October 30, 2017). "The Trump Campaign Adviser Who Pleaded Guilty Was Very Bad at Facebook" (http://www.slate.com/blogs/future_tense/2017/10/3 0/george_papadopoulos_charged_by_robert_mueller _was_suspiciously_bad_at_facebook.html). Slate. Retrieved October 31, 2017.

o Apuzzo, Matt; Schmidt, Michael S. (October 30, 2017). "Trump Campaign Adviser Met With Russian to Discuss 'Dirt' on Clinton" (https://www.nytimes.com/2017/10/30/us/poiltics/ge orge-papadopoulos-russia.html.) The New York Times.

o "Guilty Plea" (https://www.justice.gov/file/1007341/download). United States Department of Justice.

o "Statement of Facts of Guilt" (https://www.justice.gov/file/1007346/download). United States Department of Justice.

o Tanfani, Joseph (October 30, 2017). "Former Trump campaign aide George Papadopoulos pleads guilty to lying to the FBI agents in Mueller probe" (http://www.latimes.com/politics/washington/la-na-

pol-essential-washington-updates-former-trump-campaign-aide-george-1509374196-htmlstor.yhtml).
Los Angeles Times.

o "Ex-Trump Aide Papadopoulos Sentenced To 14 Days Jail For Lying To FBI" (https://headlinestoday.org/international/2456/ex-trump-aide-papadopoulos-sentenced-to-14-days-jail-for-lying-to-fb.i/)Headlines Today. Retrieved 8 September 2018.

o Matt Apuzzo; Jo Becker; Adam Goldman; Maggie Haberman (July 10, 2017). "Trump Jr. Was Told in Email of Russian Effort to Aid Campaign" (https://www.nytimes.com/2017/07/10/us/poiltics/donald-trump-jr-russia-email-candidacy.html). The New York Times. Retrieved July 11, 2017.

o "Former Soviet counterintelligence officer at meeting With Donald Trump Jr. and Russian lawyer" (http://www.nbcnews.com/news/us-news/russian-lawyer-brought-ex-soviet-counter-intelligence-foicfer-trump-team-n782851). NBC News. Retrieved July 14, 2017.

o Butler, Desmond (July 14, 2017). "Russian-American lobbyist says he was in Trump son's

meeting"
(https://apnews.com/dceed1008d8f45afb314aca6579
7762a.) Associated Press. Retrieved July 14, 2017.

o Carter, Brandon (July 10, 2017)." Trump Jr. was told
potential Clinton info came from Russian
government: repor
t("http://thehill.com/homenews/administration/34138
6-trump-jr-was-told-potential-info-on-clinton-was-
coming-from-russian). The Hill. Retrieved July 11,
2017.

o Bertrand, Natasha (July 10, 2017). "Meet the music
publicist taking credit for setting up Donald Trump
Jr.'s meeting with a Russian lawyer"
(http://uk.businessinsider.com/who-is-rob-goldstone-
donald-trump-jr-russia-2017-7). Business Insider.
Retrieved July 10, 2017.

o Becker, Jo; Goldman, Adam; Apuzzo, Matt (July 11,
2017). "Russian Dirt on Clinton? 'I Love It," Donald
Trump Jr. Said"
(https://www.nytimes.com/2017/07/11/us/poiltics/tru
mp-russia-email-clinton.html.) The New York
Times. Retrieved August 4, 2017.

o Borchers, Callum. "Donald Trump Jr.'s stunning admission to the New York Times" (https://www.washingtonpost.co m/news/the-fix/wp/2017/07/09/donald-trump-jr-s-stunningly-incriminating-statement-to-the-new-york-time.s T/)he Washington Post. Retrieved July 11, 2017.

o Becker, Jo; Apuzzo, Matt; Goldman, Adam (July 8, 2017). "Trump Team Met With Lawyer Linked to Kremlin During Campaign"(https://www.nytimes.com/2017/07/08/us /poiltics/trump-russia-kushner-manafort.html.) The New York Times. Retrieved July 12, 2017.

o Becker, Jo; Apuzzo, Matt; Goldman, Adam (July 9, 2017). "Trump's Son Met With Russian Lawyer Afte rBeing Promised Damaging Information on Clinton "(https://www.nytimes.com/2017/07/09/us/poiltics/tr ump-russia-kushnermanafort.html). The New York Times. Retrieved July 12, 2017.

o Parker, Ashley; Leonnig, Carol D.; Rucker , Philip; Hamburger, Tom (July 31, 2017). "Trump dictated son's misleading statement on meeting with Russian lawyer "(https://www.washingtonpost.com/politics/trump-dictated-sons-misleading-statement-on-meeting-with-russian-lawyer/2017/07/31/04c94f96-73ae-11e7-8f39-eeb7d3a2d304_sto.hrytml). The Washington Post. Retrieved August 1, 2017.

o Entous, Adam; Nakashima, Ellen; Mille,r Greg (March 1, 2017). "Sessions met with Russian envoy twice last yea, rencounters he later did not disclose" (https://www.washingtonpost.com/world/national-security/sessions-spoke-twicewith-russian-ambassador-during-trumps-presidential-campaign-justice-oficf ials-say/2017/03/01/77205eda-feac-11e6-99b4-9e613afeb09f_story.html). The Washington Post. Retrieved March 2, 2017.

o Lichtblau, Eric; Shear, Michael D.; Savage, Charlie; Apuzzo, Matt; Haberman, Maggie; Schmidt, Michael S. (March 2, 2017). "Jeff Sessions Recuses Himself From Russia Inquiry" (https://www.nytimes.com/2017/03/02/us/poiltics/jef fsessions-russia-trump-investigation-democrats.htm.l) The New York Times.

o Matishak, Martin (March 20, 2017)." Roger Stone takes center stage as Congress lines up Russia probe witnesses" (http://www.politico.com/story/2017/03/russia-hearing-fbi-roger-stone-236268). Politico. Retrieved April 18, 2017.

o Massie, Chris; McDermott, Nathan; Kaczynski, Andrew. "Trump adviser Roger Stone repeatedly claimed to know of forthcoming WikiLeaks dumps" (http://www.cnn.com/2017/03/20/politics/kfile-roger-stone-wikileaks-claims/). CNN. Retrieved April 23, 2017.

o Danner, Chas. "Trump Adviser Roger Stone Admits Messaging With Alleged DNC Hacker" (http://nymag.com/daily/intelligencer/2017/03/trump-adviser-roger-stone-admits-messaging-with-dnc-hack.ehrtml). New York. Retrieved April 23, 2017.

o Farley, Robert (2017-03-28). "Misrepresenting Stone's Prescience" (http://www.factcheck.org/2017/03/misrepresenting-stones-prescience/). FactCheck.org. Retrieved 2017-10-18.

o Bertrand, Natasha (2017-09-26). "Top Trump confidant points to dubious report to justify conversation with Russian cyber spy" (http://www.businessinsider.com/roger-stone-dnc-hacker-guccifer-russia-trump-2017-9.   )Business Insider. Retrieved 2017-10-18.

o Raju, Manu; Herb, Jeremy (2017-11-29)." New York radio personality was Roger Stone's WikiLeaks contact" (http://www.cnn.com/2017/11/29/politics/randy-credico-roger-stone-wikileaks/index.html).   CNN. Retrieved 2017-11-30.

o Evan Perez, Pamela Brown and Shimon Prokupecz". One year into the FBI's Russia investigation, Mueller is   on   the   Trump   money   trail" (https://www.cnn.com/2017/08/03/politics/mueller-investigation-russia-trump-one-year-financial-ti es/index.html). CNN. Retrieved April 30, 2018.

o Savage, Charlie (February 2, 2018)." Read the Nunes Memo,   Annotated "(https://www.nytimes.com/interactive/2018/02/02/u s/politics/nunes-memo-gop-fbi-annotated.html,%20https://www .nytimes.com/interactive/2018/02/02/us/politics/nune s-memo-gop-fbi-annotated.html). New York Times. Retrieved April 30, 2018.

o Nakashima, Ellen; Devlin Barrett; Adam Entous (April 11, 2017)".F BI obtained FISA warrant to monitor formerTrump adviser Carter Page" (https://www.washingtonpost.com/world/national-security/fbi-obtained-fisa-warrant-to-monitor-former-trump-adviser-carter-page/2017/04/11/620192ea-1e0e-11e7-ad74-3a742a6e93a7_sto.hrytml). The Washington Post. Retrieved April 11, 2017.

o Julie Pace (March 6, 2017). "Senate committee calls on former Trump adviser Carter Page in Russia investigation" (https://www.pbs.org/newshour/rundown/senate-committee-calls-former-trump-adviser-carter-page-russia-investigation/). Associated Press.

o Marshall Cohen & Eli Watkins (March 4, 2016). "Who is Carter Page?" (http://www.cnn.com/2017/03/04/politics/carter-page-russia-donald-trump/index.html). CNN.

o Julie Pace (April 3, 2017). "Trump campaign adviser Carter Page met with Russian spy in 2013" (http://www.chicagotribune.com/news/nationworld/p

olitics/ct-carter-page-russian-spy-20170403-sto.rhytml). Chicago Tribune. Associated Press.

- o Adam Goldman, "Russian Spies Tried to Recruit Carter Page Before He Advised Trump" (https://www.nytimes.com/2017/04/04/us/politics/carter-page-trump-russia.htm,l) The New York Times (April 4, 2017).

- o Adam Entous, Greg Miller, Kevin Sieff & Karen DeYoung, "Blackwater founder held secret Seychelles meeting toestablish Trump-Putin back channel" (https://www.washingtonpost.com/world/national-security/blackwater-founder-held-secret-seychelles-meeting-to-establish-trump-putin-back-channel/2017/04/03/95908a08-1648-11e7-ada0-1489b735b3a3_story.html), The Washington Post (April 3, 2016).

- o Filipov, David; Brittain, Amy; Helderman, Rosalind S.; Hamburger, Tom (June 1, 2017). "Explanations for Kushner's meeting with head of Kremlin-linked bank don't match up "(https://www.washingtonpost.com/politics/explanations-forkushners-meeting-with-head-of-kremlin-linked-bank-dont-match-up/2017/06/01/dd1bdbb0-460a-11e7-bcde-624ad94170ab_story.html). The Washington Post.

o "Russia inquiry expands to Trump lawyer Michael Cohen" (https://www.bbc.com/news/world-us-canada-40098658). BBC. May 30, 2017. Retrieved May 30, 2017.

o Ross, Brian; Mosk, Matthew (May 30, 2017)." Congress expands Russia investigation to include rTump's personal attorney" (http://abcnews.go.com/Politics/russia-investigation-expands-include-donald-trumps-personal-attorney/story?id=47646601). ABC News. Retrieved May 30, 2017.

o Helderman, Rosalind; Leonig, Carol; Hamburge,r Tom (August 28, 2017). "Top Trump Organization executive asked Putin aide for help on business deal" (https://www.washingtonpost.com/politics/top-trump-organization-executive-reached-out-to-putin-aide-for-help-on-business-deal/2017/08/28/095aebac-8c16-11e7-84c0-02cc069f2c37_sto.hrytml). Washington Post. Retrieved August 29, 2017.

o Harris, Shane (June 29, 2017). "GOP Operative Sought Clinton Emails From Hackers, Implied a Connection to Flynn" (https://www.wsj.com/articles/gop-operative-sought-clinton-emails-from-hackers-implied-a-connection-to-flynn-1498770851). The Wall Street Journal. Retrieved July 3, 2017.

o Cohn, Alicia (June 29, 2017)." GOP investigation sought connection between Clinton's emails and Russia: repor (t"http://thehill.com/business-a-lobbying/340166-gop-investigation-sought-connection-between-clintons-emails-and-russia). The Hill. Retrieved July 3, 2017.

o Borger, Julian (June 30, 2017). "Russia hackers discussed getting Clinton emails to Michael Flynn – repor t("https://www.theguardian.com/us-news/2017/jun/30/r ussia-hackers-clinton-emails-mike-flynn) . The Guardian. Retrieved July 3, 2017.

o Prokop, Andrew (July 1, 2017)." New reports raise some big questions about Michael Flynn and Russian hacker s("https://www.vox.com/2017/6/29/15896582/trump-russia-michael-flynn-wsj). Vox. Retrieved July 7, 2017.

o Tait, Matt (June 30, 2017). "The Time I Got Recruited to Collude with the Russians" (https://lawfareblog.com/time-i-got-recruited-collude-russians). Lawfare. Retrieved July 6, 2017.

o Skiba, Katherine; Lighty, Todd; Heinzmann, David. "Peter W. Smith, GOP operative who sought Clinton's emails from Russian hackers, committed suicide, records show "(http://www.chicagotribune.com/news/local/politics/ct-peter-smith-death-met-0713-20170713-story.html). Chicago Tribune. Retrieved July 14, 2017.

o Corn, David (October 31, 2016). "A Veteran Spy Has Given the FBI Information Alleging a Russian Operation to Cultivate Donald Trump" (https://www.motherjones.com/politics/2016/10/veteran-spy-gave-fbi-info-alleging-russian-operation-cultivate-donald-trump). Mother Jones. Retrieved January 12, 2017.

o Borger, Julian (April 28, 2017). "UK was given details of alleged contacts between Trump campaign and Moscow" (https://www.theguardian.com/us-news/2017/apr/28/trump-russia-intelligence-uk-government-m16-kremlin.)The Guardian. Retrieved April 30, 2017.

o Shane, Scott (January 11, 2017). "What We Know and Don't Know About the Trump-Russia Dossier" (https://www.nytimes.com/2017/01/11/us/politics/trump-intelligence-report-explaine.hrtml). The New York Times. Retrieved January 12, 2017.

o Wemple, Eric (January 10, 2017). "BuzzFeed's ridiculous rationale for publishing the Trump-Russia dossier" (https://www.washingtonpost.com/blogs/erik-wemple/wp/2017/01/10/buzzfeeds-ridiculous-rationale-for-publishing-the-trumprussia-dossier/). The Washington Post. Retrieved January 11, 2017.

o Bensinger, Ken; Elder, Miriam; Schoofs, Mark (January 10, 2017)." These Reports Allege Trump Has Deep Ties ToRussia" (https://www.buzzfeed.com/kenbensinger/these-reports-allege-trump-has-deep-ties-to-russia.) BuzzFeed. Retrieved December 24, 2017.

o Wood, Paul (March 30, 2017). "Trump Russia dossier key claim 'verified' " (https://www.bbc.com/news/world-us-canada-39435786) – via www.bbc.com.

o Perez, Evan; Prokupecz, Shimon; Raju, Manu (April 18, 2017)".F BI used dossier allegations to bolster Trump-Russia investigation" (http://www.cnn.com/2017/04/18/politics/fbi-dossier-carter-page-donald-trump-russia-investigation/index.html). CNN. Retrieved April 19, 2017.

o "Feinstein releases transcript of interview with Fusion GPS co-founder("https://www.politico.com/story/2018/01/09/feinstein-releases-transcript-of-interview-with-fusion-gps-co-founder-329573.) POLITICO. Retrieved 2018-01-09.

o Barrett, Devlin; Hamburger, Tom (2018-01-09). "Fusion GPS founder told Senate investigators the FBI had a whistleblower in Trump's network" (https://www.washingtonpost.com/world/nationalsecurity/feinstein-releases-testimony-of-glenn-simpson-whose-research-firm-fusion-gps-was-behindtrumpdossier/2018/01/09/15da150a-f562-11e7-beb6-c8d48830c54d_story.html). Washington Post. ISSN 0190-8286 (https://www.worldcat.org/issn/0190-8286).Retrieved 2018-01-09.

o "American Voters Back Sanctions For Russian Hacking, Quinnipiac University National Poll Finds Israel, Palestinians Not Sincere About Peace, Voters Say" (https://poll.qu.edu/national/release-detail?ReleaseID=2417.) Quinnipiac University. January 13, 2017.

o Reid J. Epstein (January 17, 2017)." About Half of Americans Think Russia Interfered With Election Through Hacking, Poll Finds" (https://www.wsj.com/articles/about-half-of-americans-think-russia-interfered-with-election-through-hacking-poll-finds-1484686800). The Wall Street Journal. Retrieved January 17, 2017.

o Shepard, Steven (March 3, 2017)." Russia investigations a 'witch hunt'? Not according to polls ("http://www.politico.com/story/2017/03/trump-russia-polls-235667.) Politico. Retrieved March 4, 2017.

- "Most Important Problem" (https://news.gallup.com/poll/1675/most-important-problem.aspx.)Gallup tracking poll. Archived (https://web.archive.org/web/20170918124707/https://news.gallup.com/poll/1675/most-important-problem.aspx) from the original on September 18, 2017. Retrieved August 6, 2018.

- Dann, Carrie (February 24, 2017)." Majority of Americans Say Congress Should Probe Contact Between rTump, Russia: Poll" (https://www.nbcnews.com/politics/first-read/majority-americans-say-congress-should-probe-contact-between-trump-russia-n725391). NBC News. Retrieved August 5, 2018.

- "Republicans Out Of Step With U.S. Voters On Key Issues, Quinnipiac University National Poll Finds; Most Voters Support Legalized Marijuana" (https://poll.qu.edu/national/release-detail?ReleaseID=2432.)Quinnipiac University. February 23, 2017. Retrieved March 4, 2017.

- "The Trump Administration and Russia "(http://apnorc.org/projects/Pages/russia-and-the-2016-election.aspx.)The Associated Press-NORC

Center for Public Affairs Research. April 14, 2017. Retrieved April 14, 2017.

o "Two-Thirds Of U.S. Voters Take Climate Personally, Quinnipiac University National Poll Finds; Opposition oT The Wall Hits New High" (https://poll.qu.edu/national/release-detail?ReleaseID=2449.)Quinnipiac University. April 5, 2017. Retrieved April 6, 2017.

o Aaron Zitner (April 24, 2017). "Poll: Americans Doubtful of Congress's Ability to Probe Russia Meddling in U.S.Election" (https://www.wsj.com/articles/poll-americans-doubtful-of-congresss-ability-to-probe-russia-meddling-in-u-selection-1493049600). The Wall Street Journal. Retrieved April 24, 2017.

o Holyk, Gregory (April 26, 2017)." Republicans and Democrats split over Russia probes: Pol l("http://abcnews.go.com/Politics/views-russian-influence-reflect-partisan-finger-pointing-poll/story?id=4700846.2 A) BC News. Retrieved May 2, 2017.

o "Does Trump-Russia Relationship Pose Security Threat? Public Split" (https://www.monmouth.edu/polling-institute/reports/MonmouthPoll_US_051817/). Monmouth University. May 18, 2017.

o Mark Murray (June 23, 2017). "Poll: More Americans Believe Comey Over Trump" (http://www.nbcnews.com/politics/first-read/poll-more-americans-believe-comey-over-trump-n776006.)NBC News.

o Jessica Taylor (July 6, 2017). "Majority Of Americans Believe Trump Acted Either Illegally Or Unethically With Russia" (https://www.npr.org/2017/07/06/535626356/on-russia-republican-and-democratic-lense-shave-a-very-different-tint). NPR.

o Langer, Gary (July 16, 2017). "6 months in, record low job approval for Trump: Poll" (http://abcnews.go.com/Politics/months-record-low-trump-troubles-russia-health-care/story?id=48639490.)ABC News.

o Jennifer Agiesta (August 10, 2017)." Poll: Trump finances fair game in Russia investigation" (http://www.cnn.com/2017/08/10/politics/cnn-poll-o russia-investigation-trump-finances/index.htm.l)CNN.

o Jeffrey M. Jones (August 9, 2017). "1 in 4 Americans Say Trump Acted Illegally With Russia" (http://www.gallup.com/poll/215648/americans-say-trump-acted-illegally-russia.aspx.)Gallup. Retrieved August 13, 2017.

o "Support for Impeachment Grows; Half of Americans Believe Russia Interfered with Electio n(h" ttps://www.prri.org/research/poll-trump-russia-investigation-impeachment-republican-party./)August 17, 2017. Retrieved September 22, 2017.

o Sauter, Vanessa (28 December 2017). "The Year in Review: L'Affaire Russe" (https://www.lawfareblog.com/year-review-laffaire-russe). LawFare. Retrieved 12 March 2018.

o Chozick, Amy (December 17, 2016)." Clinton Says 'Personal Beef' by Putin Led to Hacking Attacks ("https://www.nytimes.com/2016/12/16/us/politics/hillary-clinton-russia-fbi-come.yhtml). The New York Times. p. A12. Retrieved December 17, 2016.

o Abdullah, Halimah (December 16, 2016)." Hillary Clinton Singles Out Putin, Comey in Election Loss ("http://www.nbcnews.com/news/us-news/hillary-clinton-singles-out-putin-comey-election-loss-n69699.1 N) BC News. Retrieved December 17, 2016.

o Blake, Aaron (October 19, 2016). "The final Trump-Clinton debate transcript, annotated" (https://www.washingtonpost.com/news/thefix/wp/2016/10/19/the-final-trump-clinton-debate-transcript-annotated. /T) he Washington Post.Retrieved April 3, 2017.

o cf. Tau, Byron (September 14, 2016). "Colin Powell Blasts Donald Trump, Criticizes Hillary Clinton in Leaked Messages" (https://www.wsj.com/articles/leaked-colin-powell-emails-lambaste-donald-trump-hillary-clinton-1473862328). The Wall Street Journal. Retrieved December 11, 2016.

o Johnstone, Liz (December 11, 2016)." Priebus: "I Don't Know Whether It's True" Russia Is Responsible for Election Hacks" (http://www.nbcnews.com/politics/politics-news/despite-cia-report-russia-priebus-says-he-doesn-t-know-n694541). Meet the Press. NBC News. Retrieved March 6, 2017.

o Kaczynski, Andrew (December 19, 2016)." Trump said in 2014 that Russian hacking was a 'big problem' "
(http://edition.cnn.com/2016/12/19/politics/kfile-trump-russia-hacking./)CNN. Retrieved December 20, 2016.

o Pramuk, Jacob (September 26, 2016)." Trump: DNC hacker could have been 400 pounds and sitting in bed" (https://www.cnbc.com/2016/09/26/clinton-trump-publicly-invited-russia-to-hack-us-which-is-unacceptable.htm.l)CNBC. Retrieved December 14, 2016.

o Fox-Brewster, Thomas (October 10, 2016). "Clinton Claims Putin's Hackers Are Punting For Trump" (https://www.forbes.com/sites/thomasbrewster/2016/10/10/clinton-claims-putins-hackers-are-punting-for-trump/#4a93209c1fb.9) Forbes. Retrieved December 14, 2016.

o Eichenwald, Kurt (November 4, 2016)." Why Vladimir Putin's Russia Is Backing Donald Trump" (http://www.newsweek.com/donald-trump-vladimir-putin-russia-hillary-clinton-united-states-europe-51689.5 N) ewsweek. Retrieved December 29, 2017.

o Kessler, Glenn (December 13, 2016). "The pre-war intelligence on Iraq: Wrong or hyped by the Bush White House?" (https://www.washingtonpost.com/news/fact-checker/wp/2016/12/13/the-pre-war-intelligence-on-iraq-wrong-or-hyped-by-the-bush-white-house/). The Washington Post. Retrieved October 2, 2017.

o Flores, Reena (December 11, 2016)." Donald Trump weighs in on Russia hackinge lection, CIA intelligence" (http://www.cbsnews.com/news/donald-trump-weighs-in-on-russia-hacking-election-cia-intelligence/.) CBS News. Retrieved December 13, 2016.

o Gittens, Hasani; Dilanian, Ken (January 4, 2017)." Trump Takes Jab at 'Intelligence' Oficials for Allegedly Delaying 'Russian Hacking' Briefing" (http://www.nbcnews.com/news/us-news/trump-takes-jab-intelligence-oficials-allegedly-delaying-russian-hacking-briefing-n702906.) NBC News. Retrieved January 5, 2017.

o "Trump praises 'very smart' Putin for not expelling US diplomats"(https://www.theguardian.com/world/2016/dec/30/russia-plans-immediate-counter-measures-us-diplomats.) The Guardian. December 30, 2016.

o "Trump to order anti-hacking plan within 90 days of taking office – statement" (https://www.yahoo.com/news/trump-order-anti-hacking-plan-within-90-days-194950568.htm.l) Yahoo! News. January 6, 2017.

o "After Security Meeting, Trump Admits Possibility of Russian Hacking" (https://www.nytimes.com/2017/01/06/us/poiltics/donald-trump-wall-hack-russia.html?_r=0.) The New York Times. January 6, 2017.

o Clarke, Toni; Volz, Dustin (January 8, 2017). "Trump acknowledges Russia role in U.S. election hacking: aide" (https://www.reuters.com/article/us-usa-russia-cyber-idUSKBN14S0O6). Reuters. Retrieved January 9, 2017.

o Shear, Michael D.; Weisman, Jonathan (January 11, 2017)." Trump Says 'I Think It Was Russia' That Hacked the

o Democrats"(https://www.nytimes.com/2017/01/11/us
/poiltics/donald-trump-press-conference.html.) The
New York Times. Retrieved January 11, 2017.

o Davis, Julie Hirschfeld; Haberman, Maggie (January
11, 2017). "Donald Trump Concedes Russia's
Interference   in
Election"(https://www.nytimes.com/2017/01/11/us/p
oiltics/trumps-press-conference-highlights-
russia.htm.l) The New York Times. Retrieved April
14, 2017.

o Holmes, Oliver. "Trump on Putin's denial of
meddling in US election: 'I believe him' "
(https://www.theguardian.com/world/2017/nov/11/p
utin-and-trump-want-political-solution-to-syria-
conflict-kremlin-say.s) The Guardian. Retrieved 11
November 2017.

o Liptak, Kevin; Merica, Dan. "Trump says he believes
Putin's election meddling denials"
(http://edition.cnn.com/2017/11/11/politics/president
-donald-trump-vladimir-putin-election-
meddling/index.htm. lC) NN. Retrieved 11
November 2017.

- "Trump backs US spy agencies after Putin meddling remark" (https://www.bbc.com/news/world-us-canada-41959341). BBC News. Retrieved 12 November 2017.
- Wagner, John (November 12, 2017). "Former U.S. intelligence oficials: Trump being 'played' by Putin" (https://www.washingtonpost.com/news/post-politics/wp/2017/11/12/former-u-s-intelligence-foicfials-trump-being-played-byputin/).Retrieved 12 November 2017.
- "Mike Pence: No evidence foreign meddling efforts 'had any impact' on 2016 election outcome "(https://www.washingtonexaminer.com/mike-pence-no-evidence-foreign-meddling-efforts-had-any-impact-on-2016-election-outcome.)Washington Examiner. 2018-02-14. Retrieved 2018-07-21.
- Chait, Jonathan. "Mike Pence Says U.S. Intel Found That Russia Didn't Elect T rump. He Is Lying" (http://nymag.com/daily/intelligencer/2018/02/pence-lies-that-u-s-intel-found-russia-didnt-elect-trump.htm. lN) ew York. Retrieved February 20, 2018.

o Harris, Shane (December 11, 2016)." Donald Trump
  Fuels Rift With CIA Over Russian Hack"
  (https://www.wsj.com/articles/trump-blames-
  democrats-for-reports-of-russia-hacking-
  1481467907.)The Wall Street Journal. Retrieved
  December 12, 2016.

o Brian Ross; James Gordon Meek; Mike Levine;
  Justin Fishel (December 12, 2016")T. rump Engages
  CIA in War of Words Over Russian Election
  Hacking
  "(http://abcnews.go.com/International/trump-war-
  words-intelligence-ofifcials-amid-
  disagreementrussian/story?id=44131322.)   ABC
  News. Retrieved December 13, 2016.

o Cassidy, John (December 12, 2016). "Trump Isolates
  Himself   With   C.I.A.   Attack"
  (http://www.newyorker.com/news/john-
  cassidy/trump-isolates-himself-with-c-i-a-attack.)
  The New Yorker. Retrieved December 13, 2016.

o Ackerman,   Spencer   (December   11,   2016).
  "Intelligence figures fear Trump reprisals over
  assessment   of   Russia   election   role"
  (https://www.theguardian.com/us-

news/2016/dec/11/intelligence-agencies-cia-donald-trump-russia.) The Guardian. Retrieved December 11, 2016.

o "Morell calls Russia's meddling in U.S. elections 'political equivalent of 9/1'1" (http://www.politico.com/story/2016/12/michael-morell-russia-us-elections-232495.) Politico. December 13, 2016.

o Rebecca Savransky, "Former CIA spokesman: Trump's disrespect for intelligence community is 'shameful'" (http://thehill.com/homenews/campaign/309912-former-cia-spokesman-trump-disrespect-for-cia-intelligence-community)TheHill (December 12, 2016).

o Michael V. Hayden, "Trump is already antagonizing the intelligence community, and that's a problem" (https://www.washingtonpost.com/opinions/trump-is-already-antagonizing-the-intelligence-community-and-thats-a-problem/2016/12/12/9576a0ca-c0ad-11e6-897f-918837dae0ae_stor.yhtml), The Washington Post (December 12, 2016).

o Nelson, Louis (December 14, 2016)." McMullin: GOP ignored Russian meddling in presidential election ("http://www.politico.com/story/2016/12/evan-mcmullin-gop-russia-hacking-232625.   )Politico. Retrieved December 15, 2016.

o Munslow, Julia (July 21, 2017). "Ex-CIA Director Hayden: Russia election meddling was 'most successful covert operation in history' " (https://www.yahoo.com/news/ex-cia-director-hayden-russia-election-meddling-successful-covert-operation-history-212056443.html). Yahoo! News. Retrieved July 26, 2017.

o Hayden, Michael (November 3, 2016). "Former CIA chief: Trump is Russia's useful fool" (https://www.washingtonpost.com/opinions/former-cia-chief-trump-is-russias-useful-fool/2016/11/03/cda4f2ef-a1d5-11e6-8d63-3e0a660f1f04_story.html). The Washington Post. Retrieved July 19, 2017.

o Alex Johnson, "WikiLeaks' Julian Assange: 'No Proof' Hacked DNC Emails Came From Russia ("http://www.nbcnews.com/news/us-news/wikileaks-julian-assange-no-proof-hacked-dnc-emails-came-russia-n61654,1 N) BC News (July25, 2016).

o "WikiLeaks' Assange denies Russia behind Podesta hack ("http://www.politico.com/story/2016/11/julian-assange-russia-john-podesta-wikileaks-230676). Politico. November 3, 2016. Retrieved December 10, 2016.

o Cheney, Kyle (December 12, 2016)." Electors demand intelligence briefing before Electoral College vote ("http://www.politico.com/story/2016/12/electorsinte lligence-briefing-trump-russia-232498). Politico.

o Pelosi, Christine. "Bipartisan Electors Ask James Clapper: Release Facts on Outside Interference in U.S. Election"(https://extranewsfeed.com/bipartisan-electors-ask-james-clapper-release-facts-on-outside-interference-in-u-s-election-c1a3d11d5b7b).

o Pete Williams, "Coming Soon: The 'Real' Presidential Election "(http://www.nbcnews.com/news/us-news/coming-soon-real-presidential-election-n696556), NBC News (December 15, 2016).

- o * Gabriel Debenedetti & Kyle Cheney, "Clinton campaign backs call for intelligence briefing before Electoral College vote" (http://www.politico.com/story/2016/12/clinton-campaign-backs-call-for-intelligence-briefing-before-electoral-college-vote-232512), Politico (December 12, 2016).

- o Dan Merica, "Clinton campaign backs intelligence briefing for Electoral College electors ("http://www.cnn.com/2016/12/12/politics/hillary-clinton-electoral-college-electors,/)CNN (December 13, 2016).

- o "Electors won't get intelligence briefing: report "(http://thehill.com/homenews/news/310820-electors-wont-get-intelligence-briefing-report). The Hill. December 16, 2016. Retrieved February 12, 2017.

- o Sanger, E.; Rick Corasaniti (June 14, 2016). "D.N.C. Says Russian Hackers Penetrated Its Files, Including Dossieron Donald Trump (https://www.nytimes.com/2016/06/15/us/poiltics/russian-hackers-dnc-trump.html.) The New YorkTimes. New York City. Retrieved July 24, 2016.

- o Henry Meyer; Stepan Kravchenko (December 15, 2016)". Russia Rejects as 'Rubbish' Claims Putin Directed U.S.
- o Hacking" (https://www.bloomberg.com/news/articles/2016-12-15/russia-rejects-as-rubbish-claims-putin-directed-u-shacking).Bloomberg News. Retrieved December 16, 2016.
- o Smith, Allan (December 16, 2016)." Russia responds to reports it hacked US election: Prove i t("http://www.businessinsider.com/russia-hack-us-election-trump-2016-12). Business Insider. Retrieved December 16, 2016.
- o Yaffa, Joshua (December 20, 2016). "Russia's View of the Election Hacks: Denials, Amusement, Comeuppance" (http://www.newyorker.com/news/news-desk/russias-view-of-the-election-hacks-denials-amuesment-comeuppance).The New Yorker. Retrieved January 14, 2017.
- o Filipov, David (Dec">ber 23, 2016). "Putin to Democratic Party: You lost, get over it" (https://www.washingtonpost.com/world/europe/tru

mp-syria-hacking-and-terrorism-in-play-as-russias-putin-meets-the-press/2016/12/23/28ead25a-c878-11e6-acda-59924caa2450_story.html). The Washington Post. Retrieved December 26, 2016.

o Pagliery, Jose; Chance, Matthew; Burrows, Emma (February 1, 2017). "Russian spy purge after suspected leaks toU.S. intelligence" (http://money.cnn.com/2017/02/01/news/fsb-kaspersky-arrests/). CNN. Retrieved July 18, 2017.

o Kramer, Andrew E. (January 25, 2017). "Top Russian Cybercrimes Agent Arrested on Charges of Treason" (https://www.nytimes.com/2017/01/25/world/europe/sergei-mikhailov-russian-cybercrimes-agent-arrested.htm.1)The New York Times. Retrieved July 18, 2017.

o Alexander Smith, Alexan Putin on U.S. election interference: 'I couldn't care less ('https://www.nbcnews.com/news/w orld/putin-u-s-election-interference-i-couldn-t-care-less-n855151,)NBC News (March 10, 2018).

o Putin says Jews, Ukrainians, Tatars could be behind U.S. election meddling

(https://www.usatoday.com/story/news/world/2018/0
3/10/putin-says-jews-russian-citizenship-could-
behind-u-s-election-meddling/413321002,
/A)ssociated Press (March 10, 2018).

o Alana Abramson, Putin Criticized for Remarks
Insinuating Jews and Other Minority Groups Could
Be Behind U.S. Election Interference
(http://time.com/5194830/vladimir-putin-jews-tatars-
ukrainians-u-s-election-interference, /T) ime (March
11, 2018).

o Avi Selk, Putin condemned for saying Jews may
have manipulated U.S. electio
n(https://www.washingtonpost.com/news/worldview
s/wp/2018/03/11/putin-condemned-for-saying-jews-
may-have-manipulated-u-s-election, /W) ashington
Post (March 11, 2018).

o Zengerle, Patricia (September 19, 2017)." Trump
choice for Russia ambassador: 'No question' Russia
meddled" (https://www.reuters.com/article/us-usa-
diplomacy-russia/trump-choice-for-russia-
ambassador-no-question-russia-meddled-
idUSKCN1BU20V). Reuters. Retrieved September
19, 2017.

o Cohen, Zachary; Sciutto, Jim (October 20, 2017)." CIA corrects director's Russian election meddling claim "(http://www.cnn.com/2017/10/19/politics/cia-pompeor-ussia-meddling-election/index.html.) CNN. Retrieved October 21, 2017.

o Andrew Weisburd; Clint Watts; JM Berger (November 6, 2016). "Trolling for Trump: How Russia is Trying to Destroy

o Nance, Malcolm (2016). The Plot to Hack America: How Putin's Cyberspies and WikiLeaks Tried to Steal the 2016

o Election. Skyhorse Publishing. ISBN 978-1-5107-2332-0. OCLC 987592653.

o Lichtman, Allan J. (2017). The Case for Impeachment. Dey Street Books. ISBN 978-0-06-269682-3.

o Beauchamp, Zach; Zarracina, Javier; Mark, Ryan; Northrop, Amanda (December 1, 2017A). visual guide to the key events in the Trump-Russia scandal. Vox.

o Miller, Greg; Jaffe, Greg; Rucker, Philip (December 14, 2017). "Doubting the intelligence, Trump pursues Putin and leaves a Russian threat unchecked". The Washington Post.

o Entous, Adam; Nakashima, Ellen; Jaffe, Greg (December 26, 2017). "Kremlin trolls burned across the Internet as Washington debated options". The Washington Post.

o Frank, Thomas (January 12, 2018). "Secret Money: How Trump Made Millions Selling Condos To Unknown Buyers". BuzzFeed News.

o U.S. Department of Justice federal indictment against 13 Russian individuals and 3 Russian entiti,e 1s6 Feb 2016

    o Joint Statement from the Department Of Homeland Security and Ofifce of the Director of National Intelligence on Election Security, October 7, 2016

    o McCain, Graham, Schume,r Reed Joint Statement on Reports That Russia Interfered with the 2016 Electio,n 11 Dec 2016

    o The New York Times. Retrieved October 19, 2016.

    o Kaczynski, Andrew (October 22, 2016)." Trump Jr. says conversations like his father's

2005 hot mic comments are 'a fact of life' " (http://edition.cnn.com/2016/10/21/politics/trump-jr-facts-of-life./)CNN.

o Wolfgang, Ben (October 23, 2016)." Eric Trump: Sexual assault accusations just' dirty tricks' from Clinton campaign" (http://www.washingtontimes.com/news/2016/oct/23/eric-trump-sexual-assault-accusations-just-dirty-t./)The Washington Times.

o Folkenflik, David (October 13, 2016). "Feeling Burned by Media, Trump Turns Up Heat" (http://www.houstonpublicmedia.org/npr/2016/10/13/497850278/feeling-burned-by-media-trump-turns-up-hea.t /H) ouston Public Media. Retrieved October 13, 2016.

o Reilly, Katie (October 13, 2016). "Read the New York Times' Response to Donald Trump's Retraction Demand" (http://time.com/4530428/new-york-times-donald-trump-lawsuit./)Time. Retrieved October 13, 2016.

o "Donald Trump's Attorney Says Trump's Accusers 'Aren't Women He'd Be Attracted To' " (http://nymag.com/thecut/2016/10/trumps-lawyer-accusers-arent-women-hed-be-attracted-to.htm.1)New York. October 19, 2016. Retrieved October 19, 2016.

o "Donald Trump's attorney: Trump's sexual assault accusers 'aren't even women he'd be tatracted to' " (http://nymag.com/thecut/2016/10/trumps-lawyer-accusers-arent-women-hed-be-attracted-to.htm. lB) usiness Insider. October 19, 2016. Retrieved October 19, 2016.

o Wagner, John. "All of the women who have accused Trump of sexual harassment are lying, the White Housesays"(https://www.washingtonpost.com/news/post-politics/wp/2017/10/27/all-of-the-women-who-have-accused-trump-of-sexual-harassment-are-lying-the-white-house-says/.) The Washington Post. Retrieved 17 December 2017.

- o Korte, Gregory. "White House on sex assault allegations: 'Franken has admitted wrongdoing and the presidenthasn't'(https://www.usatoday.com/story/news/politics/2017/11/17/white-house-sex-assault-allegtaions-franken-hasadmitted-wrongdoing-and-president-hasnt/875394001/.) USA Today. Retrieved 17 December 2017.

- o Alemany, Jacqueline. "Sanders rebuffs sexual harassment allegations against Trump" (https://www.cbsnews.com/news/sanders-rebuffs-sexual-harassment-allegations-against-trump/). CBS News. Retrieved 17 December 2017.

- o Emanuella, Grinberg (October 14, 2016)." Tweets show why women don't report sex asault" (http://edition.cnn.com/2016/10/13/health/why-women-dont-report/.) CNN. Retrieved October 15, 2016.

- o Plank, Liz (October 13, 2016). "Donald Trump is giving us a master class in why #WomenDontReport"

(https://www.vox.com/2016/10/13/13274972/
donald-trump-is-giving-us-a-master-class-in-
why-womendontrepo.r   tV)ox.   Retrieved
October 15, 2016.

o Kliff, Sarah (October 18, 2016). "Trump,
Cosby, Ailes: it took celebrity accusers to
make us listen to sexual assault victims"
(https://www.vox.com/identities/2016/10/18/1
3306300/trump-cosby-ailes-sexual-
harrasment.) Vox.

o Kliff, Sarah (October 14, 2016). "A cop who's
spent 30 years fighting sexual assault explains
why victims often wait to come forward"
(https://www.vox.com/identities/2016/10/14/1
3275786/sexual-assault-victims-reporting.)
Vox. Retrieved October 15, 2016.

o Dominus, Susan (October 13, 2016)." After
Donald Trump, Will More Women Believe
Their   Own   Stories?
"(https://www.nytimes.com/2016/10/14/magaz
ine/afterd-onald-trump-will-more-women-
believe-their-own-stories.htm.l   )The   New

York Times Magazine. Retrieved October 15, 2016.

- o "Fox News Contributor Warns Sexual Assault Allegations May "Backfire" And Turn Trump Into A "Victim" " (http://mediamatters.org/video/2016/10/13/fox -news-contributor-warns-sexual-assault- allegations-may-backfire-and-turn-trump- victim/213810). Media Matters for America. October 13, 2016. Retrieved October 19, 2016.
- o Kludt, Tom (October 14, 2016). "At Fox News, Donald Trump allegations bring echoes of recent scandal" (http://money.cnn.com/2016/10/14/media/fox-news- donald-trump-roger-ailes-allegations/index.html.) CNN. Retrieved November 18, 2017.
- o "Scarborough questions timing of Trump accusations" (http://thehill.com/blogs/ballot- box/presidential-races/300763-scarborough-if-i-had- been-sexually-harassed-by-trump-.i) The Hill. October 16, 2016. Retrieved November 18, 2017.
- o Cillizza, Chris (October 13, 2016). "Michelle Obama's speech on Donald Trump was remarkable"

(https://www.washingtonpost.com/news/the-fix/wp/2016/10/13/michelle-obama-just-put-a-huge-and-emotional-exclamation-point-on-trumps-hot-mic-tape/). The Washington Post. Retrieved October 20, 2016.

o Louis, Errol (October 14, 2016). "Michelle Obama's devastating speech" (http://edition.cnn.com/2016/10/14/opinions/what-michelle-obamas-trump-speech-accomplished-louis./)CNN. Retrieved October 20, 2016.

o Gambino, Lauren (October 14, 2016)." Michelle Obama speech crushes Trump with weight of women's experience" (https://www.theguardian.com/us-news/2016o/ct/14/michelle-obama-speech-donald-trump-women.) The Guardian.Retrieved October 20, 2016.

o Gambino, Lauren (October 14, 2016)." Michelle Obama denounces Donald Trump's rhetoric: 'It has shaken me to my core' " (https://www.theguardian.com/us-news/2016/oct/13/michelle-obama-donald-trump-misconductfrightening). The Guardian. Retrieved November 11, 2016.

o Liptak, Kevin (October 14, 2016). "How Michelle Obama's speech denouncing Donald Trump came together" (http://edition.cnn.com/2016/10/14/politics/michelle-obama-speech./)CNN. Retrieved November 11, 2016.

o Moore, Peter (November 19, 2017)." Most Republicans don't think sexual assault would disqualify rTump from the presidency"(https://today.yougov.com/news/2016/10/18/most-republicans-dont-think-sexual-assault-would-d/).YouGov. Retrieved October 18, 2016.

o Savransky, Rebecca (November 16, 2017). "Poll: Majority of Hillary Clinton voters think Bill Clinton allegations'credible' " (http://thehill.com/homenews/news/360722-poll-majority-of-hillary-clinton-voters-think-bill-clinton-allegations-credible). The Hill. Retrieved November 18, 2017.

o "TIME Person of the Year 2017: The Silence Breakers" (http://time.com/time-person-of-the-year-2017-silence-breakers/). Time. Retrieved 4 February 2018.

www.ingramcontent.com/pod-product-compliance
Lightning Source LLC
Chambersburg PA
CBHW031047250726
48655CB00004B/1333